# Learning to Teach,
# Teaching to Learn

# Learning to Teach, Teaching to Learn

A CORE TEXT FOR PRIMARY STUDENT
TEACHERS IN IRELAND

Tony Bonfield and Kathleen Horgan

GILL

Gill Education
Hume Avenue
Park West
Dublin 12
www.gilleducation.ie

Gill Education is an imprint of M.H. Gill & Co.

Design and print origination by O'K Graphic Design, Dublin
Illustrator: Derry Dillon
Cover design: Lisa Dynan

At the time of going to press, all web addresses were active and contained information relevant to the topics in this book. Gill Education does not, however, accept responsibility for the content or views contained on these websites. Content, views and addresses may change beyond the publisher or author's control. Students should always be supervised when reviewing websites.

*The paper used in this book is made from the wood pulp of managed forests. For every tree felled, at least one tree is planted, thereby renewing natural resources.*

ISBN: 978-0-7171-62444

# Acknowledgements

The authors wish to acknowledge the support they have received from the management and staff of Mary Immaculate College and from colleagues in the field of education in other institutions of learning.

We also appreciate the invaluable input of our students, whose experiences, honesty and insights have contributed greatly to this publication.

We also thank our partners and families for their love and support during the creation of what we hope is a worthwhile resource to help inform and inspire future generations of teachers.

# About the Authors

**Tony Bonfield**, BEd, MEd, EdD, is a lecturer in Philosophy of Education at Mary Immaculate College, Limerick. His research interests include the exploration and analysis of concepts pertinent to social inclusion and exclusion in education, national and international identities as embedded in curriculum, the investigation of aspects of comparative education, and the review of a range of concepts attending the nature of educational studies when conceptualised as a field of knowledge. He has worked at many levels of education and has considerable experience in the primary sector.

**Kathleen Horgan,** BEd, MEd, PhD, is a member of the Department of Reflective Pedagogy and Early Childhood Studies, Faculty of Education, Mary Immaculate College, Limerick. She has been awarded a National Teaching Excellence Award and a Government of Ireland Senior Research Scholarship in recognition of her contributions to teaching and research. Her professional interests embrace reflective practice, teacher learning, social justice and early childhood education. She has published and presented her work nationally and internationally and has collaborated with educational institutions, government agencies and philanthropic organisations in Dubai, the UK, the US, Zambia, India, Bangladesh and Sri Lanka.

*We dedicate this book to*
*Peadar Cremin and Noel Moloney,*
*two inspiring teacher educators, mentors, colleagues and friends.*

# Contents

## Chapter 8  Lesson Planning 143

## Chapter 9   Fostering Classroom Dialogue 167

## Chapter 10   Establishing a Positive Classroom Climate 188

## Chapter 11    Assessment and Learning                                   212

# List of Figures

# Overview

This book is essential reading for all student teachers preparing for work in Irish Primary classrooms, and offers valuable support during the taught and school placement components of initial teacher education programmes. It provides an accessible yet thought-provoking introduction to the processes of learning and teaching that every student teacher needs to acquire. The book is divided into 12 chapters, which provide theoretical and practical insights into the following key topics: becoming a teacher, reflective practice, the professional portfolio, learning theories, the child-centred classroom, approaches to research, classroom observation, lesson planning, classroom dialogue, establishing a positive classroom climate, assessment and classroom relationships.

Opportunities to engage more deeply with the core issues in each chapter are provided through a range of activities – Tasks or M-Level Tasks. Tasks cater for undergraduate students and M-Level Tasks for master's level students. The M-Level Tasks provide greater challenge and point to further reading for those who wish to pursue topics in greater detail.

The book is intended for student teachers, lecturers, mentors and tutors involved in initial teacher education. It is particularly relevant to students undertaking BEd and PME degrees in primary education, and students entering school placements and other professional experiences. It is envisaged that university teachers will utilise this book in their classrooms and that pre-service teachers will draw upon it in seeking to understand their practice in the light of educational theory.

This book offers support to student teachers who wish to develop flexible, responsive and creative approaches to teaching and learning. It highlights the importance of the research base underpinning teaching and teachers' own creative engagement, providing a wealth of innovative ideas to enrich pedagogy and practice. It addresses many of the current needs of student teachers involved in initial teacher education and supports them in progressing through their trajectories of learning; it aims to help them to become more skilful and artful in their enactment of teaching as they become more aware of the complex dynamic between learner, teacher, context and curriculum.

The objective of this book is to support lecturers and their students in exploring learning to teach in the primary school. The book explores the philosophy and tenets of the Irish Primary School Curriculum 1999 and conceptualises teaching and the process of learning as personal, social, intellectual and emotional endeavours.

# CHAPTER ONE

# Becoming a Teacher: Current Issues in Education

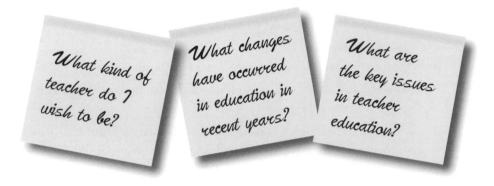

What kind of teacher do I wish to be?

What changes have occurred in education in recent years?

What are the key issues in teacher education?

**Once you have worked through this chapter, you will have:**

- Gained insight into some of the changes that have influenced Irish education in recent years.
- Recognised the significance of critical reflection and reflective practice as central aspects of teacher education.
- Developed an appreciation and understanding of teacher identity as an evolving and significant concept in your development as a teacher.
- Come to recognise the significance of working positively within a diverse and constantly changing society with varied social and educational needs.
- Developed an appreciation of the key contribution of educational research to teacher education.
- Gained a degree of understanding in respect of the concept of leadership, and its intrinsic and ineluctable role within teacher education.

## THE PRIMARY SCHOOL CURRICULUM 1999

---

### TASK 1.1: 'THE SABER-TOOTH CURRICULUM'

J. Abner Peddiwell wrote his essay 'The Saber-Tooth Curriculum', published in *The Saber-Tooth Curriculum and Other Essays* (1939), as a humorous observation outlining how unquestioned customs of schooling could lead to a reluctance to embrace badly needed changes. Peddiwell believed education needed to be receptive to the developing needs of life and he thought education and curriculum in his time were adhering unduly to outdated needs instead of embracing necessary changes.

Read 'The Sabre Tooth Curriculum' (widely available online) and address these questions:

- What would you consider to be the fish-grabbing, horse-clubbing and tiger-searing of our time?
- What motivated New-Fist to design a curriculum?
- How do the aims of education today differ from those of the Paleolithic era outlined in the essay?
- If you were to design a new primary school curriculum for the twenty-first century, what areas would you prioritise and why?

---

The Irish Primary School Curriculum (PSC), published in 1999 and gradually implemented over a number of subsequent years, amounted to a substantial revision of the 1971 curriculum (Department of Education 1971). You may have experienced several aspects of the 1999 curriculum in the course of your education. The 1999 publication was the outcome of a lengthy process of collaborative curriculum design undertaken by representatives from a broad range of partners within primary education (Looney 2001).

The PSC 1999 was the second major curricular initiative in Irish primary education in a period of thirty years. The 1971 curriculum had initially outlined the first clear statement of child-centred principles for all national schools (Department of Education 1971). The 1999 documentation claims 'to incorporate [those] principles and develop them' (NCCA 1999: vii). That intention is maintained in several key ways. There is a similarity in aims, with both curricula advancing aspirations firmly located in the child-centred tradition. Emphasis in both cases is placed on 'enabling the child to live a full life as a child' (Department of Education 1971: 12; NCCA 1999: 7) and preparing the child for further education. Stress is placed in both curricula on the importance of a rounded development for each child, individual difference, activity methods, the principle of subject integration and the importance of environment-based learning (Department of Education 1971; NCCA 1999).

> ## TASK 1.2: THINKING ABOUT BROAD AIMS
>
> In pairs, discuss and develop two broad aims for a group of learners. Choose the age group you wish to focus on. Keep the aims broad rather than subject specific and prepare a rationale for your choice of aims.

However, the authors of the PSC 1999 are keen to emphasise the impact of a broad range of recent influences on society, and the need to incorporate and prioritise these in the curriculum (NCCA 1999). Developments within child-centered understandings of education are to the fore, with an emphasis on the developmental and aesthetic aspects of learning (NCCA 1999). Moreover, greater emphasis is placed on language development and on incorporating other 'key issues…of relevance to primary education' (NCCA 1999: 9). These key issues are presented as representing the landscape of change in education, culture, society and spirituality in Ireland and elsewhere. Changes and issues in these areas are seen as having a considerable ongoing influence on all our lives, not least on children in school. In the area of education we see matters relating to quality of education, the enhancement of literacy and numeracy, the crucial role of early childhood education, the role of information and communications technology (ICT) in schools and society, the importance of catering for children with special needs, and the role of the curriculum in contributing to equality of access to education. Equally, considerable importance is also placed on questions of our national identity within the European and global dimensions of our modern society, the development of pluralism in our schools and society, along with developing tolerance and nurturing the spiritual dimensions of life (NCCA 1999).

> ## M-LEVEL TASK 1.1: REVIEWING KEY ISSUES IN THE PSC 1999
>
> Review the 'Key Issues in Primary Education' outlined in the *Primary School Curriculum: Introduction* (NCCA 1999: 25–31) (http://www.curriculumonline.ie/Primary/Curriculum).
>
> - How significant are these issues now?
> - Have they stood the test of time?
> - Could you suggest some further issues that merit attention now?
> - Can a curriculum exert a considerable impact on the shaping of society?

Specifically, the PSC 1999 puts to the fore the importance of enabling 'children to meet, with self-confidence and assurance, the demands of life both now and in the future' (NCCA 1999: 6) and this aspiration finds further expression in three broad aims:

1. To enable the child to live a full life as a child and to realise his or her potential as a unique individual
2. To enable the child to develop as a social being through living and co-operating with others and so contribute to the good of society
3. To prepare the child for further education and lifelong learning

(NCCA 1999: 7)

---

### TASK 1.3: AIMS IN ACTION

Read and reflect on the aims of the PSC 1999, outlined above (NCCA 1999: 7).

In a group discussion, choose one of these three broad aims and tease out some implications of this aim for classroom atmosphere, the role of the teacher and the significance of subject content.

Draw on your own schooling experiences, which may have been gained through your encounter with the PSC 1999, with other curricula in other societies or in non-formal educational settings.

---

The PSC 1999 provides a broad set of learning experiences and endorses a variety of approaches to teaching and learning with a focus on catering to the varying needs of individual children. The aims of the curriculum aspire to all children being introduced to a range of learning opportunities that acknowledges the learner's uniqueness, develops their full possibilities and enables them to meet the challenges of present and future living. The emphasis is on the child as an active learner, and, by means of a diversity of teaching methodologies, the ambition is to nurture the development of significant skills in communication, inquiry, problem-solving, investigation and analysis, critical thinking, social and personal awareness, and interaction (NCCA 1999).

While the curriculum emphasises the need for greater attention to be paid to students with special educational needs and also the needs of gifted children, it also seeks to facilitate the growth of the individual child in all aspects of his or her life; these aspects are cited as spiritual, moral, cognitive, emotional, imaginative, aesthetic, social and physical (NCCA 1999).

According to the authors of the PSC 1999, the curriculum is reflective of the educational, cultural, social and economic aspirations and concerns of Irish society. It also wishes to take into account the evolving nature of our society and seeks to enable children to adapt to these changes. Specifically, the curriculum is divided into the following broad key areas, which are again further divided into 11 subjects:

- Language (Gaeilge, English)
- Mathematics
- Social, Environment and Scientific Education (History, Geography, Science)
- Arts Education, Visual Arts, Music and Drama
- Physical Education
- Social, Personal and Health Education

Initially, the PSC 1999 was set out in 23 documents, consisting of an introduction, 11 curriculum statements associated with each subject and the same number of teacher guidelines. These are now available online: http://www.ncca.ie/en/Curriculum_and_Assessment/Early_Childhood_and_Primary_Education/Primary-Education/Primary_School_Curriculum/.

In the case of each curriculum statement there is an outline of its rationale, aims and objectives; very structured content and assessment approaches for each of the four class levels are also laid out. These class levels are presented as Infants; First and Second; Third and Fourth; and Fifth and Sixth. The teacher guidelines are intended to provide a comprehensive range of resource materials to support a variety of approaches to teaching and learning.

---

### TASK 1.4: CURRICULUM STRUCTURE

As a very comprehensive curriculum document, you will encounter the entire Primary School Curriculum 1999 many times throughout your training as a teacher. Gaining an initial understanding of its structure is worthwhile. Choose any one subject and familiarise yourself with the structures employed in presenting that subject within the curriculum. In particular, take note of aims, objectives, strands and insights on evaluation.

## KEY DEVELOPMENTS SINCE 1999

> ### TASK 1.5: SOCIETAL CHANGES, EDUCATION AND THE CURRICULUM
>
> In the course of your own experience of schooling and society, you may have noticed and lived through many changes. Identify a number of societal changes that you have encountered and assess the extent to which schools, curricula, and education structures and services have accommodated these changes.

In the years since 1999, Irish schools have encountered considerable challenges; ones that have demanded previously untried responses. Some merit consideration in this book, particularly as they inexorably influence your pre-service education, your sense of a growing professional identity and your prevailing understanding of the role of teachers in Irish society. To the fore are challenges around the inclusion of children with special learning needs in mainstream classrooms, the early and prompt identification of children with special learning needs, the need for schools to adjust to a significant increase in the number of children entering schools from a wide variety of ethnic backgrounds, the requirement to build a new sense of partnership with parents, and an emphasis on enhancing a sense of social inclusion (Teaching Council 2011). Significantly, there has also been acceleration in ICT research and the availability of new technologies developed for classroom usage and the advancement of teaching and learning strategies. The period has also seen the enactment of an assortment of legislation that continues to influence the daily work of teachers in significant ways. Significant pieces of legislation include the Education Act 1998, the Education (Welfare) Act 2000, the Equal Status Act 2000–2004, the National Qualifications Authority Act 2001, the Teaching Council Act 2001, the Education for Persons with Special Education Needs Act 2004 and the Disability Act 2005. Some of the spirit of this legislation might be gleaned from a key aspiration set out in the Preamble to the Education Act 1998; one that brings to the fore a key objective of giving practical effect to the rights of all children as they engage in education, ensuring that a quality of education appropriate to their needs and abilities be provided while also advancing equality of access to and participation in education. The Preamble contains the aspiration that

> the education provided respects the diversity of values, beliefs, languages and traditions in Irish society and is conducted in a spirit of partnership between schools, patrons, students, parents, teachers and other school staff, the community served by the school and the state.

In January 2010, the Free Pre-School Year (FPSY) was introduced with the specific purpose of making early learning opportunities available to all children aged more than three years and two months on 1 September in the relevant preschool year (Ring 2015). Another significant development was the introduction of the Primary Language Curriculum in September 2016.

All told, the rapid nature of change within society and the aforementioned background of legislative and education initiatives have also had a significant and lasting impact on this society's understanding of teacher education. It became increasingly obvious that in order to embrace these and other changes in society and schooling, a significant reconceptualisation of teacher education across its entire spectrum was required (Teaching Council 2011). The Teaching Council, which was charged with this reconceptualisation, took the view that

> innovation is essential at all stages of the continuum if teacher education is to be effective in meeting the changing needs identified.... The Council sees the concept of innovation as encompassing those processes whereby fresh thinking is applied to teacher education with the aim of renewing and improving it. Initial teacher education must be reconceptualised so that it is fit-for-purpose in preparing 21st century teachers.... (Teaching Council 2011: 8)

Deficiencies in older models of teacher education were noted, including a need to create a new balance and dynamic between theory and practice (Teaching Council 2011). An over-reliance on pre-service teacher education with clear insufficiencies evident in ongoing career and professional development, as well as notable inadequacies within the induction process for newly qualified teachers were cited (Teaching Council 2011). The limited exposure of prospective teachers to the ever-widening spectrum of school experiences in the form of pre-service school placement became evident, and it was advocated that the school placement

> should take place in a variety of settings and incorporate a variety of teaching situations and school contexts: different age groups of students; different sectors... various socio-economic and cultural environments; multi-class and mixed ability teaching situations; and team teaching/co-teaching situations. (Teaching Council, 2011: 13)

Addressing these issues has come to be viewed as essential, particularly so as 'to ensure that tomorrow's teachers are competent to meet the challenges that they face and are life-long learners, continually adapting over the course of their careers to enable them to support their students' learning' (Teaching Council 2011: 11–15).

## TASK 1.6: EXAMINING OUR ASSUMPTIONS

'Your assumptions are your windows on the world. Scrub them off every once in a while, or the light won't come in.'

Alan Alda, actor

Undoubtedly we all make many assumptions every day and assumptions are made about us. In the school situation, our assumptions can be very influential in our engagement as teachers with learners. In this exercise, choose a school setting that differs from your own primary school (e.g. single sex, multi-denominational, religious, urban, rural, DEIS, etc.) and pursue the following lines of inquiry:

- What assumptions could I make about my learners' families?
- What assumptions might I make based on where these learners live?
- What assumptions could I make about the gender of my learners and about what's 'appropriate' for different genders?
- What assumptions might I make about the kind of content my learners can manage?
- What assumptions could I make about my learners' values, way of life and life experiences?
- What other assumptions might come to mind?

(Adapted from Institute for Humane Education 2015)

## M-LEVEL TASK 1.2: THREE PILLARS OF TEACHER EDUCATION

Read the Teaching Council's policy document entitled *Policy on the Continuum of Teacher Education* (2011a). This document argues that policy on teacher education should be based on three pillars: innovation, integration and improvement. Assess how well the document manages to integrate these pillars into the policy as a whole.

## TEACHER EDUCATION: CHANGES AND CONSTANTS

Teacher education in Ireland has seen considerable review and reconfiguration in recent years at all levels of teaching: primary, secondary and further education. Reviews have been undertaken and are ongoing across many undergraduate and postgraduate programmes in teacher education. Attempts are being made to address issues such as an apparent theory–practice dichotomy, as well as the quality, duration and diversity of school placements and the length of pre-service education. At a more specific level, it is arguable that addressing many of the following issues, as they relate to the education of a prospective teacher, has emerged as a central concern in a number of key reviews (Teaching Council 2011; Teaching Council 2013a; Teaching Council 2013b; Teaching Council 2013c):

- Making critical reflection and reflective practice central to teacher education
- Developing and exploring our sense of teacher identity
- Recognising, appreciating and working positively within a diverse and constantly changing society with varied social and educational needs
- Recognising the essential contribution of educational research to teacher education
- Understanding that leadership is an intrinsic and ineluctable part of teacher education

These five themes are treated as deeply interrelated in this book and should also be seen as such in your journey within teacher education. While they are not listed in any particular order here, it is intended that the initial attribute of critical reflection will provide a strong basis for all other concerns and act as a key touchstone for the development of your teacher education programme. However, the attributes are best understood as being interwoven and interdependent, with the potential for incremental development in a wide variety of contexts. Tasks, problems and activities within this book will seek to develop these attributes in a manner relevant to your experience as student teachers and future teachers.

## Developing Reflection and Criticality in Teacher Education

**M-Level Task 1.3: The Place of Educational Theory**

Theory has often received a mixed reception within the teaching community. Speculate on why that may be the case. Develop some ideas in respect of what theory might or might not contribute to your identity as a teacher, drawing on Inglis's view below.

Those who refuse all theory, who speak of themselves as plain, practical people, and virtuous in virtue of having no theory, are in the grip of theories which manacle them and keep them immobile, because they have no way of thinking about them and therefore of taking them off. They aren't theory free; they are stupid theorists.

(Inglis 1985: 40)

The discourse of 'reflection', which is explored as a central and recurring theme throughout this book, has a lineage in teacher education. John Dewey was among the first theorists in this area to explore the concept of 'reflective practice' by examining the dynamics that exist between experience and reflection (Dewey 1933). He was motivated by the concern about a culture of dependency among teachers – a dependency on textbooks and other external authorities. This dependency, he believed, prompted many teachers to 'flock to those persons who give them clear-cut and definite instructions as to how to teach this or that' (Dewey 1902: 152). The development of professional judgements and decision-making skills were neglected to a point where teachers might 'accept without inquiry or criticism any method or device which seems to promise good results' (Dewey 1902: 152).

In addressing the question of reflection, Dewey sought to distinguish between actions that are merely routine and those that are reflective, with those described as routine often finding their sole justification in tradition and authority (Dewey 1933). Reflective actions, on the other hand, are seen as involving processes which actively, continually and thoughtfully address routines, rituals and beliefs in a manner that is holistic, open-minded, wholehearted and responsible (Dewey 1933). Significantly, the process is not to be restricted to the application of a ready-made set of techniques. Instead, Dewey argued that reflection 'enables us to direct our activities with foresight and to plan according to ends-in-view or purposes of which we are aware, to act in deliberate and intentional fashion, to know what we are about when we act' (1933: 17).

We shall see later in this book how Dewey's work acted as a basis for others, particularly Schön (1983) (See Chapter 2), who managed in different ways to locate the concept of reflection at the heart of discourse within teacher education, where it remains to the present day.

One key concern within the discourse of reflective theory is that of the integration of theory and practice. Integrating theory and practice involves your analysis of meaningful, recurring patterns of experience, the deliberative application of those examined experiences to your practice and then making further modifications based on those experiences in the light of your continued, systematic and regular critical reflection.

Since there are many definitions and claims made in respect of critical thinking and reflection, their consideration in this initial chapter has limitations. We will therefore consider a broad set of insights in relation to critical thinking and reflection. Critical thought will be viewed as an inextricable feature of teacher reflectiveness and as *the* 'abiding attitude or disposition' (Dunne 1993, cited by Kelleghan 2002: 45) that underpins teachers' identity and engagement in their classrooms and schools. This adherence to critical reflection within teacher education is based on the argument that

(h)uman existence, because it came into being through asking questions, is at the root of change in the world. There is a radical element to existence, which is the radical act of asking questions. At root, human existence involves surprise, questioning and risk. And because of this it involves actions and change. (Freire, cited in hooks 2009: 183)

It is indisputable that the development of critical thinking is key to our identity as reflective teachers or prospective teachers. For some, this may raise doubts or evoke a certain fear. Our experiences of schooling to date may not have encouraged it. American author and feminist bell hooks offers some reassurance; she contends the naturalness of criticality to the human condition, its rootedness in our humanity and its availability to us when we take the time and trouble to seek it:

> Children are organically predisposed to be critical thinkers. Across the boundaries of race, class, gender and circumstance, children come into the world of wonder and language consumed with a desire for knowledge. Sometimes they are so eager for knowledge that they become relentless interrogators – demanding to know the who, what, when, where and why of life. Searching for answers, they learn almost instinctively how to think. Sadly, children's passion for thinking often ends when they encounter a world that seeks to educate them for conformity and obedience only. Most children are taught early on that thinking is dangerous. (hooks 2009: 7–8)

---

### TASK 1.7: A CRITICAL THINKER

The following is a description of a critical thinker by Paul and Elder, prominent authorities on critical thinking. Assess their perspective. There may be factors within critical thinking that the authors have omitted. You might also identify areas where you have specific strengths and indeed accomplishments that require further work and development. Finally, you might offer a conjecture on how critical thinking might underpin worthwhile teaching.

A critical thinker:

- Raises vital questions and problems, formulating them clearly and precisely
- Gathers and assesses relevant information, using abstract ideas to interpret it effectively
- Comes to well-reasoned conclusions and solutions, testing them against relevant criteria and standards
- Thinks open-mindedly within alternative systems of thought, recognizing and assessing, as need be, their assumptions, implications, and practical consequences
- Communicates effectively with others in figuring out solutions to complex problems.

(Paul and Elder 2009: 11)

## DEVELOPING OUR IDENTITIES AS TEACHERS

Argyris and Schön (1974) argue that all humans require a developed disposition of reflective action as a prerequisite to the full development of their very humanity. If so, it is tenable that the exploration and development of our own identity, and, specifically, our teacher identity, should be a primary concern within this book.

Your time as a student teacher is a vital opportunity for you to develop your teacher identity. Throughout this book, we will seek to explore and discuss your experiences, recollections, perceptions, stories and situations. Such an approach will hopefully enrich the development of your sense of teacher identity. Student teachers can typically adopt some received notions of teacher identity that they may have gleaned from what they witnessed themselves in their years of schooling. However, exploring what it means to be a teacher with the support of critical guidance from teacher educators is crucial. Student teachers have the dual role of both students and teachers and may, therefore, 'labour under the responsibilities of independent and demanding roles that require a reformulation of identity' (Gaudelli and Ousley 2009: 936).

Developing Our Identities as Teachers

The very process of developing sustainable personal and professional identities is quite a complex and demanding one. By acknowledging Palmer's view that 'good teaching cannot be reduced to technique; good teaching comes from the identity and integrity of the teacher' (1998: 2), we can't avoid the seriousness of the issue of identity. One primary understanding of identity is that it is fluid and open to change: who we are now, how we think, what we feel, the values we hold, the perspectives we advance are not fixed forever. Our very identities, as they encounter changes, challenges and varying critical perspectives, can be seen to be in a process of continual renegotiation. Reflecting on emerging situations, and on how each individual's 'self' is challenged in fluid and varying contexts as it seeks to develop its own sense of authenticity and sustainability, is something to be welcomed. This concept of identity seems perennial, lacking finitude, and requires us to return, renew and reconsider with regularity, since

> teacher professional identity…stands at the core of the teaching profession. It provides a framework for teachers to construct their own ideas of 'how to be', 'how to act' and 'how to understand' their work and their place in society. Importantly, teacher identity is not something that is fixed, nor is it imposed; rather, it is negotiated through experience and the sense that is made of that experience. (Sachs 2005: 15)

In his book entitled *The Courage to Teach* (1998), Palmer asks teachers to undertake an expedition toward connecting with themselves, their vocation and their learners by examining their own lives and identities. He argues that the 'what' (content), the 'how' (our methods), and the 'why' (our justifications) of education have been discussed for years in various ways in education discourse; however, discussion of the 'who' or the identity of the teacher has been neglected since this has been seen as intrusive and overly personal for public sharing. Palmer argues that this inner self deserves our wholehearted attention. Three constituent and deeply interwoven elements of identity come from his analysis – the intellectual, the emotional and the spiritual – and he argues that each must be embraced equally (1998). If teaching was to be seen purely in terms of intellect, it might be reduced to an unemotional abstraction. Seeing teaching as an entirely emotional enterprise might be viewed as self-indulgent, and may reduce it to a solely spiritual quest, where some of its connectedness to reality might suffer. Consequently, all three elements are interdependent in teaching, simply because they are so interwoven within our humanity. Palmer explains all three as follows:

> By intellectual I mean the way we think about teaching and learning – the form and content of our concepts of how people know and learn, of the nature of our students and our subjects. By emotional I mean the way we and our students feel as we teach and learn – feelings that can either enlarge or diminish the exchange between us. By spiritual I mean the diverse ways we answer the heart's longing to be connected with

the largeness of life – a longing that animates love and work, especially the work called teaching. (Palmer 1998: 4–5)

Palmer goes much further than just examining a range of professional skills involved in being a teacher and in this way addresses the idea of teacher identity from a holistic viewpoint. His key question is: 'Who is the self that teaches?' (1998: 4), and he maintains that good teaching emanates from the identity and integrity of the teacher. He describes identity and integrity in the following ways:

> By identity I mean an evolving nexus where all the forces that constitute my life converge in the mystery of self: my genetic makeup, the nature of the man and woman who gave me life, the culture in which I was raised, people who have sustained me and people who have done me harm, the good and ill I have done to others and to myself, the experience of love and suffering – and much, much more.... By integrity I mean whatever wholeness I am able to find within that nexus as its vectors form and re-form the pattern of my life. Integrity requires that I discern what is integral to my selfhood, what fits and what does not – and that I choose life-giving ways of relating to the forces that converge within me: Do I welcome them or fear them, embrace them or reject them, move with them or against them. (Palmer 1998: 13–14)

Of significance, therefore, are questions about values and how you develop ethical dispositions in relation to both your own sense of self, and to other people and their ongoing professional engagement. It may seem that no artificial divide between different aspects of your life can prevail, nor can a generic teaching 'template' be applied when you, as an individual self, enter with integrity into the turbulent milieu of human learning, as this very profound encounter with learners can be seen as nothing less than participating in the 'building of true human life' (Buber 1947: 113).

This approach to identity can therefore challenge your present conceptions of yourself and your choices, your understanding of your so-called fixed traits, your personal understanding of continuity and habits, your conformity to others' ideals and ultimately your ideas of what constitutes 'you'. It raises provocative, uncomfortable and challenging questions about freedom of choice, and the possible fallibility of some of your traditions and precedents; it may point you towards a more critical interrogation of your comfortable routines, and supports a view of the self as 'a continuous reflexive project' (Hargreaves, 1994: 71), involving struggle, reassessment and openness to change.

### TASK 1.8: DEVELOPING AN IDENTITY JOURNAL

Developing an identity journal should take place over a lengthy period of time. The process is not prescriptive and the thoughts expressed in your journal are private and should not be intended for others. You can return to your journal as ideas develop, and are challenged and overtaken by other insights. You may wish to consider some of the following questions as prompts to your thinking.

Why have I decided to become a teacher? Did I really choose it? Did other people tell me it 'would be a good idea' and did I then do what others expected of me? Did I long to do otherwise and develop another career? If I say I decided to become a teacher 'to get a job', why do I say that? How do my motivations to become a teacher influence my perceptions of teaching?

What are my key values and beliefs and how do they influence my perception of teaching? How does the learning context I'm living through as a student teacher impact on my ability to put these beliefs and values into practice? Should I explore my teaching identity and give it expression in the classroom? In what ways is my identity evolving over the course of time? How do I match my evolving personal identity with my learners' evolving needs, interests and identities?

## Societal Change and Student Teachers

The pace of change in Ireland's educational, social and cultural landscape has accelerated considerably throughout the last two decades. Analyses have critiqued older assumptions about societal homogeneity and have indicated that the integration of children from diverse cultural and linguistic backgrounds and the associated implications require considerable attention in this society (Condon 2015). The effect of integration on schools is ongoing, sometimes major and often quite varied. Information amassed during the Department of Education and Skills' (DES) annual census for the school year 2013–2014 indicates that 23 per cent of Irish schools educated almost 80 per cent of children of newcomer families (cited by Duncan 2015). Clearly this period has seen demographic changes within many school communities, with considerable challenges and opportunities afforded by the integration of many different newcomer families.

---

**TASK 1.9: US AND THEM**

A report suggests that 'research shows there is a conception of "us" and "them" among some students, identifying white, settled, Catholic students as the "norm" and those from minority groups as "other". This perception can come across in the language of students and of teachers' (Devine 2005, cited in Carey *et al.* 2008: 26).

Explore this viewpoint by drawing on and sharing your own experiences in recent years, paying particular attention to intercultural education.

---

Pertinent to these considerable changes has been the need for teachers to develop a growing awareness of such opportunities and challenges, and teachers have been informed by publications such as *Guidelines on Intercultural Education in the Primary School* (NCCA 2005), in which intercultural education is defined as having two focal points:

> [In the first instance, it is an education that] respects, celebrates and recognises the normality of diversity in all areas of human life. It sensitises the learner to the idea that humans have naturally developed a range of different ways of life, customs and worldviews, and that this breadth of human life enriches all of us. [Second]…it is education [that] promotes equality and human rights, challenges unfair discrimination, and promotes the values upon which equality is built. (3)

Equally, the ongoing inclusion of children with special learning needs within mainstream schooling, the development of various programmes to counter inequality in education, the initiation of debate regarding the ownership and patronage of schools, the adoption of newer technologies, changes in family structures and hierarchies, and other developments would all indicate that the education of teachers requires the development, and the incorporation and application, of criticality and reflection in respect of established and emerging policy positions. Such a pathway of reflective criticality may be seen as central to the development of engaged professionalism and responsible citizenship, both of which identities are informed by and reflective of the view that 'critical thinking means that the critical person has not only the capacity (the skills) to seek reasons, truth, and evidence, but also that he or she has the drive (disposition) to seek them' (Burbules and Berk 1999: 48).

How do you prepare as a student teacher to understand and address the diversity of learners' needs, especially when this diversity may differ considerably from your own experience of schooling? Currently, there is little agreement in the literature on teacher education regarding a recommended singular approach for you to take (Churton, Cranston-Gingras and Blair 1998; Cochran-Smith 2004; Darling-Hammond and Bransford 2007).

Even the very language we use in this sphere needs scrutiny. Words such as 'diversity', 'inclusion', 'integration' and 'needs' are contested and may mean different things to different people. Considering the ongoing trend towards diversity among our school-age population, some discontinuity of culture, language, experiential backgrounds, expectations, values, and patterns of communication and interaction between teachers (including student teachers) and the learners in their classrooms may exist. To explore this further, you might begin by asking yourself the following questions:

- What is my understanding of diversity?
- How open am I to cultures, perspectives and ways of life other than my own familiar patterns?
- How can I develop my understanding of other cultures and ways of life?
- How might that benefit my development as a person and as a teacher?
- What might I surmise from this about entry to teacher education in Ireland?
- If I conclude that entry is less reflective of diversity than I might prefer, can I seek to explain that? How might it be addressed? Indeed, should it be addressed?
- What is my view of the following aspiration in respect of schools in Ireland from the NCCA report *Diversity and Inclusion*?

> An inclusive school welcomes, recognises, respects and celebrates diversity. A commitment to achieve equality of access, opportunity, participation and outcome for all its students is a foundational principle of an inclusive school. From the perspective of the learner, it is a school where the learner feels comfortable engaging with all aspects of schooling; where he/she has a strong sense that the school is working for them, in their interest; where she/he feels a genuine sense of belonging and well-being. (NCCA 2009: 8)

Questions in relation to the above aspiration might be:

- How is such an all-inclusive school to be achieved?
- How do I as a student teacher recognise my own strengths, talents, prejudices, fears and limitations, and how can that knowledge assist me in contributing to such a school?
- How does my own education influence me in respect of this statement?
- How am I challenged by this perspective?

In asking the above questions, we are exercising our innate sense of criticality and ability to think critically. Central to this book is the view that critical thinking empowers us, is based on discernment, is inherently democratic, helps to ensure a strong link between theory and practice, requires a willingness to detach ourselves from our established views and maintain the belief in the fallibility of our inquiry, and reminds us that none of us has a monopoly on the answers. Re-examining some of our previously held views may be difficult or troubling, and yet may yield a sense of freedom and deep insight. bell hooks, while writing in terms of the classroom, posits the view that such a sense of criticality is deeply inherent to our own development and the development of societal well-being:

> The classroom with all its limitations remains a location of possibility. In that field of possibility we have the opportunity to labour for freedom, to demand of ourselves and our comrades an openness of mind and heart that allows us to face reality even as we collectively imagine ways to move beyond boundaries, to transgress. This is education as the practice of freedom. (hooks 1994: 207)

---

**M-LEVEL TASK 1.4: WHAT DOES IT MEAN TO BE IRISH?**

Give some in-depth consideration to the following ideas and questions:

What does it mean to be Irish in the Ireland of today? Within the Irish population there is a great deal of diversity in terms of ways of living, beliefs and values. Yet, do we maintain and uphold a narrow definition of Irishness in the Irish primary classroom of today? Do culture and tradition define who we are? Is it necessary to define what it means to be Irish before we can understand the ethnicity of others? (adapted from INTO 2004).

---

## Student Teachers and Research

Historically, much has been written about the relationship between teachers and research. This relationship has, at times, been seen as ruptured, underdeveloped and in need of considerable reinvigoration (Hargreaves 1999). The debate has often focussed on the dichotomies apparent between theory and practice in education. Many teachers, it has been contended, viewed 'theory (as) the soft-centre, not the hard-core around which their everyday practice revolves' (Richmond 1970: 23). Engaging with theory might have been viewed as either a form of 'philosophical abstruseness' or its very opposite: namely an indulgence in 'small talk about the tricks of the trade' (Richmond 1970: 23). Some perceived educational theory as being possibly detrimental to teachers and that it served only to obfuscate 'such natural understanding and seriousness as they might have' (Wilson 1975: 119). In many cases, however, teachers felt a skills deficit in respect of the rigours of undertaking research. In other instances, institutional and research traditions seemed to exclude the teacher practitioner. However, an emerging and discernible shift in emphasis can be noted. This has involved a move from a degree of over-reliance on the non-teaching expert in the sphere of research towards the idea of the teacher–researcher, a concept wherein the activity of ongoing research is inherent to the teacher's identity, so much so that

> (t)here can be no educational research if teachers play no important role in the process of articulating, analysing and hypothesising solutions to complex educational problems. The specialist inquiries of professional researchers should be viewed as subordinate to this fundamental process. (Elliott 1990: 16)

It is clear that classrooms and schools are abundant with possibilities for worthwhile research. Equally, every student teacher and practising teacher has a rich set of experiences that they have garnered in school settings, including impressions, fixed ideas, recollections, notions about teaching, perspectives, recalled conversations, tentative theories and assumptions. Within the long continuum of becoming and practising as a teacher, it is significant to note that you can pursue what Cochran-Smith and Lytle call an 'inquiry stance' toward your own endeavours, a position that is 'critical and transformative'. This is linked not just to high standards for all learners but to 'social justice' and 'the individual and collective professional growth of teachers'. Teachers are empowered by such a stance because it 'talks back to, and challenges, many of the assumptions that define teaching and research on teaching in the current era' (Cochran-Smith and Lytle 2009: 44).

Therefore, as a student teacher, you will encounter progressive challenges in the acquisition and development of research competencies. As you progress in teacher education, you will also encounter the opportunity to engage in a sustained piece of demanding and reflective research in the form of an undergraduate dissertation. It is envisaged that the incremental development of research competencies will ultimately contribute to the development of a research-based profession; one that is self-sustaining, resourceful and imbued with the view that 'theory is lived in practice and practice becomes a form of living theory' (McNiff and Whitehead 2002: 35). Towards this achievement, the qualities of critical reflectivity emerge as essential, and the benefits are multiple. A research consciousness among teachers allows adaptability in terms of engagement with learners, an ability to interpret, evaluate and adapt evidence from a broad spectrum of sources, an enhanced capacity to make decisions based on evaluated evidence, and a capacity to compare, differentiate and ultimately inform situations in a reflective and critical manner. In that sense teaching will move from being a dependent role to being one of engaged praxis, characterised by confidence among teachers 'that their kind of theorizing, relating closely and dialectically with practice, is actually the core of educational studies and not just the endpoint of a system for adapting and delivering outside theories' (Walsh 1993: 43). In this book, readers will be introduced to some of the intricacies of research and some viable opportunities for inquiry (see Chapter 6). At the core of such an introduction lies the key touchstone of developing our sense of critical reflection, an attribute that challenges and disturbs previously held opinions with regularity and insightfulness.

---

### Task 1.10: What Is the Place of Educational Research?

Place the following benefits of educational research in your preferred rank order and offer some reasons to support your choice. You might then attempt to add at least three further benefits of educational research to your list. Before doing this, you might read the passage below, which offers a rationale for educational inquiry.

The benefits of educational research:

- Research insight can shape understanding.
- Research can inform action.
- Research should have inferences for broader project and policy implementation.
- Research can solve existing problems.
- Research should inform decision-making.
- Research can allow us to develop an in-depth analysis of complex problems.

A rationale for educational research:

> Teachers are more than technicians or purveyors of information. Accordingly, they must be committed to lifelong intellectual, personal, and professional growth. Because both faculty and teacher candidates must continually develop these habits of mind, teacher education programs must stimulate the exploration and development of the full range of human capabilities. Thus, all our teacher education programs foster intellectual curiosity and encourage an appreciation of learning through the sustained analysis of ideas, values, and practices; and through intuition, imagination, and aesthetic experience. Teacher candidates are expected to develop a philosophy of teaching and learning. This philosophy and continuous professional growth should include values, commitments, and professional development.... This commitment means that undergraduate instructors rarely tell teacher candidates what it means to be an effective teacher, but instead provide guidance along with intellectual and practical entry points into the range of literature, scholarly debates, and experiences that help define contemporary education. Candidates, as a result of this inquiry orientation, will

develop the understandings necessary to become effective teachers. In other words, 'inquiry' and 'practice', 'research' and 'teaching', 'thinking' and 'doing' are expected to be integrated concepts and activities, rather than oppositional ones. (Indiana University Bloomington 2015)

## Student Teachers as Leaders

### TASK 1.11: TEACHING AS LEADERSHIP

Review the following extract and discuss how the school situation described might differ from your experiences as a learner in primary school. Equally, you might speculate on the significant challenges such an approach would imply for you as a prospective teacher. How would you define teacher leadership? What hinders you from leading at times? Can you describe any experiences or situations where you were hindered from leading? Have you observed examples of good leadership in your past experiences (from students, teachers, support staff, parents, the community, etc.). In your opinion, what typifies these examples as noteworthy?

'I expect all the teachers in our school to think of themselves as pedagogical leaders,' said Martti Hellström, the principal of Aurora Primary School. All teachers are actively engaged in designing the school curriculum and setting the learning goals for their pupils. It's also up to teachers to assess how well their pupils achieve the learning goals because there are no external standardized tests in Finland. When asked about his role as the leader of the school, Hellström replied that he was 'like the leader of an orchestra. I try to get the best out of each and every person in our school.' Although teacher leadership is not a commonly used term in Finland, most teachers have a sense of leadership as members of a professional learning community in their schools. (Sahlberg 2013: 37)

Excellent leadership qualities are now seen as key features of a teacher's profile and are judged to be central to the development of learning, the development of schools, the undertaking of initiatives, the advancement of change and the formulation of policies within schools. It is envisaged that leadership capacity, based on reflective criticality, a keen research consciousness and an understanding of the dynamics of leadership, will further the professional capacity of teachers. Critically, the concept of leadership is one that now permeates all teachers' engagement and is no longer just the concern of principals and other promoted teachers. Teachers display leadership in a variety of ways.

Some roles are formal and have designated responsibilities, while other more informal roles can emerge as teachers develop greater competence as a result of interacting with their learners and peers. The variety of leadership roles ensures that teachers can provide leadership in a manner that is congruent with their talents and interests. Irrespective of the roles they assume, teacher leaders contribute to the culture of their schools, improve learning and influence practice among their peers. Teacher leaders model and promote the use of systematic inquiry as a critical component of teachers' ongoing learning and development. Fullan does not overstate the importance of this ongoing learning and development when he asserts:

> (t)o go down the path towards excellence requires a high-capacity teaching profession and school leaders to work collectively in focused ways on the consolidation of current success, and on the further development of the innovative learning methods essential for a complex but exciting global world. (Fullan 2013: 5)

As an inherent aspect of teacher identity, leadership underpins all aspects of school management, assessment, mentoring, collaborative work, curriculum development, in-service provision, methodological research and innovation, evaluation and implementation of technological and other advances, as well as many other emerging areas within education. As mentioned, teachers demonstrate leadership in varied, sometimes interwoven, ways. Education programmes for aspiring teachers seek to incorporate the development of leadership and its attributes as a key element, thus launching pre-service teachers on a leadership pathway that aims to ensure that they

> continue their professional growth throughout their careers [and] they also continue developing the knowledge, skills, and dispositions of teacher leaders even as they serve as change agents in their schools. By beginning the process earlier in their careers, they will be better prepared to grow into and assume greater and greater teacher leadership roles as practicing teachers. (Bond 2011: 294)

---

**M-LEVEL TASK 1.5: OVERCOMING OBSTACLES TO LEADERSHIP**

Download and review the article entitled 'Overcoming the Obstacles to Leadership' by Moore, S. and Donaldson, M.L. (2007) (http://www.ascd.org/publications). Seek out parallels and differences between your experiences and those cited in the article. Evaluate the article on the basis of different cultural understandings and traditions of leadership. Assess the relevance of its recommendations to your situation and your disposition in terms of the demands of leadership.

## A SUMMARY OF KEY POINTS

- In recent times, teachers in Ireland have encountered many changes that are the result of a rapidly altering society, particularly the inclusion of learners with special educational needs in the mainstream system and the previously unparalleled rate of integration of learners from different ethnic and cultural backgrounds.
- In this more diverse society, the teacher's role has required considerable re-examination; foremost to this is the concept of the teacher as a life-long learner in an era of continuing change and professional reassessment.
- Critical reflection and reflective practice are deeply intertwined with the idea of teachers as life-long learners and are also central concepts in teacher education.
- As reflective practitioners, we can bring recognition of the essential contribution of educational research to our work and help to ensure that our teaching is engaging, vitalised and informed by meaningful and appropriate insight and knowledge.
- A rich and varied understanding of leadership is an intrinsic and ineluctable part of our evolving identity as reflective and responsive educators.

# CHAPTER TWO

# Becoming a Critically Reflective Teacher

*What is reflective teaching?*

*Are there different levels of reflection?*

*How can theory help me develop as a reflective teacher?*

Once you have worked through this chapter, you will have:

- Reviewed your own beliefs about learning and teaching.
- Been introduced to some key theorists in the field of reflective practice.
- Developed your understanding of reflection and critical thinking.
- Seen the connections between reflective practice and professional learning.
- Been introduced to the core perspectives and skills of the reflective practitioner.
- Explored a number of frameworks to promote structured reflective thinking.
- Engaged with reflective writing at different levels of depth.

## INTRODUCTION

Teaching is a complex and often puzzling endeavour. As a teacher starting out, there is a lot to learn. Reflecting on your teaching experiences and interactions is an essential part of the process of becoming a teacher. By reflecting, we mean interrogating formative moments that occurred in your learning and teaching experiences through the lens of your current knowledge of educational theory, with a view to deepening your awareness and improving your practice. A reflective approach to teaching will help you to become flexible, self-analytical and responsive to the complex dynamics of classroom interaction. It will help to liberate you from limiting assumptions that you may hold about learners, learning and teaching. It will enable you to act in a more deliberative and intentional manner while taking responsibility for your actions and their effects. Your school placement experiences will require you to respond appropriately to students of different backgrounds, abilities, motivations and learning styles. Accommodating such differences requires you to be skilful and reflective.

An explicit goal of reflective practice is to create deeper understanding and insight, which forms the basis for continually improving your teaching practice throughout your career. Becoming a reflective practitioner involves a commitment to growth and professional development, and being aware of a range of possible choices and responses to every classroom situation. Building the habit of reflective practice will help you to remain adaptable in the ever-changing environment of the classroom.

## STARTING WITH YOUR BELIEFS

The literature on teacher learning acknowledges that prior to embarking on your teacher education programme you developed views about learning and teaching as a result of your experiences a student. In other words, long before you commenced your programme of teacher education, you were already engaged in an 'apprenticeship of observation' for at least 13 years during your time in primary and post-primary school (Lortie 1975). This 'apprenticeship of observation' promotes the formulation of beliefs or personal theories about the nature of teaching and learning. Identifying and reflecting on these theories and beliefs will help you to recognise within yourself certain dispositions that may either augment or limit your capacity to understand, accommodate and engage your learners appropriately. From research and experience we have found that student teachers tend to assume that their prospective learners will have orientations towards learning and emotional needs similar to their own (Hollingsworth 1989; Knowles and Holt-Reynolds 1991). For example, student teachers who found certain aspects of learning enjoyable during their schooling often assume that this will also hold true for their learners. Student teachers who were isolated or bullied by their peers tend to have a particular sensitivity towards learners who are affected by such behaviours.

While predispositions that derive from our own experiences may benefit certain learners within our classes, these perspectives are usually too narrow and limited to meet the diverse needs of all the learners in any one classroom. Hence, a key aspiration within teacher education is to provide opportunities for student teachers to identify and interrogate their prior conceptions, beliefs and experiences of learning and teaching. This will help to expand, balance and contextualise these beliefs, thereby rendering them more responsive to the varying needs of learning and teaching. Such focus is highlighted by the Teaching Council in its policy document on teacher education:

> Initial teacher education should be mindful of, and challenge as appropriate, the attitudes and beliefs about teaching and learning which student teachers carry with them and which inform and guide their professional practice. (Teaching Council 2011: 11)

## Personal Learning Timeline

In order to expand and modify our beliefs, research has shown that reflection and inquiry are necessary. Reflection helps to challenge our well-worn commonsensical ideas through a process of systematic inquiry, thereby promoting professional growth and development.

---

**TASK 2.1: TIMELINE AS A LEARNER**

As a starting point to looking at your latent beliefs about learning and teaching, draw a timeline of your own experiences as a learner, highlighting key moments, experiences and insights that you derived along the way. This can include relationships with certain teachers and/or classmates, achievements, disappointments, extracurricular activities, etc. Do not include personal names or details that could identify anyone in your timeline. Figure 2.1 presents a sample of a personal learning timeline.

---

Figure 2.1: Example of a Personal Learning Timeline

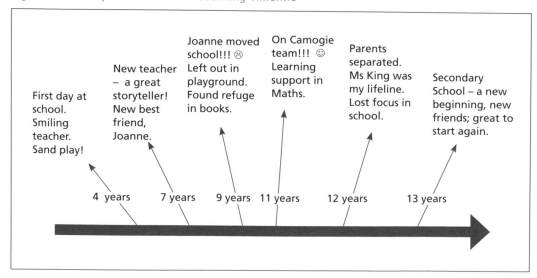

**TASK 2.2: PERSONAL BELIEF FORMATION TIMELINE**

Having drawn your timeline described in Task 2.1 in as much detail as possible, revisit each experience that you have marked and ask yourself what belief about yourself, learning or teaching was created, consolidated or challenged as a result of each experience. See Figure 2.2 for an example of a personal belief formation timeline.

Recall an incident from your primary or post-primary schooling that had an impact on you either positively or negatively. Explain why it was significant and what you learned from this experience.

Write a paragraph beginning with each of the following:

- Given my current understanding of teaching, I would like to be a teacher who...
- My current understanding of learning means that, as a teacher, I will...
- A personal metaphor that illustrates my current understanding of teaching: In my view, teaching can be compared to...

Figure 2.2: Example of a Personal Belief Formation Timeline

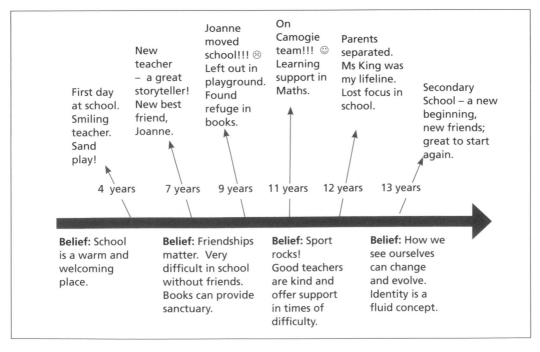

## Student Teachers' Beliefs about Learning and Teaching

According to recent research, the following key beliefs were held by Irish student teachers at the point of entry to their teacher education programmes (Horgan 2015).

Learning is facilitated when learners:

- Feel safe.
- Are praised by the teacher.
- Are contented in class.
- Are trusted and treated fairly.
- Are motivated and challenged.
- Have their needs and abilities addressed.

Effective teachers:

- Are liked and remembered.
- Create a positive atmosphere in class.
- Are confident.
- Promote participation.
- Are patient and maintain a sense of calm.
- Make learning an enjoyable experience.

---

### TASK 2.3: EXPLORING OUR PERSONAL BELIEFS ABOUT LEARNING AND TEACHING

Read the statements from Horgan (2015) above and rank them in order according to your personal understandings of learning and teaching.

- Do you have other beliefs that you can add to this list?
- How can we know if our beliefs are true?

Beliefs about learning and teaching such as the above read like rules of thumb. Can you think of exceptions to these rules?

Write exceptions to the beliefs that you hold most strongly and think of situations or contexts where this opposite belief might also be true. For example, take the belief that effective teachers are liked. An exception is that effective teachers are not always liked; effective teachers sometimes have to make difficult decisions for which they may not be liked by their learners.

---

## REFLECTIVE PRACTICE

There are many definitions of reflective practice. But before we explore some of these, we would like you to consider how you might define reflective practice. What does the term reflective practice mean to you? How would you define it?

## Task 2.4: Defining Reflective Practice

Consider the following definitions of reflective practice from a range of different authors. Choose the definition/s that resonate/s strongly with your own views. Outline your reasons for your choice.

Teaching, like any truly human activity, emerges from one's inwardness, for better or for worse. As I teach, I project the condition of my soul onto my students, my subject, and our way of being together. The entanglements I experience in the classroom are often no more or less than the convolutions of my inner life. Viewed from this angle, teaching holds a mirror to the soul. If I am willing to look in that mirror and not run from what I see, I have a chance to gain self-knowledge – and knowing myself is as crucial to good teaching as knowing my students and my subject. (Palmer 1998: 2)

Reflective practice is viewed as a means by which practitioners can develop a greater level of self-awareness about the nature and impact of their performance, an awareness that creates opportunities for professional growth and development. (Osterman and Kottkamp 2004: 2)

The practitioner allows himself to experience surprise, puzzlement, or confusion in a situation which he finds uncertain or unique. He reflects on the phenomenon before him, and on the prior understandings which have been implicit in his behaviour. He carries out an experiment which serves to generate both a new understanding of the phenomenon and a change in the situation. (Schön 1983: 68)

Reflection is a window through which the practitioner can view and focus self within the context of her own lived experience in ways that enable her to confront, understand and work towards resolving the contradictions within her practice between what is desirable and actual practice. (Johns 2000: 34)

Reflective thinking is not a new concept. Socrates, in Plato's *Meno*, saw reflection as 'the discovery of what is within, which is brought to consciousness by questioning' (Plato 1956: 130–9). The writings of many theologians and philosophers throughout the ages contain references to reflection, meditation and contemplation. In the decade 1970 to 1980, a small number of international scholars and teacher educators wrote about reflection. Their work was based, in large part, on John Dewey's (1909, 1933) concept of reflective teaching. Dewey's view of teaching offered an alternative to the competency-based approach to teacher education, which considered teaching as a formulaic, technical endeavour that focussed solely on the development of certain skills.

More recently, the concepts of reflection and reflective teaching have received wide interest and application in the field of teacher education. Below, we present a brief overview of the contributions made by some key figures to our understanding of reflective practice.

## John Dewey

In his book *How We Think*, published in 1933, Dewey suggests that a primary purpose of education is to develop the habit of reflection so we can engage in intelligent thought and action rather than routine thought and action. For Dewey, routine thought is not reflective. It is based on taken-for-granted assumptions and responds to what is expected in the situation. Routine thought does not challenge the status quo of our internal or external realities.

Dewey (1933, 1938) presents reflection as a form of thought that arises from a puzzling or confusing situation and leads to a search for new information. In other words, Dewey argues that the process of reflection is ignited in response to an unanticipated situation. According to Dewey, reflective thinking generally addresses practical problems or problems of practice.

Developing the Art of Reflection

---

### TASK 2.5: HOW WE THINK – APPLYING DEWEY'S IDEAS

Read the following application of Dewey's ideas on thinking. Can you identify the stages of the reflective process here that align with those outlined by Dewey?

In life, we are often faced with situations that require us to problem-solve. Have you ever lost your keys or misplaced something valuable? What mental processes do you typically go through? Maybe initially you experience confusion and upset. This may be followed by a wide array of ideas as to the whereabouts of the lost item. Gradually, you may begin to evaluate a range of possible locations for the lost item that will lead to the elimination or retention of some possibilities. The remaining options may be tested hypothetically as to their feasibility. Eventually, a limited number of possible solutions may be favoured and then tested in the reality of experience.

---

Dewey maintains that reflective thinking requires us to evaluate our beliefs and assumptions continuously in order to consider other plausible interpretations of events and experiences (Dewey 1933). Our resulting decisions should always remain open to further scrutiny and reformulation. He defines reflection as:

> active, persistent and careful consideration of any belief or supposed form of knowledge in the light of the grounds that support it and the further conclusions to which it leads…it includes a conscious and voluntary effort to establish belief upon a firm basis of evidence and rationality. (Dewey 1933: 9)

According to Dewey, reflective thinking involves a combination of *rational thought*, where we reach a conclusion based on reasoning, and *intuitive thought*, where we allow new ideas, solutions and insights to arise spontaneously. Dewey highlights that reflection is an active cognitive process, involving sequences of interconnected ideas, which take account of underlying beliefs and knowledge. He states that the attitudes we bring to reflection can either open up the possibility of gaining insight into our practice or shut it down. The attitudes he considers essential to reflective thought are open-mindedness, wholeheartedness and responsibility.

Open-mindedness involves a willingness to listen to and consider viewpoints that are different to our own and an openness to the possibility that even our most embedded beliefs may be limited or erroneous (Dewey 1933). Wholeheartedness involves a dedication to the process of inquiry, regardless of any personal cost so that:

Teachers who are wholehearted regularly examine their own assumptions and beliefs and the results of their actions, and approach all situations with the attitude that they can learn something new. (Zeichner and Liston 2014: 12)

Dewey's final prerequisite, responsibility, involves questioning what we are doing and why we are doing it. It requires us to consider both the intended and unintended results of our actions. Responsibility asks us to question, not just if our methods are working, but also who they serve and who they do not serve. This kind of inquiry might lead us, for example, to a realisation that our instruction is not culturally appropriate or sufficiently differentiated to address the needs of some learners within our classes, leading to the unintended consequence of frustration or low self-esteem on the part of those whom our teaching does not serve.

## Max van Manen

van Manen (1977) identified three levels of reflection: (a) technical, (b) practical and (c) critical. van Manen's model is sequential and hierarchical, with each level being a prerequisite for the next.

The first level, *technical reflection,* is concerned with the effectiveness of strategies or methods to achieve certain objectives or goals. Here we are concerned with what works and what doesn't, but we do not question the appropriateness or suitability of our methods or learning goals. Typical questions we might ask ourselves when reflecting at this level might be:

- How can I get all the learners to listen to me?
- How can I ensure that the learners move quietly to the PE hall?
- Did I have the correct amount of activities in my Maths lesson?
- How can I get Marie and Ruth to pay better attention?
- How can I effect smooth transitions between activities?

The second type of reflection, *practical reflection*, allows for examination not only of means but also of goals. In contrast to technical reflection, this involves an examination of the assumptions that we are making with regard to a particular situation or experience. For example, the question that we raised above – 'How can I get all the learners to listen to me?' – might lead to a review of our assumptions about learning. Does this question assume that learning cannot occur without listening? Or, conversely, can learning be taking place when it appears that the learners are not listening to me? Why might they not listen to me? The lens of consideration now expands to embrace not just what we are doing as teachers but also what our learners might be doing, and why.

Are my expectations that Marie and Ruth pay attention at variance with their need for active learning? Are my expectations regarding behaviour age appropriate? In exploring a situation from this perspective we clarify our assumptions and expectations, consider new ideas and assess the educational consequences of our actions. At this level, we analyse both teacher and learner behaviours to see if and how our goals are met. We also check if there is a consistency between what we say we believe (our espoused theories) and what we actually do in the classroom (our theories in use). In other words, we reflect on whether we practise what we preach. For example, our espoused theories might embrace constructivism and problem-solving methodologies, yet we may use a didactic, teacher-directed style that allows for diminished opportunities for active engagement on the part of our learners. If, through reflection, we notice this discrepancy and explore the reasons for it, we may find that the underlying cause is a fear that we may be unable to manage the class if learners are given more freedom to move and engage actively. Now our focus is appropriately directed towards the need to build our confidence and competence in classroom management so that the disequilibrium between how we want to teach and how we actually do is brought into balance, ensuring more congruence between our values and our practice.

Typical questions we might reflect on at the practical reflection level are:

- Am I giving my learners sufficient opportunities to develop decision-making skills?
- How can I build in better accountability on the part of learners for collaborative learning tasks (see Chapter 5)?
- What can I do to help students make connections to their prior knowledge?
- Are my learning goals appropriate?

The third level, *critical reflection*, embraces and develops from the previous two levels. At the level of critical reflection, we are also called to review moral and ethical considerations, such as judgements about whether or not our teaching is equitable, just and respectful of all. Critical reflection locates our analysis of personal action within the wider socio-historical and sociocultural contexts. Here we strive to uncover the spectrum of intended and unintended consequences of our actions and to consider the many dilemmas we face on a daily basis in the classroom. The following excerpt from a student teacher's reflective journal while on school placement highlights an example of one such dilemma:

> *Discipline was another big challenge for me. Challenge in that I set up a reward system and it worked really, really well. But it was only halfway through the teaching practice that I realised that I didn't like the reward system, even though it was working – that I didn't like what it was relaying to the children. I realised that I was using a stimulus–response approach to classroom management, and this was at variance with my belief in child-centred and constructivist approaches. (Fionn)*

So, like Fionn, to move to the level of critical reflection, we need to query the 'givens' or the taken-for-granted assumptions of our practice. Larrivee and Cooper delineate the key aspects of critical reflection as follows:

> Questioning of underlying assumptions, biases, and values one brings to bear on their teaching.
>
> Conscious consideration of the ethical implications and consequences of practices on learners and their learning.
>
> Examination of how instructional and other classroom practices contribute to social equity and to the establishment of a just society.
>
> Extended awareness beyond immediate instructional circumstances to include caring about democratic foundations and encouraging socially responsible actions.
>
> (2006: 12)

## Donald Schön

In the early 1980s, the concept of reflective practice was popularised by the work of Schön. Schön (1983, 1987) criticised the prevalent perception of practitioner as technician, replacing it with a portrayal of practitioner as decision maker, or reflective practitioner. According to Schön, reflective practitioners continually learn by reconstructing experience through reflection. He describes 'knowing-in-action' as the predictable response to familiar situations. However, when an event or situation does not accord with expectations and the experience is unfamiliar, professionals respond by thinking while doing. This on-the-spot response he termed 'reflection-in-action'. Compared to Dewey's notion of reflection, this type of activity does not rely on a series of conscious steps in a decision-making process. Instead, the knowledge is inherent in the action. It is based, in part, on the past experiences of the practitioner being brought to bear on the particular situation. This brings forth and expands upon a tacit knowledge in an individual that is not consciously articulated at the time.

In contrast to reflection-in-action, which occurs during the teaching event, 'reflection-on-action' is the form of reflection that occurs after action. In other words, its role in the learning process is retrospective, helping to inform action and develop theory.

While Schön's work has inspired many models of reflection and categories of reflective practice, it has also drawn criticism for lack of clarity (Eraut 2004), for ignoring the context of reflection (Boud and Walker 1998) and even because the pivotal concept of reflection-in-action is deemed unachievable (Moon 1999).

---

### M-Level Task 2.1: How Feasible Is Reflection-in-Action?

Read and reflect on the following article:

van Manen, M. (1995), 'On the Epistemology of Reflective Practice,' *Teachers and Teaching: Theory and Practice*, 1(1): 33–50, available from: http://www.maxvanmanen. com/files/2011/04/1995-EpistofReflective-Practice.pdf.

In this article, van Manen questions the feasibility of Schön's concept of reflection-in-action.

Having read the article, consider the following questions:

- How reflective is the active moment in which the teacher is engaged with the learners in her/his charge?
- How valid is the concept of reflection-in-action (thinking about doing something while doing it) as evoked by Schön?

---

## Stephen Brookfield

Brookfield (1998) maintains that critically reflective teaching occurs when we identify and interrogate the assumptions that underpin how we work. Brookfield acknowledges that this is difficult work and 'very few of us can get very far on our own' (197).

No matter how much we may think we have an accurate sense of ourselves, we are stymied by the fact that we are using our interpretive filters to become aware of our own interpretive filters. This is the equivalent of a dog trying to catch its tail, or trying to see the back of your head while looking in the bathroom mirror (Brookfield 1998).

Those of us who have persisted in our quest to see the back of our head or to view an outfit from behind know the value of other strategically placed mirrors to provide that 360-degree view that is needed! In a similar way, Brookfield (1998) coined the term 'critical lenses' to denote different perspectives that 'reflect back to us a stark and differently highlighted picture of who we are and what we do' (197).

### Critically Reflective Lens 1: Our Autobiography as a Learner

Brookfield considered this lens as 'one of the most important sources of insight into practice to which we have access' (1998:198). Our biographies as learners have significant implications for how we teach because our experiences are remembered and felt at a visceral level, which is much deeper than at the level of thought. We might think that we have developed our teaching style and orientation towards learners as a result of our study of education, only to find that 'the foundations of how we work have been laid down in our autobiographies as learners' (Brookfield 1998: 198). Analysing our autobiographies as learners often helps us to understand why we are so deeply committed to certain ideals and values. As Pirsig said in *Zen and the Art of Motorcycle Maintenance*: 'You look at where you're going and where you are, and it never makes sense, but then you look back at where you've been, and a pattern seems to emerge.'

Through my own autobiographical writing, I (Horgan) was surprised to discover that the genesis of my commitment to social justice education and reflective practice was strongly influenced by a challenging experience in a particular class in primary school.

> *When I was ten years old and in the first term of Fifth Class in primary school, my class teacher divided our class arbitrarily into two groups, deemed to be sheep and goats. The sheep were the 'workers'. The goats were the 'idlers'. The sheep were asked to move to the top of the class and the goats to the back. The goats were instructed not to engage in any way with the teacher, the other children or the work that would be conducted in the class from that point forward. Their only duty was to stay quiet.*
>
> *One afternoon, Breda, a 'goat/idler', was fiddling with her hair. Our teacher found this most irritating and told her to stop. Sometime later, Breda absentmindedly or nervously began playing with her hair again. In a storm of fury, our teacher ordered Breda to the top of the class. She removed her scissors from the desk and cut Breda's long blond hair straight across at the level of her ears. Long golden tresses fell to the floor mixed with tears of outrage and dismay. Despite many pleas from parents and school managers, the 'sheep' remained separate from the 'goats' and educational apartheid prevailed in this class for the rest of the year.*

As a teacher and teacher educator, I have revisited this experience on many occasions and from many perspectives. It has taught me a number of valuable lessons about the power of the teacher to empower or disempower learners; the choice that teachers have to see the best or the worst in their learners; and the importance of attending to the emotional and psychological well-being of teachers and learners. In complete contrast to the account above, I also encountered in my schooling so many wonderful and inspiring teachers who encouraged us as learners to reach for greatness, to see the best in ourselves and to constantly strive to realise our full potential.

---

### TASK 2.6: PERSONAL AUTOBIOGRAPHY AS A LEARNER

Write your autobiography detailing your own experiences as a learner. You may observe certain formative moments that left an indelible imprint and continue to inform who you are and what you value.

---

## Critically Reflective Lens 2: Our Learners' Eyes

Brookfield (1998) states that seeing ourselves through our learners' eyes helps us to teach more responsively. Without this information, 'it is hard to teach well' (199). However, a key concern in seeking out feedback is ensuring confidentiality so that learners feel safe to express their opinions without fear of retribution. Brookfield proposes five questions:

- At what moment in the class this week were you most engaged as a learner?
- At what moment in the class this week were you most distanced as a learner?
- What action that anyone in the room took this week did you find most affirming or helpful?
- What action that anyone in the room took this week did you find most puzzling or confusing?
- What surprised you most about the class this week?

(Brookfield 1998: 201)

In your teacher education programme, you may have opportunities to experience teaching from the perspective of the learner in contexts such as peer teaching and peer learning. These occasions provide excellent opportunities to reflect on the subtleties of teaching as perceived from the perspective of the learner.

## Critically Reflective Lens 3: Our Peers' Perspectives

Although critical reflection often begins alone, participating in critical conversations with peers can often reflect back to us some images that may help us to go deeper into our process of learning. Much has been written about how critical friendships amongst peers can promote professional learning. Critical friends may play different roles, depending on what is required in any given situation. The roles can include:

- **The confidence booster**, who affirms, highlights your strengths and picks you up when you are down.
- **The inspirer**, who challenges, provokes and inspires.
- **The equity consciousness raiser**, who explores your assumptions and taken-for-granted beliefs.
- **The resourcer**, who provides information and connections.
- **The planner**, who suggests possible next steps to take in the inquiry process.

A critical friend has an ongoing relationship with you based on mutual trust and professional respect. The following guidelines may be helpful in defining the nature of the relationship between critical friends:

- You engage reciprocally and supportively.
- You ensure confidentiality.
- You commit time to developing the relationship.
- You explore individual goals and expectations at the outset.
- You set agendas for meetings, ensuring opportunities for mutual planning, feedback, discussion and evaluation.
- You examine relevant materials, e.g. lesson plans, schemes, lesson observations and reflections, literature, etc.
- You engage in exploration and analysis that enables both of you to broaden your perspectives, engage in reflection and learn new strategies.
- You evaluate the impact of this reflective process on professional learning and outcomes for practice.

### Critically Reflective Lens 4: Theoretical Literature

The theoretical literature can help to expand our perspectives and understandings, and to draw insight from the experiences of others. It offers multiple perspectives on familiar situations so that our frame of reference expands beyond the personal to encompass other ways of interpreting and responding to situations. Consulting the literature can also offer comfort as it can 'help us to realize that what we thought were signs of our personal failings as practitioners can actually be interpreted as the inevitable consequence of certain economic, social and political processes. This stops us falling victim to the belief that we are responsible for everything that happens in our classrooms' (Brookfield 1998: 200–201).

## Reflective and Unreflective Teachers

Hillier (2005) points out that reflective thinking involves challenging the comfortable, taken-for-granted parts of our professional selves. Reflective teachers spend a lot of time thinking about classroom interactions and consider both the intended as well as the unintended consequences of their actions. They operate in a perpetual learning spiral in which dilemmas surface, continuously initiating a new cycle of planning, acting, observing, reflecting and adapting. They engage in the thoughtful reconsideration of events that happen in their classroom with a constant view to improvement.

Unreflective teachers uncritically accept ideas that are handed down by figures of authority and that are implicit in the cultural norms and hidden curricula of schools. Unreflective thinking can become embedded within a school, leading to a flimsy rationale such as 'This is the way it is done in this school.'

Unreflective teachers usually accept just one explanation for a situation or behaviour and choose from a narrow range of solutions. They are reactive and tend to ascribe blame to others (learners, parents, colleagues, etc.) rather than looking inwards and exploring their role in the situation. They tend to view events and situations as isolated and not connected to wider issues and processes. Unreflective teachers defend their opinions and methods without questioning them or exploring alternatives. This restricts professional development and growth, and promotes teaching stagnation, with some teachers adopting the same methods, approaches and even the same style of classroom layout and decoration throughout their careers.

---

### TASK 2.7: LEGACY OF UNREFLECTIVE TEACHERS

Perhaps you can recall some unreflective teachers or examples of unreflective thinking from your own experiences of school. For instance, certain learners might have been labelled as difficult or disruptive, leading to a consistency of response from teachers without proper consideration of how teaching approaches, relationships, ethos or dominant school culture might have contributed to the alienation of these learners.

Describe the impact of this unreflective teaching on learners, other teachers, parents and the school ethos in each situation.

---

## Levels of Reflectivity in Student Teacher Thought

Research into the nature of student teachers' reflections acknowledges the existence of varying degrees of reflectivity in student teacher thought, with few achieving a level of critical reflection (Hatton and Smith 1995). Most student teachers reflect on their experiences in a 'descriptive and technical' manner (Collier 1999: 179), often 'reporting' what occurred rather than moving to a level of 'analysing' their experiences (Richert 1992: 189).

Korthagen (1985) and Korthagen and Wubbels (1991) identified two distinctive student orientations: one external and non-reflective; the other internal and more reflective. Those in the latter group tend to ask questions about what is happening and why, find it easy to identify what they want to learn, have sound interpersonal relationships, exhibit personal security and self-efficacy, and demonstrate concern for their impact on learning. Fletcher (1997) concurs with the view that some students have a greater capacity for reflection, stating that 'some students are clearly more adept at reflection and already apply it constructively to all aspects of their life, not just to their early steps in teaching' (240).

---

### TASK 2.8: HOW REFLECTIVE AM I?

Think about and write your responses to each of the following questions:

- Would you describe yourself as a naturally reflective person?
- In what contexts do you find it easier to reflect on your experiences? For example, on your own or with trusted friends? Through writing a diary?
- What resistance do you have to reflection?

---

## Some Frameworks for Reflective Practice

Reflection, especially critical reflection, is a challenging activity for student teachers. It benefits from a structured approach that enables you to tap into your own experiential bank, to make connections and to construct personal meaning to inform your developing practice. The provision of frameworks for reflective practice has been found helpful, especially at the beginning stages, as they can help you to reflect on the appropriate issues and encourage you to 'move on' in your thinking and learn from the reflective process (Moon 1999: 194).

The following section presents some frameworks to help structure your reflective analysis. In more formal reflective writing, where your work is being assessed, it may be helpful to use a framework to ensure that you are reflecting at a sufficient level of depth. Before using any model of reflection in an assignment, check if your college provides guidance regarding preferred models.

Consider which of the frameworks outlined below might work best for you and in which contexts they might be most useful.

### *Experiential Learning Cycle*

Gibbs (1988) presented what he called the Reflective Cycle, a six-stage experiential learning cycle comprising the following stages (see Figure 2.3).

1. **Description:** in this section, you describe the incident or event that you are reflecting on. Keep your description succinct and to the point.

2. **Feelings:** describe your reactions and feelings. How did you feel at the time/ afterwards? What did you think at the time/afterwards?

3. **Evaluation:** evaluate the effectiveness of the actions taken. What was good and bad about the experience? On what basis are you making your evaluation? Support your argument with references to relevant educational theory.

4. **Analysis:** what sense can you make of the situation? What might have helped or hindered the event? Draw on a broad range of evidence and theory to help you analyse what was really going on in the situation. Look for multiple sources of evidence to build a cohesive analysis. This section is crucial, particularly for higher level writing. Many student teachers receive poor marks for reflective assignments by not integrating theory and experience. This is a cyclical process where theory informs your understanding of practice, but practice also informs and develops theory.

5. **Conclusion:** what can be concluded from this experience and the analysis you have undertaken? Could you have done anything differently? What have you learned from the experience? If you are reflecting on a positive experience, consider what aspects of the experience might transfer to another, similar situation in the future. Also, consider if there is anything you could change to improve things even further. If the incident was negative, suggest how you might have intervened to prevent this adverse occurrence and how you plan to prevent such a thing from happening in the future.

6. **Action plan:** what action will you undertake to ensure that you will be better equipped to cope with a similar event in the future?

Figure 2.3: The Reflective Cycle

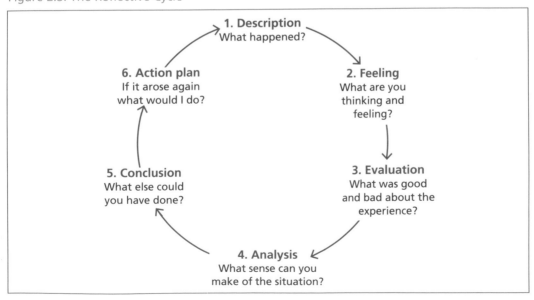

Source: Gibbs, G. (1988), *Learning by Doing: A Guide to Teaching and Learning Methods*, Oxford: Further Education Unit, Oxford Polytechnic.

---

### TASK 2.9: APPLYING THE REFLECTIVE CYCLE (GIBBS 1988)

You may be familiar with the model devised by Gibbs (1988), or it may be the first time you have encountered a reflective framework. Whatever your experience, Gibbs's model is a good place to start when writing reflectively as its stages are clear and accessible.

Choose an experience from your school placement and explore it using the steps outlined by Gibbs.

Having applied all stages of the Reflective Cycle in your exploration, consider how effective the framework was in helping you to explore and understand your experience.

---

## Personal and Professional Empowerment Model

Francis (1995) developed the following model that is based on Smyth (1989). She found this a useful approach to reflection that promoted personal and professional learning for student teachers.

Table 2.1: Stages in Personal and Professional Empowerment

| DESCRIBING | WHAT DO I DO? |
|---|---|
| Detailed observational description without judgement | |
| INFORMING | WHAT DOES THIS MEAN? |
| Search for patterns or principles underpinning the described practice | |
| CONFRONTING | HOW DID I COME TO BE THIS WAY? |
| Examination of the broad historical, social and cultural context | |
| RECONSTRUCTING | HOW MIGHT I VIEW/DO THINGS DIFFERENTLY |
| Consideration of alternative views and generation of goals for future critical action | |

*Source*: Francis, D. (1995), 'The Reflective Journal: A Window to Preservice Teachers' Practical Knowledge,' *Teaching and Teacher Education*, 11(3), May: 231.

---

### TASK 2.10: APPLYING FRANCIS (1995): STAGES IN PERSONAL AND PROFESSIONAL EMPOWERMENT

Reflect on an issue, experience or dilemma that you experienced while teaching, applying the stages outlined by Francis (1995) in Table 2.1.

Consider the value of this framework as an aid to reflective thinking and writing.

Francis (1995) describes her reflective framework as being a model for personal and professional empowerment. How do you think this might be the case?

## *What? So What? Now What?*

Another structured framework for reflection that has considerable value in the field of teaching is that developed by Rolfe *et al.* (2001). This reflective model is based on three simple questions: What? So what? Now what? Below is a list of questions adapted from Rolfe *et al.* (2001) that you may choose to answer in response to the three elements.

### What?

- What is the issue?
- What was my role?
- What was I trying to do?
- What did I do?
- What was the response of others?
- What were the consequences for the learner(s)? Myself? Others?
- What feelings did it evoke in the learner(s)? Myself? Others?
- What were the positive and negative aspects of the experience?

### So What?

- What can I learn from this experience?
- What was my thought process as I acted?
- What knowledge can I bring to the situation now?
- What could I have done to prevent it or make it better?
- What is my new understanding of the situation?
- What wider issues arise from this experience?

### Now What?

- What do I need to do now?
- How can I learn from this experience?
- What theoretical insights can inform my learning?

---

### TASK 2.11: WHAT? SO WHAT? NOW WHAT?

Use the questions developed by Rolfe *et al.* (2001) to help guide your critical reflections on a teaching experience or occurrence. The questions encourage you to go to the literature to underpin your reflections with relevant theory.

You can start by responding to the 'What?' and 'So What?' questions and later begin to use the 'Now What?' questions.

Having used this framework, consider how the framework has helped you to uncover deeper meanings to assist your understanding of an event.

## A HIERARCHY OF REFLECTIVE WRITING

Writing your reflections on experiences and events helps to deepen your capacity for reflection. Committing your reflections to paper allows you to observe patterns in your thinking and provides some distance between you and your experiences, leading to greater objectivity in your analysis. Writing also helps to integrate different ideas by connecting current experiences with past experiences, old knowledge with new knowledge, theory with practice. Reflective writing is personal, exploratory and tentative and, as such, is different from the traditional academic writing with which you may be familiar.

Researchers have attempted to devise rubrics for analysing the quality of reflective writing. Many of these rubrics highlight similar features, which we can group hierarchically under the following headings: *descriptive reflection*, *comparative reflection* and *critical reflection* (see, for example, Hatton and Smith 1995; Jay and Johnson 2002; Lee 2005). When assessing your reflective writing, your tutors will require more than a superficial review of your experience. They will seek evidence of deeper reflection. This means moving beyond the descriptive and subjecting your experience to scrutiny from a range of different perspectives.

## Level 1: Descriptive Reflection

This first level of reflecting involves describing an incident or 'puzzle of practice', typically drawn from your own school placement experiences. Descriptive reflection involves describing an experience, event or concern. It could be something that went particularly well or didn't go well at all. It could involve reflecting on a response or reaction from an individual or group, or it could involve reflecting on your own responses or reactions. Fundamentally, descriptive reflection involves answering the question, 'How can I make sense of what happened?' It entails more than just reporting the facts. It involves finding significance in an experience so that you can recognise the salient features, become aware of causes and consequences, and inform your understanding. Figure 2.4 illustrates some questions to guide your descriptive reflection.

Let's consider the following example of descriptive reflection written by Maedhbh, a student teacher. Maedhbh is reflecting on an English reading lesson she taught during school placement:

*I had planned my lesson around a written text. Once I had distributed copies of the text, I became aware very quickly that one group of learners immediately began to talk and act up. I tried to regain their attention by asking some simple comprehension questions to refocus them on the task, but this only made the*

*situation worse. Despite my desire to be an understanding and approachable teacher, I raised my voice in frustration and threatened sanctions if they did not pay attention. This caused them to become quiet, but I was not able to engage them in the rest of the class.*

Figure 2.4: Questions to Guide Your Critical Reflection

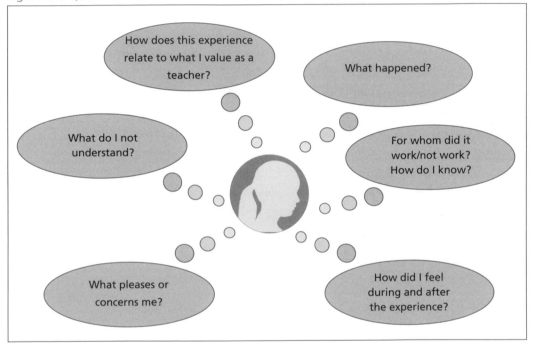

## Level 2: Comparative Reflection

The next level of reflective writing, comparative reflection, involves comparing different interpretations of the same event. While your reflective writing will be based on your personal experience, it will draw on other sources and types of evidence to help you interrogate your experience fully, leading to new levels of understanding and awareness. Within any given situation, different perspectives yield different results. Earlier we explored Brookfield's (1998) critical lenses, which seek lines of inquiry and insight from the varied perspectives of our autobiographical experience, our learners, our peers and the theoretical literature. All of these sources of evidence are relevant and necessary at the level of comparative reflection in order to paint a more reliable and powerful picture. Moon (2001) refers to this requirement for different sources of evidence as the need for 'multi-dimensionality'. When we consider alternative perspectives or diverse ways to approach a problem, we discover meaning we might otherwise miss. Figure 2.5 provides some questions to guide you on your comparative reflection.

Maedhbh revisited her experience and re-framed her interpretation through the lens of comparative reflection:

> *Thinking back over it, I now realise that there may have been several reasons for what happened. The group of learners who resisted the reading text were L2 English speakers who, while reasonably proficient in English, may have lacked confidence in handling the level of language in the reading text. Brophy (2010) found that when readability levels are too high some students feel overwhelmed, and this emotional response causes them to react negatively to the tasks. I spoke to the class teacher afterwards, who was present, and she indicated that there were problems not just with the readability of the text but also [with] the appropriateness of the content and my methods of exploration. I also spoke with some of the children involved. They said that they didn't like the reading text. My angry response to the class was based on my emotional feeling of rejection, that they did not value me or the effort I had put into my preparation. I now feel that I may have jumped to an incorrect analysis of the situation. I now realise that I need to take the abilities and interests of the learners into consideration more in my planning.*

Figure 2.5: Questions to Guide Your Comparative Reflection

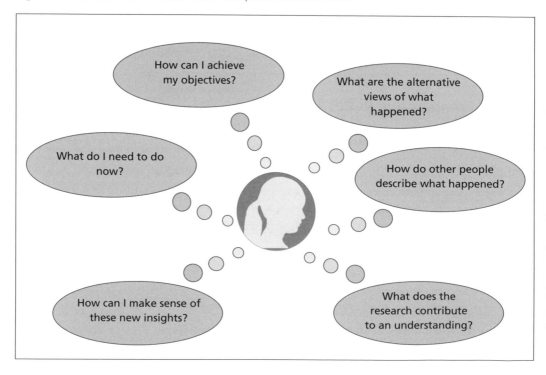

## Level 3: Critical Reflection

At the level of critical reflection, we consider whether or not our teaching is equitable, just and respectful to all. When writing at the level of critical reflection, you will demonstrate an awareness that actions and events can be understood from a range of different perspectives and are influenced by social, cultural, historical or political contexts. From this multi-dimensional perspective, we acknowledge, not just the intended consequences of our actions, but the unintended consequences also. This necessarily raises questions about the ethical and moral aspects of our work. Perhaps what we formerly considered best practice may not meet the needs of a particular learner; what we take for granted in one culture may be unacceptable in another. By taking the broader context into consideration, we come to see ourselves as agents of change, capable of understanding what is, but also working to create what should be. Figure 2.6 illustrates some typical questions for you to ask at the level of critical reflection.

Figure 2.6: Questions to Guide Your Critical Reflection

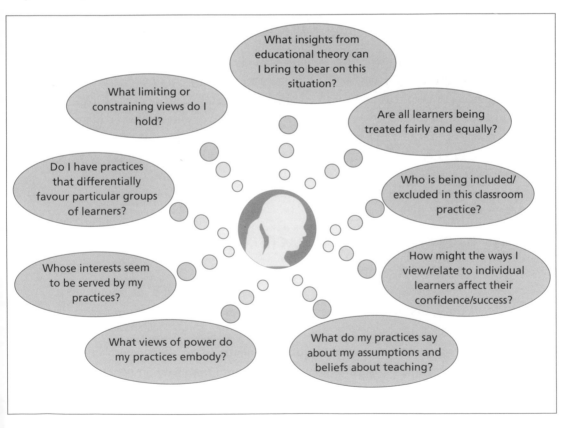

When Maedhbh reflected critically on her English lesson, this is what she found:

*Thinking about the 'hidden curriculum' of the class, I can now see that the group of children who acted up during the lesson were not members of the dominant cultural group in the class, as Bourdieu would have said. As such, they had little educational or cultural 'capital'. I can now see how my choice of the reading text reflected my own biases and assumptions about the children, their ways of learning and their abilities. I also know from my reading of the literature in Sociology of Education that these children are disadvantaged in school as a result of this mismatch. I realise now that the reasons they said that they 'did not like' the text was due to its cultural inappropriateness. I feel I need to acquaint myself with the culture and background of these children so that I can live my belief that all children are equal and should be treated as such.*

---

**TASK 2.12: REFLECTING CRITICALLY ON THE LEARNERS' EXPERIENCE**

To encourage critical reflection you might identify two learners as a focus for your reflection: one for whom the lesson content and being in school are positive experiences; one for whom the lesson content and being in school are problematic. In addition, one of the learners could be of a gender, race or culture that is different from your own. Each learner can then 'sit on your shoulder' and 'whisper' what went well and what did not and how the experience of school affects them, either positively or negatively.

---

## POINTS TO REMEMBER WHEN PRACTISING REFLECTIVE WRITING

- Avoid too much description and too little analysis.
- Reflective writing requires practice and constant standing back from oneself.
- Try writing about the same event from different people's perspectives. Refer to Brookfield's critical lenses.
- Deepen your reflective writing through collaboration. Work with critical friends and reflective peer groups to get the support and the viewpoints of others.
- Include the ethical, moral, historical and socio-political contexts and considerations as they are relevant to the issue under scrutiny.
- It is important to remember to include references to the relevant literature in your reflective writing. It will be helpful if you can explain why you acted in a particular

way with reference to the literature. Alternatively, you might consult theory to find solutions to help you to overcome the problems you identified in your reflection.

- While you are writing a personal account, it is still important to adopt a formal, academic style.
- Reflective writing often requires the use of past and present tenses, depending on whether you are recounting events or making more general comments. Past tense is used to recount a particular experience or incident. When referencing the literature or making general comments, the present tense is usually used.
- Avoid being judgemental about other people's behaviour. Ensure you exclude any identifying markers that might point to particular individuals or institutions.

## A SUMMARY OF KEY POINTS

- Reflecting on your teaching experiences and interactions is an essential part of the process of becoming a teacher.
- Reflection helps to challenge well-worn commonsensical ideas through a process of systematic inquiry, thereby promoting professional growth and development.
- Dewey (1933) maintains that reflective thinking requires us to continuously evaluate our beliefs and assumptions in order to consider other plausible interpretations of events and experiences.
- Van Manen (1977) identified three levels of reflection: (a) technical, (b) practical and (c) critical.
- Schön (1983, 1987) maintains that reflective practitioners continually learn by reconstructing experience through reflection. He uses the terms 'knowing-in-action', 'reflection-in-action' and 'reflection-on-action' to describe different ways of responding to experiences of practice.
- Brookfield (1998) uses the term 'critical lenses' to denote different perspectives that can be employed in reflective practice. These include our autobiography as a learner of practice, our learners' eyes, our colleagues' experiences and the theoretical literature.
- Reflective frameworks can help to ensure that experiences are explored at increasing levels of depth.
- There are norms and conventions associated with reflective writing.

# CHAPTER THREE

# Developing Your Professional Portfolio

What is a professional portfolio?

How can I learn from the process of developing my portfolio?

What should I include in my portfolio?

---

**Having worked through this chapter you will:**

- Understand what a professional portfolio is, its purpose and how it can assist in your development as a teacher.
- Recognise the stages involved in portfolio development.
- Be able to draft your personal autobiography as a learner and your personal philosophy of teaching.
- Appreciate the process involved in selecting and reflecting on portfolio artefacts.
- Know how to write an integrative narrative.

---

## WHAT IS A PROFESSIONAL PORTFOLIO?

A professional portfolio tells the story of your developing understanding of learning and teaching, from embarking on your pre-service programme to emerging as a qualified teacher. The Teaching Council defines a professional portfolio as follows:

The term professional portfolio is used…to denote an instrument which is used by the student teacher to document his or her work, to support the process of reflection on his or her practice and to identify areas in which he/she may need support or guidance. The portfolio also facilitates students to become more conscious of the theories and assumptions that guide their practice, and provides a basis for collaborative dialogue about teaching. (2011: 6)

Your professional portfolio will illustrate your philosophy of learning and teaching, and will serve as a record of your teaching experiences and reflections on practice. Preparing a professional portfolio involves interrogating your teaching beliefs and practices in order to make explicit your tacit knowledge and assumptions. It will require you to approach teaching as scholarly inquiry (Boyer 1990; Schön 1995; Lyons *et al.*, 2002).

Portfolios serve a variety of purposes, such as helping with formative and summative assessment, stimulating metacognitive reflection and providing evidence of competency (Lyons 1999; Wolf and Dietz 1998). Good professional portfolios provide a coherent narrative of your professional journey and use evidence to substantiate your reflections on the impact of formative experiences on your learning. In other words, your portfolio will not only record what you have done but also how you understood, evaluated and solved problems at particular junctures during your teacher education programme. Developing a reflective portfolio will provide an opportunity for you to record, preserve and present your effort, progress and achievement as a student teacher through purposeful reflection on selected aspects of your work and learning over time. Portfolios can be presented in hard copy or electronic forms. Electronic portfolios are popular on many teacher education programmes as they promote the development of student teachers' ICT skills, facilitate the highlighting of connections between different aspects of the portfolio through hyperlinking and allow artefacts, or items which you deem significant, to be presented in many different formats (e.g. audio, video, graphics and text). When drafting your portfolio, you will encounter the term 'artefact' and may be unsure what constitutes an artefact in this context. An artefact is a term that is used to refer to items of evidence that you may choose to include in your portfolio to exemplify an aspect of your teaching or to demonstrate learning or mastery.

Your pre-service portfolio can evolve into a professional biography that you could continue to use and update throughout your career in education. Your portfolio will provide an opportunity for you to present your individuality and achievements, and to highlight your growth in cognition and performance. Hence, in summary, your portfolio will:

- Document your progress as a learner and teacher.
- Provide a forum for developmental reflection.

- Allow you to take ownership of your learning.
- Encourage critical thinking.
- Record, preserve and present your work and achievements.

## WHAT IS INCLUDED IN A PROFESSIONAL PORTFOLIO?

While the guidelines regarding the compilation of professional portfolios are unique to each teacher education programme, most portfolios contain the following:

- Personal autobiography as a learner
- Personal philosophy of teaching
- Artefacts to demonstrate competence in each of the professional standards
- Rationale and reflection statements to accompany each artefact
- An integration reflection – a capstone reflection that demonstrates the interrelationships between the artefacts and presents an overview of your professional development during the portfolio process

The Teaching Council specifies that a professional portfolio 'may include: class teaching and other school experiences; planning for teaching, learning and assessment; personal and professional reflections; recording of pupils'/students' work (written, video, audiotaped, photographic, etc.); recording of professional conversations with the Co-operating Teacher, HEI Placement Tutor, fellow students, etc.' (2011: 17).

## Autobiography as a Learner

Compiling your portfolio is a developmental process (Giuliano 1997). Portfolios often begin with an autobiographical account of your experiences of learning and teaching. The ability to recognise and describe formative experiences that have shaped your understanding of education is a significant dimension of self-understanding and reflective practice. Writing your educational autobiography will provide an opportunity for you to reflect critically on the following:

- Key experiences that have shaped your views of learning and teaching
- Social and cultural experiences that have informed your world view
- Ideological and philosophical constructs that have influenced the way you perceive education
- Your inspiration to become a teacher
- Your teaching goals and aspirations

The following steps may help you to draft your autobiography as a learner.

## Step 1: Recalling

Think about and write freely in response to the questions below. Jot down your thoughts as a stream of consciousness. Do not worry about punctuation, grammar or spelling at this stage. Just get your memories on paper.

- What was your overall experience as a learner during childhood and adolescence?
- Can you recall occasions when you found learning particularly easy or particularly difficult? Describe one such occasion. What emotions do you recall?
- What motivated you to learn?
- What assisted you in learning (include strategies used by you and by your teachers)?
- What learning obstacles did you encounter?
- Think of a teacher who inspired you as a learner. Describe their inspirational qualities.
- Think of a teacher with whom you found it difficult to learn. Reflect on why this was so.
- How did your early life experiences (cultural, social, educational) contribute to your development as a person and your perspectives on education?
- Can you recall when you decided to become a teacher? What was your motivation?

## Step 2: Connecting

Now read back over what you have written. Try to identify the dominant themes that emerge most strongly in your writing. A key theme may be the joy of learning, or the satisfaction of achievement, or a desire for praise or affirmation, or fear of getting it wrong, or an awareness of the needs of others in the class, or the appropriateness or inappropriateness of teaching approaches used, or the social dynamics of the class and their impact on you, etc.

## Step 3: Reflecting

Reflect on how significant personal  experiences may have influenced your choice to become a teacher. Perhaps you decided to become a teacher when you were already in college or working. Through this process, you may see connections between your childhood and adolescent learning experiences and your decision to become a teacher. Now, in the form of a personal narrative, write about the formative experiences that impacted your understanding of learning and teaching and your decision to embark on an educational career.

- Begin with an introductory paragraph, highlighting the key themes of your educational autobiography.
- Present your autobiography in the first person.

- Reflect on how the events you have alluded to have informed, or will inform, your perspectives as a student teacher.
- Conclude your autobiography with a brief summary statement.

The following are opening paragraphs from two student teachers' personal narratives:

### Lisa's Autobiography as a Learner

*I recall that my early education was very difficult for me. Most of the time, I just didn't get it and was often in trouble. My time in Fifth Class was a defining year for me. We had a new teacher – Mr Murphy. He was a very kind and encouraging teacher. After small break, he would sit down and have a chat with us for a couple of minutes each day. He always told us interesting stories. We all got the work done, and then we would sit down and have a little rewarding chat before we carried on working. There was a great sense of industry, purpose and enthusiasm in that class, and I don't remember any bad behaviour. My decision to become a teacher was very much inspired by my experience in Mr Murphy's class. It felt like an oasis of calm, a place where we could go to engage with ideas and learning in a way that was very open-ended and enjoyable. Having experienced learning difficulties and problems with other teachers in the years prior to this, it was in that classroom that I realised I was capable.*

### Alexandra's Autobiography as a Learner

*As a child of immigrant parents, where English was not spoken in our home, learning was a source of both struggle and opportunity for me. Looking back on my learning journey from where I stand today, I am overwhelmed to think that I have made it this far. Certain people and events have been very formative influences on my life and have shaped my understanding and experience of learning, teaching and myself as a learner. Reflecting on key events and experiences, I observe a number of themes that have been constant, like a soundtrack to a movie. I will present my learning autobiography chronologically while highlighting the key themes as they emerged.*

---

### TASK 3.1: REVIEWING AUTOBIOGRAPHY NARRATIVES

Having completed steps 1–3 above, and using Lisa and Alexandra's biographies as guides, draft the first paragraph of your learner's autobiography. Exchange your draft with a peer and, using sticky notes, write comments, questions and suggestions on each other's drafts. The following rubric may be used as a guide. Remember to be affirming and constructive in your commentary.

| | What worked well? | Suggestions for improvement |
|---|---|---|
| Portrayal of the experiences and interests that led to the choice of teaching as a career | | |
| Outline of key areas of focus and special interest | | |
| Style and accuracy | | |

## Personal Teaching Philosophy

A teaching philosophy is a reflective statement that outlines your values, beliefs, aspirations and inspirations regarding learning and teaching. Your teaching philosophy will usually derive from or be influenced by your educational autobiography. As such, the issues and themes that you have identified in your autobiographical narrative will underpin your teaching philosophy. Writing your teaching philosophy is a formative process. It helps you to reflect on and clarify your motivation to teach, your beliefs about learning and teaching, and the values that serve as your navigational compass. Brookfield points out that your teaching philosophy is '... a distinctive organizing vision – a clear picture of why you are doing what you are doing that you can call up at points of crisis – [that] is crucial to your personal sanity and morale' (2006: 16).

Writing a teaching philosophy will help you to connect with the inner aspect of yourself that was 'called' to teach. Again, to quote Brookfield:

> Teaching is about making some kind of dent in the world so that the world is different than it was before you practiced your craft. Knowing clearly what kind of dent you want to make in the world means that you must continually ask yourself the most fundamental evaluative questions of all – what effect am I having on students and on their learning? (Brookfield 2006: 16)

Your teaching philosophy is also a yardstick against which you can check the degree of congruence between your espoused theories (i.e. your beliefs, values, ideals, etc.) and your theories-in-use, which are reflected in your selection of teaching methods, content, resources, assessment strategies and classroom management techniques. Goodyear and Allchin (1998: 106–107) explain:

A clear vision of a teaching philosophy provides stability, continuity, and long-term guidance.... A well-defined philosophy can help them remain focused on their teaching goals and to appreciate the personal and professional rewards of teaching.

Locating your beliefs within, or in opposition to, certain educational theories such as constructivism, behaviourism, social cognition or multiple intelligence theory will help to expand your discussion and demonstrate your ability to engage meaningfully with education theory (see Chapter 5). The following is a sample opening paragraph from a student teacher's philosophy.

### Hugh's Teaching Philosophy

*I believe that learning is a search for meaning. Therefore, as a teacher I need to be cognisant of the issues about which children actively try to construct meaning. I need to pay attention to their questions and try to uncover the assumptions that lie behind these questions. I concur with Nel Noddings (2003, 2004, 2005) who advocates the ethic of caring, rooted in receptivity, relatedness, and responsiveness, as a foundation on which to base my approach to teaching. I believe in the pastoral dimension and that each child is a unique individual, with unique needs for personal, social, intellectual, physical, emotional and spiritual growth. I intend to do my best to help children meet their potential by providing an environment that is safe, encourages risk-taking, and welcomes diverse ideas. Three key themes underpin my philosophy of learning and teaching: (1) scaffolding children to construct meaning, (2) encouraging curiosity and (3) promoting respect for self and others.*

In this opening paragraph, the student teacher prioritises the ethic of caring as a key teaching value. His philosophy statement leans towards a constructivist view of learning and states the general goals of inspiring, empowering and supporting growth. The paragraphs that follow (not included here) highlight how the three themes he identifies above inform his relationships with learners and his general approach to planning, teaching, curriculum and assessment.

As well as broad statements of purpose such as those outlined by Hugh above, the main body of a teaching philosophy should also demonstrate how you plan to put your beliefs into practice by highlighting examples of what you do, or plan to do, in the classroom.

### Teaching Philosophy as a Living Document

Developing a teaching philosophy is an ongoing process as it will change and evolve throughout your pre-service programme and teaching career. Many pre-service teachers find that classroom observation and practicum experiences greatly influence their teaching philosophy (Sheridan and Moore 2009). This was true in the case of a student teacher, Lisa, who found her belief that a warm, friendly teaching personality would win over the learners' affections on school placement was incorrect:

> *Something I always relied on when I was teaching was being able to engage them with a warm manner and just being friendly with them. But it turned out that I was constantly checking them.*

This experience prompted Lisa to expand her philosophy of teaching to embrace the need to modify her attitudes and approaches to accommodate learner resistance. Maynes, Allison and Julien-Schultz (2012) state that there is a correlation between personal beliefs, pedagogy and classroom practice, whereby 'experiences influence beliefs and beliefs influence practice' (69). Hence, there is great value in revising your teaching philosophy in response to key learning experiences. Presenting different iterations of your teaching philosophy, written at key points during your pre-service programme, is an excellent way of highlighting the evolution of your cognitions about learning and teaching, and of demonstrating your professional growth and development.

To summarise, your philosophy of learning and teaching:

- Is a concise and coherent presentation of your beliefs, goals, motivations, understandings and feelings regarding learning and teaching.
- Positions your unique beliefs about learning and teaching within (or in opposition to) appropriate paradigms of educational theory.
- Sets the tone and identifies the key themes and issues that will be adverted to throughout your portfolio.
- Discusses how you put your beliefs into practice by including concrete examples of what you do or anticipate doing in the classroom.
- Is a living document that will be revised and modified in the light of your professional learning experiences.
- Is the foundation on which the substance of your portfolio is built. Hence, the development of the content of the portfolio should extend logically from the principles, beliefs and goals that you outlined in your philosophy statement.

As a living document, your professional portfolio will be carried forth and further developed during your induction years as a teacher: 'Student portfolios begun during the teacher education programme should provide the focus for personal and professional development during the newly qualified teacher's induction period. They should further provide the framework for the teacher's ongoing reflection and professional development' (Teaching Council 2011: 23).

Figure 3.1: The Portfolio Process

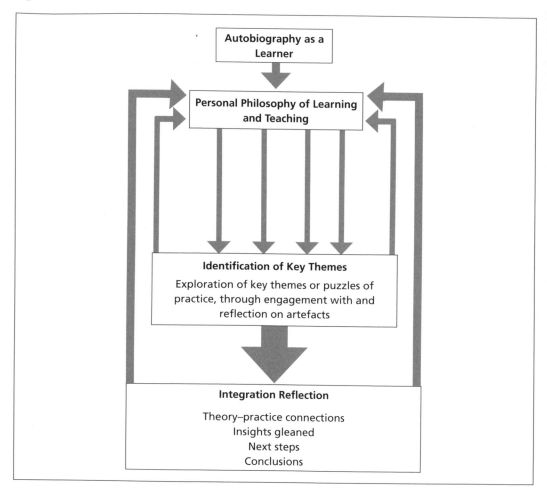

## Drafting Your Teaching Philosophy

Drafting a teaching philosophy is a reflective task that encourages student teachers to consider what teaching means to them and challenges them to explore new ways of teaching (Weber 1997). Reflecting on your philosophy of learning and teaching will inevitably raise questions about how you believe learning occurs, what your role as a teacher might be, and how you might plan, enact and assess your teaching interactions. Below we have listed a range of areas that could meaningfully be explored in your teaching philosophy statement. Take some time to reflect on and write in response to the prompts in each of the six areas. Contemplate the ideas that you generated in this first draft, and revise and refine them until you have a statement that clearly and succinctly represents your beliefs and ideas.

## Your Personal Theory of Learning

Brainstorm the images that come to mind when you think of 'learning'. Consider the location in which learning takes place, those present, the stimulus for learning, the learning duration, the disposition of the learner, etc.

Now imagine yourself as a teacher. How do you see yourself interacting with the learners? Draft a paragraph in response to the prompt 'Learning occurs most effectively when…'.

## Your Personal Theory of Teaching

Note the images that come to mind when you think of 'teaching'. What does an ideal teaching situation look and feel like to you? As you sketch the mental picture of your teaching ideal, consider the setting, approaches used, the learners, the teacher's role, relationships, motivation, etc. Can you think of a metaphor that describes your ideal teaching situation? For example, 'Good teaching is like gardening/baking/building/ mountain climbing/coaching a team/entertaining, etc.' Explain why you chose that metaphor.

## Your Aspirations for Learners

How do you want learners to feel as a result of your teaching? What do you want them to know and be able to do?

## Your Preferred Pedagogical Approaches

What are your beliefs regarding learning theory and the specific learning strategies you would use, such as individual or collaborative tasks, problem-based learning, project work, thematic learning, etc.?

## Your Assessment of Learning

What different types of assessment do you favour: assignments, tests, projects, presentations, portfolios, etc.? How do you plan to differentiate your assessments to suit individual learners' needs and abilities?

## Your Professional Growth

How will you ensure your continued growth as a teacher? What is your attitude towards reflective practice? What are your professional aspirations and how will you support yourself in reaching them? How do you collaborate with others?

## Artefacts and Reflections

When preparing a professional portfolio, bear in mind that you are trying to make explicit what you know about learning and teaching. You are also attempting to make visible how you plan, enact, evaluate and reflect on your teaching experiences. As mentioned at the beginning of this chapter, an 'artefact' in the context of a portfolio is an item of evidence that demonstrates an aspect of your teaching, your learning or your mastery. Artefacts should be selected carefully to illustrate your teaching skills, reflections, accomplishments and interests. They may include:

- Teaching materials that you have devised.
- Recordings of your teaching. Ensure adherence to child protection protocols regarding the use of images of children.
- Lesson plans, schemes, learner assessments and reflections. Ensure that all identifiers are removed from your writing so that information relating to learners, teachers and schools remain confidential.
- Classroom observation summaries.
- Inquiry/research projects.
- Written commentaries that demonstrate your thinking.
- Examples of mentor feedback: commentaries by course instructors, university supervisors, teachers, principals and others.
- Certificates and awards.
- Involvement in professional organisations and leadership roles.

As you can see from the list above, devising a portfolio will require you to keep a record of all aspects of your work. We strongly advise that you develop a dedicated folder (either hard copy or virtual) where you store relevant work and documentation from which you can select representative artefacts for inclusion in your portfolio.

Takona (2002: 87) suggests that what you place in the portfolio should be determined by four key questions:

- What is your absolute best work that demonstrates the degree of your mastery of a given competency?
- What work best shows the diversity of your preparation as a teacher?
- What honours or awards have you received?
- Is there any related non-course work experience that should be mentioned in a separate area?

## TASK 3.2: SELECTING ARTEFACTS THAT DEMONSTRATE ATTAINMENT OF TEACHING COUNCIL LEARNING OUTCOMES FOR INITIAL TEACHER EDUCATION (ITE) GRADUATES

The grid below contains a list of the key areas of focus in the Learning Outcomes for Graduates of Programmes of ITE (Teaching Council 2011: 23–7). Work individually or with a partner to list artefact types in the second column that might demonstrate engagement with each standard. In the third column, suggest areas of potential overlap, where the artefacts may address more than one standard.

| Learning Outcome | Artefact Type | Areas of Integration |
|---|---|---|
| knowledge-breadth; knowledge-kind; ethical standards and professional behaviour; education and the education system; key principles of planning, teaching, learning, assessment, reflection and self-evaluation; subject knowledge and curriculum process and content; communication and relationship building | | |
| know-how and skill range; know-how and skill-selectivity; analytical and critical thinking, problem-solving, reflection and self-evaluation skills; planning, teaching, learning and assessment skills; classroom management and organisational skills; communication and relationship-building skills | | |
| competence context; competence role; integration and application of knowledge skills, attitudes and values in complex and unpredictable educational settings | | |
| competence learning to learn; the teacher as lifelong learner | | |
| competence insight; professional and ethical teaching | | |

### Selecting Artefacts

Select artefacts that demonstrate your professional growth and development, with reference to the learning outcomes outlined by the Teaching Council (see Task 3.2) and/or the evaluation criteria outlined in your teacher education programme.

Ensure that you provide a variety of types of evidence to demonstrate each professional standard/evaluation criterion. Consider your intent in selecting each artefact. Do you wish to highlight a particular teaching skill or illustrate professional learning? Which items from your collection are the best examples for your intended purpose?

Questions to consider when selecting each artefact:

- Which professional standard/evaluation criterion does this artefact exemplify?
- How effectively does it demonstrate that I have mastered this standard/criterion?
- How well does it exemplify key aspects of my philosophy of teaching?
- Is it the same or different in type to other artefacts that have already been selected?

Figure 3.2 is an example of a student teacher's e-portfolio. While the structure may vary from institution to institution, the components will be broadly similar.

Figure 3.2: Sample E-portfolio

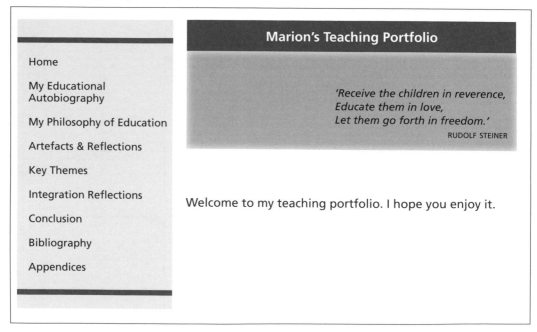

### Reflecting on Artefacts

A portfolio is essentially a reflective project, so the quality of your reflections will determine, to a large extent, the overall quality of your portfolio. The ability to describe the relevant characteristics of an artefact and to explain how these features demonstrate your achievement of key learning goals or relate to the purpose of the portfolio as a whole is a core feature of portfolio development.

In Chapter 2, we explored the topic of reflective practice in some detail and provided a range of suggestions and ideas to help you to understand and practise reflective thinking and writing. We recommend that you write a reflective commentary to accompany each artefact selected for inclusion in your portfolio. Reflective commentaries give substance and meaning to your chosen artefacts and give you the opportunity to chronicle the narrative of your learning. Review the frameworks for reflection that we explored in Chapter 2 and identify a format that best supports the focus and orientation of your portfolio.

You should write a brief reflective commentary to accompany each artefact included in the portfolio, in which you explain what the item is, why it was selected, how it exemplifies your teaching philosophy and how it helps you to meet the evaluation criteria for the portfolio as a whole.

## Integration Reflection

Having presented your chosen artefacts and reflected on your rationale for including them, it is beneficial to write an integration reflection that demonstrates the interrelationships between the artefacts and provides an overview of how you have developed professionally with reference to the professional standards and/or the specific evaluation criteria highlighted by your teacher education programme. This capstone reflection should highlight aspects of your learning and teaching that you consider particularly effective and point to the next steps to further enhance your professional development.

When writing this final reflection, it may be helpful to:

- Refer to your initial philosophy statement and indentify the aspects that are still relevant and the aspects that have changed, indicating what has caused your thinking to change.
- Summarise what the portfolio highlights about your key areas of professional strength, including disposition, attitudes, skills and knowledge. You may wish to highlight particular abilities you have developed in fields such as research, planning, classroom management, facilitating classroom interaction and discussion, differentiation, integration, collaborative learning, problem-solving, assessment, special educational needs, early years, etc.
- Outline how you intend to facilitate continued professional growth. For example, by engaging in ongoing professional development; joining professional associations; pursuing further studies in education; collaborating with teachers, parents and the community, etc.

General points to keep in mind when developing your portfolio:

- Show coherence between the ideals and goals you highlight as important to you in your teaching philosophy and the artefacts you choose to display in your portfolio.
- Demonstrate how your engagement with the theoretical foundations of education has enriched your understanding of practice, which in turn has deepened your understanding of theory.
- Present a range of artefacts of different types that demonstrate your engagement with and reflections on relevant categories within the Code of Professional Conduct for Teachers (Teaching Council 2012), notably, values and relationships, integrity, conduct, practice, professional development, collegiality and collaboration.
- Ensure adherence to codes of child protection and professional confidentiality.

## A SUMMARY OF KEY POINTS

Your professional portfolio:

- Presents the narrative of your developing understanding of learning and teaching.
- Documents your progress as a learner and teacher.
- Provides a forum for developmental reflection.
- Enables you to take ownership of your learning.
- Encourages critical thinking.
- Catalogues, preserves and presents your work and achievements.

Portfolios usually contain:

- A personal autobiography as a learner and a personal philosophy of teaching narratives.
- Artefacts to demonstrate competence in each of the professional standards.
- Rationale and reflection statements to accompany each artefact.
- A capstone reflection that demonstrates the coherence within the overall portfolio and highlights your professional development during the portfolio process.

# CHAPTER FOUR

# Learning Theories and Educational Applications

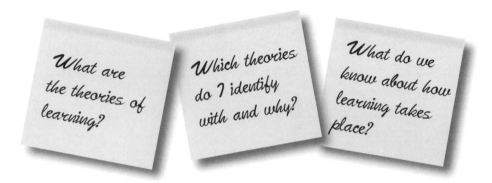

*What are the theories of learning?*

*Which theories do I identify with and why?*

*What do we know about how learning takes place?*

Once you have worked through this chapter, you will have:

- Encountered theories of learning as posed by behaviourists.
- Explored the basis of constructivist learning theories.
- Gained insight into Piaget's theory of cognitive development, including the concepts of stages and readiness.
- Acquired insight into Vygotsky's sociocultural theory of development.
- Evaluated Gardner's theory of multiple intelligences and insights on differing learning styles.

## INTRODUCTION

---

### TASK 4.1: LOOKING AT OUR OWN EXPERIENCES OF LEARNING

Consider the following questions:

- Have you thought about how you learn?
- Do you learn in a different way to others?
- Do you find it easier to learn using concrete, practical examples rather than from theories?
- Is it easier to learn when the learning is closely related to your experiences and interests?
- What situations involving learning have been most satisfactory for you and why?
- What situations involving learning have you found to be unsatisfactory and why?
- Is learning always a deliberate undertaking for you or can it be incidental or, indeed, accidental?
- Focus on a recent experience of sustained learning: what can you recall of your own processes of learning, particular difficulties you had, approaches you took? How would you describe your overall learning approach in this case?

---

For centuries, people have speculated about the processes of learning. Contending viewpoints and theories have been advanced, disputed, dismissed and reworked over many years. In this chapter, we will introduce a number of significant theories in respect of human learning and speculate on their possible impact on current education practice, and the teaching and learning environments that prevail in modern schools.

## BEHAVIOURIST LEARNING THEORY

### Edward Thorndike

The scientific study of learning began in earnest in the nineteenth century, with Edward Thorndike (1874–1949) as the dominant theorist. He posed a crucial question: 'Is the human simply a very advanced mammal that operates by a stimulus–response mechanism, or actually a cognitive creature that uses its brain to construct knowledge from the information received by the senses?' (cited in Darling Hammond *et al.* 2001: 5).

Thorndike attempted to apply scientific approaches to understanding learning. He saw learning as being based on continual trial and error, with the construction of mental connections based on positive responses to specific stimuli such as reward. Learning, he asserted, was the result of the incremental construction of connections or the building of associations between our sense impressions and our instinctual impulses to act. Thorndike endorsed active learning on the part of students and attempted to create an environment where particular stimuli would guarantee learning. This early understanding of learning became known as behaviourism and was taken much further by B.F. Skinner (1904–1990).

## B.F. Skinner

Skinner augmented and developed Thorndike's stimulus–response learning theory and assisted in the design of programmed learning or programmes of learning that sought to give a positive reward for what were viewed as the correct responses. This form of programmed learning provided appropriate reinforcement to the learner, placed an emphasis on reward rather than punishment and moved the learner through incremental phases of learning while incorporating distinct skills. In the classroom, reinforcement might occur as the teacher manages the environment so that learners are encouraged to repeat desired ways of behaving or acting. Indeed, Skinner supported the use of teaching machines for a broad range of learners (e.g. preschool to adults). The teaching machine was a mechanical device the purpose of which was to administer a syllabus of programmed learning. This allowed the learner to respond and, on the basis of this response, be rewarded or otherwise.

Moreover, Skinner argued that any skill could be taught as long as it was age appropriate for the learners in question. He advocated the dissection of skills into the following steps:

1. A very clear specification of the actions that the learner is to learn to do.
2. The deconstruction of the task desired into small steps, progressing from the simplest to the most complex.
3. The learner undertakes each step with the reinforcement of correct actions.
4. A pathway of success for the learner is maintained until the goal is reached.
5. Occasional reinforcement, such as regular rewards, ought to be ensured so as to maintain consistency in the learner's mastery of the task.

(Adapted from Hilgard and Bower 1975)

Behaviourist learning theory had some impact on practices in schools in some societies. The design of very tightly organised curricula with very specific objectives, and the regular reinforcement of skills and ideas through the use of specific activities and other approaches were often a direct outcome of the application of behaviourist learning theory. Undoubtedly, behaviourism often impacts on spheres of learning where rote learning and rigorous reinforcement and repetition are dominant. In more complex spheres of learning, where higher levels of thought are involved, behaviourist approaches appear less effective. In those realms of higher order thinking, the processes of perceiving, experiencing, processing and evaluating material, and making sense of ideas and concepts require us to see learning as a much more intricate process that can only be fully understood through very different theoretical lenses. Interestingly, behavioural learning theory suggests that both adaptive and maladaptive human behaviour are learned and that learning occurs as a result of the consequences of behaviour (Alberto and Troutman 2006).

---

### TASK 4.2: A PLACE FOR BEHAVIOURISM?

Review the following questions. Your own experience in education may be a valuable resource in this discussion.

- Perhaps this may evoke some memories for you. In some early years settings (such as a crèche or a preschool), there may have been a reward chart and children who behaved in the manner expected received a sticker or place on the chart. The reward was deemed to encourage further good behaviour. It was also intended to improve the behaviour of others by promoting positive role models. In primary school the use of rewards, whereby learners accumulated points or tokens that could be exchanged for desirable activities, subjects, classroom tasks or for less homework, may have also been a feature. How effective do you think these approaches were?
- In some cases, learners may have been denied access to tasks, activities or subjects that they clearly enjoyed and such deprivation was used to reinforce a desired behaviour. What is your view of such an approach?
- Have you experienced learning that was characterised by a strict adherence to pre-specified outcomes, either set by you or a teacher?
- How might some school activities, lessons, routines and tasks be undertaken well in the context of a behaviourist approach.

---

## Piaget's Cognitive Theory, Stages and Readiness

Jean Piaget (1896–1980) was one of the most significant investigators in the area of developmental psychology during the twentieth century. He was principally concerned with the major influences on how children come to know. Over his lifetime, he came to the view that learning is a developmental cognitive process and that learners construct knowledge rather than simply absorbing it from the teacher or parent. Piaget depicts two significant processes used by every child in his or her attempt to adapt to the world. These processes are called *assimilation* and *accommodation*. Through assimilation, we absorb new information or experiences and incorporate them into our existing schemas or cognitive framework. The process of accommodation involves altering our existing schemas as a result of new data or new experiences. New schemas are also developed during this process.

Both of these practices are employed throughout life as a person continuously adjusts to their environment in more multi-faceted ways. Very often we can even notice the ways in which we adapt to novel insights, situations and information in our lives. Assimilation is the process of changing the external situation so that it can be positioned in our pre-existing mental structures or schemas. Accommodation is the process of altering our internal cognitive or mental structures in order to accept something new from the environment. Both processes occur concurrently and interchangeably throughout life. An apposite example of a situation in which both processes might be used would be our approach to the new challenges of college life.

Piaget suggests that we build or construct knowledge and meaning based on our own experiences and senses, and that the manner in which we do this is strongly connected to our particular stage of development in biological, mental and physical terms. In arguing this, Piaget shifts our understanding of learning away from a *tabula rasa* (or blank slate) conception of learning, as suggested by behaviourism, and posits the process as an active, exploratory and vibrant one. He maps how children's responses to learning differ considerably depending on their mental, physical and biological growth, and he argues for a sequential model of development based on stages. Children progress through age-related steps and are only able to advance when they are cognitively ready, or reach a point of 'readiness'. Piaget underpins his viewpoint of learning by describing four key stages in development and growth, with all ages cited being approximate rather than rigidly fixed. These stages are as follows: sensorimotor (0–2 years), preoperational (2–7 years), concrete operations (7–14 years) and formal operations (11–15years) (Santrock 2008).

## M-Level Task 4.1: Observing Learner Development

Choose a learner at one of Piaget's stages, as outlined in the grid below. Undertake some further research into the stage and summarise some further key features of this developmental stage in the column headed 'Additional Features of Each Developmental Stage'. In the column headed 'Your Learner's Engagement with Learning' describe how your chosen learner's engagement with learning concurs or otherwise with the broad description for the developmental level in question.

| Piaget's Stages of Development | General Characteristics of Each Stage | Additional Features of Each Developmental Stage | Your Learner's Engagement with Learning |
|---|---|---|---|
| Sensorimotor (0–2 years) | Involving the coordination of senses with a motor response | | |
| Preoperational (2–7 years) | Symbolic thinking is possible and evident, as in the use of syntax for expression. However, abstract thought remains challenging. | | |
| Concrete operational (7–11 years) | Concepts linked to tangible situations or objects | | |
| Formal operations (11+ years) | Speculative, theoretical and alternative thinking are present, as are deduction and induction. Strategic planning is feasible. Concepts can be applied to other situations. | | |

Piaget's theory proved to be quite influential on practice and thinking within a broad range of preschool and primary education systems from the 1960s onwards, and his insights delivered part of the basis for a set of understandings of learning now called constructivist learning.

---

### TASK 4.3: ASSIMILATION AND ACCOMMODATION

Read the following and reflect on your own sense of assimilation and accommodation when confronted with a new experience in life, particularly one that disturbed your previous perceptions of a situation. This may be a recent occurrence or drawn from your past.

> Accommodation is a process that involves altering one's existing schemas as a result of new information or new experiences. It may also involve the development of new schemas.
>
> For example, a young child may have a pre-existing schema in relation to dogs. Dogs all have four legs. And so the child may immediately consider that all animals with four legs are dogs. Because of this, when the child sees a cat for the first time she may well call it 'doggy', as she is focussing on its four legs. However, she will gradually undertake a process of accommodation by which her current schema in regard to dogs will change and she will also develop new schemas in relation to four-legged animals that embrace not only dogs but also cats, foxes, etc.

---

Based on Piaget's work, a great deal of educational practice has endorsed the concepts of discovery learning and supporting the developing interests of the child as two key primary principles. The processes of assimilation and accommodation were readily linked to the process of discovery, leading to the term 'discovery learning'. Piaget suggests that teachers should challenge the learner's capacities but refrain from introducing content or tasks that are excessively beyond the child's stage of development (Santrock 2008).

## TOWARDS CONSTRUCTIVISM: VYGOTSKY'S SOCIOCULTURAL THEORY OF DEVELOPMENT

It has been suggested that Piaget did not place sufficient 'emphasis on the social, on interaction with others, on emotion or on context' (Cremin and Arthur 2014: 57) and for that reason we will give some consideration to Lev Vygotsky's sociocultural theory of development, which had a critical impact on the field of psychology and education (Woolfolk 2004). The Russian scientist Vygotsky (1896–1934) extended Piaget's developmental theory of cognitive abilities of the individual to include the idea of social–cultural cognition, which espouses that all learning occurs in a cultural context and involves social interactions. Vygotsky's theory purports that children learn by means of social relations and from their surrounding or ambient culture, a view that somewhat digresses from Piaget's view that children act independently of their environment in order to learn. By means of what Vygotsky entitles 'dialogues', children relate with others to learn the cultural beliefs or values of humanity. Vygotsky's central argument, therefore, is that 'human activities take place in cultural settings and cannot be understood apart from these settings' (Woolfolk 2004: 45). In this way, the ambient culture is of major significance in constructing our cognitive and learning processes.

In Vygotsky's view, children come to comprehend their surroundings through their engagements with more experienced persons, both other children and adults. By encountering and using many varied but shared cultural tools such as language, signs, music, symbols and art, children's understanding of their world is enhanced and strengthened.

Through these social engagements, children progress in the direction of more personalised thinking or cognition. Because of its deeply social quality, learning might be termed a co-constructed process, meaning that it inherently comprises of people interrelating while engaged in common activities, usually to unravel a problem. When children obtain assistance from adults or peers through this process, they may be capable of employing enhanced learning capabilities in their approach to subsequent and similar problems. Co-constructed dialogues and solutions are therefore internalised, prompting the child to greater autonomy of thinking.

## Scaffolding of Learning

The idea of the scaffolding of learning (and please note the building metaphor) lies at the heart of Vygotsky's work and is intrinsic to his sociocultural theory of learning. Having stressed the role that culture and language occupy in developing learners' learning, Vygotsky also placed an emphasis on the means by which teachers and others might support learners in developing innovative ideas and abilities. Vygotsky, therefore, proposed the theory known as the zone of proximal development (ZPD). As a perspective, this suggests that learners learn best that which is incrementally beyond their existing experiences, but do so with assistance from the teacher or another (Vygotsky 1978). In this manner, scaffolding involves providing the child with structured leads, prompts and pathways in undertaking problem-solving, so that he or she accumulates better approaches to the problem, and can bridge the gap between what they know or can undertake independently and what they can know or undertake with some structured assistance.

Since its publication in the 1960s, Vygotsky's work has enthused many educators and influenced them to focus on approaches that place emphasis on structured scaffolding in problem-solving, within contexts of organised cooperation and in situations often typified by the use of systematic, interventionist and supportive approaches.

## Zone of Proximal Development: A Challenge to Piaget?

Some research has disputed Piaget's view that all children will inevitably move to the next stage of development as they mature. It is suggested that environmental and cultural factors also play a very significant role in progressing through the stages. Vygotsky's zone of proximal development challenges aspects of Piaget's view on learning. Vygotsky contends that, given appropriate assistance and structuring, children could solve problems that Piaget would deem to be outside the child's present cognitive capacity. Such a zone is one in which a child can perform a challenging task, but only with apt and well-structured support (Woolfolk 2004). For Vygotsky, the role of the teacher is to be aware of when and how to become involved so that the child can be assisted onwards and thereby bridge the gap between present undertakings and actual capability.

Table 4.1: Zones of Development

| What the learner can potentially attain | Zone of Potential Development |
|---|---|
| Describes the area between a child's level of independent performance (what he/she can do alone) and the child's level of assisted performance (what he/she can do with support) | Zone of Proximal Development |
| What the learner can do without assistance | Zone of Actual Development |

In tandem with Piaget, Vygotsky believes children to be active learners. However, in believing that learning occurs optimally through the interactions children have with more experienced others, his view clearly has a much more communal or relational quality. Vygotsky sees the relational aspects that attend learning as core, particularly when he defines the 'zone of proximal learning' (Vygotsky 1978) as a sphere in which learners address and solve problems beyond their actual developmental level (though accessible to their level of potential development) while under adult assistance or in partnership with more accomplished peers.

## TASK 4.4: PERSPECTIVES ON SCAFFOLDING

Examine the following perspectives on Vygotsky's sense of scaffolding, as argued by Silver (2011). What do you think of some of the assertions made? Reflect on one example of successful classroom learning you have experienced as a learner and how it correlates or otherwise with the advice outlined below.

In the classroom, scaffolding can be performed with just about any task. Consider these guidelines for scaffolding instruction.

- Assess the learner's current knowledge and experience for the academic content
- Relate content to what students already understand or can do
- Break a task into small, more manageable tasks with opportunities for intermittent feedback
- Use verbal cues and prompts to assist students

(Silver 2011: 28–31)

## MULTIPLE INTELLIGENCES AND LEARNING STYLES

At this point, it is important to consider a perspective that learners differ in how they learn. Intrinsic to that perspective is the view that an onus lies with teachers to understand the ways in which different learners come to terms with learning and make sense of the world, their environment, curriculum, classroom challenges and problems. Such a view of learning, namely one that advances the idea of a multiplicity of learning styles and types of intelligence, claims that teachers should understand the different means by which learners process information, gain insights and accommodate their new experiences.

## TASK 4.5: EXERCISE – A REFLECTION ON YOUR OWN APPROACH TO LEARNING

- Recall some aspect of your learning that you feel happy about: how did you achieve that sense of competence?
- Recall a disappointment in your learning journey: why do you think your learning was unsuccessful in this instance?
- Can you recall your manner of learning in school?
- Are you learning in a different way now in college?
- Try to identify differences between how you learn now and how you learned previously.

- Could you describe your approach to learning as having a particular style?
- What is your key motivation when attempting to learn now?
- What factors obstruct your learning?

In terms of assisting teachers in addressing learners' differing styles of learning, in this introductory text we will focus briefly on Gardner's work on multiple intelligences (1983), and on Silver, Strong and Perini's (2000) developments in the area of learning styles. It is important to note that both sets of insights should be viewed as theories and consequently as being subject to further analysis, review and revision, particularly as research deepens in the area. It is also noteworthy that Silver *et al.* and Gardner argue that all learners have capacity in all learning styles and forms of intelligence, but display particular strength in one or possibly two.

## TASK 4.6: HOW DOES CHRISSY LEARN BEST?

Read this description and discuss the questions that follow.

> Chrissy has a love of books and reading. Reading books is one of the ways that Chrissy sometimes transitions into the classroom. She has an extensive vocabulary and is very detailed in her descriptions when she is telling or retelling stories. Once when Chrissy was reading a book about animals, she [acted] out the sounds of the animals in the book. Chrissy also takes reading books as an opportunity to socialize with her peers. She enjoys teaching others and if one of the other children got an animal wrong, Chrissy would correct them and tell them the correct name. She enjoys participating as several different characters through her dramatic play experiences. Some examples are dinosaurs, kitty cats and different roles while playing house. She works well alone and is in touch with her feelings. Using her linguistic skills, Chrissy can tell her teachers how she is feeling and can differentiate between her emotions well. When Chrissy wants to be alone, she will tell us and when she wants or needs someone to be with her, she will let us know. (Mehta 2002: 30).

- In terms of learning, how does Chrissy learn best of all?
- What gives her greatest satisfaction in learning?
- How might a teacher work with Chrissy in order to assist her learning?
- What are her strongest characteristics in terms of engaging with her environment?
- Finally, read through the section below on Howard Gardner's theory of multiple intelligences, and then review your first responses to these questions about Chrissy in the light of any new insights gained.

## Howard Gardner's Theory of Multiple Intelligences

Howard Gardner's theory of multiple intelligences was originally proposed in 1983 in his text *Frames of Mind: The Theory of Multiple Intelligences*. He argued against the traditional perspective of viewing intelligence as a singular capacity, and instead advanced a perspective on intelligence as differentiated and multi-faceted. Gardner based his theory on the substantial amount of work undertaken within the sphere of cognitive research and on re-examining much prior work in experimental psychology. In this initial articulation of his views, Gardner outlined seven particular abilities or forms of intelligence:

- Visual–spatial
- Verbal–linguistic
- Logical–mathematical
- Bodily–kinaesthetic
- Intrapersonal
- Interpersonal
- Musical–rhythmic

He was later to argue that further abilities should also be considered, namely existential intelligence, naturalistic intelligence and moral intelligence. The case for all is set out in considerable detail by Gardner, but for the moment we will give some brief consideration to his original seven forms of intelligence.

### Visual–Spatial Intelligence

Visual–spatial intelligence is deeply connected to a person's observation of the visual world around them: their ability to view the world accurately, to note patterns in that environment and to differentiate between different forms and objects. It is basic to our orientation, movement and anticipation of change in the environment. It is inherent to the successful recognition of objects and differences between them, and to building our sense of visual memory.

### Verbal–Linguistic Intelligence

Verbal–linguistic intelligence entails an awareness of language in oral and written forms. More precisely, Gardner (1983) clarifies that it comprises sensitivity to the importance of words and to their order, and to the sounds, rhythms, variations and cadences of words, along with an understanding of the different purposes of language, such as its capacity to influence, encourage or deliver information in order to realise precise goals. People with verbal–linguistic intelligence may exhibit considerable ability in reading, writing and recounting stories, and a dexterity with words.

## Logical–Mathematical Intelligence

Logical–mathematical intelligence involves having the ability to examine problems logically, undertake mathematical processes and examine issues methodically. An individual demonstrates logical–mathematical intelligence when perceiving patterns, thinking deductively and thinking logically. This form of intelligence does not have its origin in the auditory–oral sphere, as in the case of the linguistic sphere above or musical intelligences below, but instead its roots are in the world of objects. It is in the course of ordering and reordering objects and in evaluating their quantity that we gain our primary and most important knowledge about the logical–mathematical capacity.

## Bodily–Kinaesthetic Intelligence

Bodily–Kinaesthetic intelligence encompasses the usage of one's body in ways that combine expressiveness and goal orientation, such as those involved in the largely unrefined motor skills of running, lifting objects and climbing, and also in the more precise motor skills needed for considerable manual dexterity, such as engaging hands and fingers in handling or using objects. These unrefined and precise motor activities are the basis of bodily intelligence.

## Intrapersonal Intelligence

According to Gardner (1983), intrapersonal intelligence involves the growth of the inner characteristics of a person and an individual's understanding of their spectrum of emotions. It involves the capability to recognise feelings, and to accommodate them and encompass them in symbolic systems as a way of comprehending and regulating one's actions. Most basically, intrapersonal intelligence is the capability to discriminate between emotional states of pleasure and pain. In more complex contexts, it is the capability to identify and denote intricate sets of feelings. According to Gardner, these abilities are particularly evident in novelists, who are perhaps more responsive to internal experiences and emotional states (Gardner 1983: 239).

## Interpersonal intelligence

Interpersonal intelligence comprises the capability to discern and note differences among other persons in terms of their personalities, impulses, attitudes and intentions. At its most basic level, interpersonal intelligence is the ability of a child to detect the moods of the individuals around him or her. At a more advanced level, it permits a skilful discernment of the desires and intentions of other individuals, even when they may be somewhat obscure, and the incorporation of this understanding into one's behaviour.

Gardner cites teachers and others within the caring professions as persons in need of, and perhaps often exemplifying, advanced forms of interpersonal intelligence.

### Musical–Rhythmic Intelligence

This sphere of intelligence is clearly connected with the recognition and composition of musical tones, pitches and rhythms. In Gardner's view (1983), pitch (melody) and rhythm are the central components of musical intelligence. He contends that rhythmic capability exists apart from any auditory capacity, which means that deaf people are included in this sphere of intelligence. Though pitch and rhythm are both central to developing musical intelligence, the emotional repercussions of music also have a profound impact on individuals.

---

#### M-LEVEL TASK 4.2: THE FIRST THIRTY YEARS

Read and discuss Gardner, H. (2011), 'Multiple Intelligences: The First Thirty Years,' Harvard Graduate School of Education, available from: www.multipleintelligencesoasis. org – click on 'Resources' and then 'The 30th Anniversary Introduction to *Frames of Mind*'.

---

As mentioned, it is imperative that theories such as Gardner's be regarded as insightful rather than as the final word. Theories on intelligence and learning styles may provide us with some useful perspectives on our learners, but they continue to evolve and are subject to revision and the findings of further research and study. It is essential, therefore, that we refrain from any superficial categorisation of learners on the basis of such insights, particularly as increasing insight reveals the complex, multi-faceted and interconnected ways in which humans encounter ideas, concepts and knowledge.

However, all reflective teachers know that not all learners encounter new things and approach ideas, notions, concepts and knowledge in the same manner. Learners clearly have different styles. Some researchers studying these differences have tried to develop theories of learning styles, which attempt to describe the manner in which individual learners gain data, appraise it and incorporate it into their previous understandings. Such theories often lead to generalisations. Learners are categorised according to some general underlying principles and teachers are encouraged to modify their approaches to individual learners on the basis of these findings.

Attempts to assist teachers in engaging with distinct dissimilarities between learners have relied upon many bases, including insights from Jung (1933) and Gardner's theory of multiple intelligences, briefly outlined above (1983).

## A MODEL OF LEARNING STYLES

One model of learning styles that has considerable currency in current education discourse was originated by Silver, Strong and Perini (1997) and could be seen as representative of the genre. In a book called *So Each May Learn* (Silver *et al.* 2000), they combine insights from Jung and Gardner to identify the existence of four distinct learning styles. These are as follows:

- **Mastery style:** this has been described as the sensitive–thinking style and Silver *et al.* characterise it as being typified by sensitivity to details, a sense of order, good planning abilities and good organisation, and as being based on good memory.
- **Understanding style:** known also as the intuitive–thinking style, a learner in this category is known by their ability to identify patterns and reoccurrences, raise queries, make connections and develop arguments about new concepts and ideas.
- **Self-expressive style:** this has been called the intuitive–feeling style and involves a predisposition in the learner towards developing original solutions based on imagining possibilities, developing hypotheses, engaging in speculation and evaluating possible outcomes.
- **Interpersonal style:** as its other title – the sensing–feeling style – might indicate, this learner learns in a predominantly experiential manner with a considerable reliance on creating trust, personalising material and ideas, building empathy with persons and their contexts, and offering an emotional response in learning situations.

---

### M-Level Task 4.3: Further Study

Undertake some further study into Silver *et al.*'s theory (1997, 2000) of learning styles with an emphasis on both identifying your own learning approaches and developing a critique of the theory.

---

## CONCLUSION

It is important to note that there are many critiques of current developments in learning theory from different quarters. As your exploration of the sphere develops, you will encounter viewpoints that seek to challenge these perspectives on learning. It is important to note that all learning theories have contributed to our current understanding of the processes of learning and are effective at some level. However, Winch (2006) alerts us to the perils of rigid certainty, over-categorisation and a reliance on neat schemata when dealing with as complex an area as human learning:

Despite the enormous contemporary interest in human learning and the amount of research that is done on it, we are in danger of knowing even less than we knew at the beginning of this century. This is not because we have failed to accumulate information about the subject, but because we have too much, a lot of it misleading, and we have been obsessed with theory-building at the expense of attention to particular cases. The rapid growth of the study of learning as a branch of psychology has been largely responsible both for the increase in information and the decline in clarity on the topic. (vii)

## A SUMMARY OF KEY POINTS

- Our understanding of child-centred education is enriched by engaging with a broad range of insights from the field of child psychology.
- Learning is posed as a multi-dimensional process that makes considerable demands on teacher reflection and adaptability.
- Intrinsic to teaching is the need to understand the ways in which different learners come to terms with learning and make sense of the world, their environment, curriculum, classroom challenges and problems.
- Learning is a complex process, the understanding of which necessitates an awareness of new and emerging research along with continuous reflection on and adaptation of our practices as teachers.

# CHAPTER FIVE

# Learning and the Child-Centred Classroom

When you have worked through this chapter you will have:

- Analysed the basic tenets of child-centred education.
- Encountered the perspective of John Dewey that education is a socially interactive process.
- Engaged with Jerome Bruner's view that children be regarded as active learners who construct their own knowledge and understandings.
- Critically reviewed some differences between a didactic and constructivist classroom.
- Gained some insights into problem-based learning.   .
- Understood the possibilities for collaborative learning in the classroom.

## INTRODUCTION

Piaget's thoughts on child development and Vygotsky's views on socially-situated learning, the construction of knowledge and the emphasis on experience as a basis for learning became central ideas for those who advocated what is known as 'child-centred education' in the twentieth century. Child-centred curricula and schools were established with an emphasis on learning that centred on learners' own experiences and environments. It is likely that most of you have experienced elements of a child-centred education, as it was formally instigated in Irish primary schools in 1971. In some instances of schooling, a clear breach with traditional didactic approaches was made, and many forms of rote memorisation and direct teacher-led instruction were abandoned in favour of group work and project-led teaching based on a spectrum of topics of intrinsic interest to children. This proved controversial at times.

A debate on education, which continues today, is concerned with locating a balance between two perspectives: the traditional school's focus on a teacher-led transmission of 'essential' knowledge and a child-centred philosophy of learning based on personal experience with facilitated situations in which to search, ascertain and construct knowledge by means of a broad range of discovery learning approaches.

In the twentieth century, child-centred education, in seeking to strengthen its position, has drawn considerably on the work of two further theorists, namely, John Dewey (1859–1952) and Jerome Bruner (1915–). A brief overview of their theories may assist our understanding of the evolution of child-centred education in our own society, as represented within official curricula.

## JOHN DEWEY: EDUCATION AS A SOCIALLY INTERACTIVE PROCESS

You have already encountered Dewey's insights on reflective thinking in Chapter 2. Here, we revisit Dewey as we explore his views on learning. His educational theories were advanced most explicitly in 'My Pedagogic Creed' (1897), *The School and Society* (1900), *The Child and the Curriculum* (1902), *Democracy and Education* (1916) and *Experience and Education* (1938).

Some key ideas emerge as consistent in Dewey's writing. First, Dewey maintains that education, learning and schooling, properly conceived, are always socially interactive processes. The school occupies a unique position in which to advance democracy, social change and personal growth. Its very status as a social institution poses a dilemma for all involved. Does the school perpetuate previously adopted mores and ways of doing things or should it be an active agent in social reconstruction? For Dewey, the answer is clear. The school should provide an environment where all learners can actively engage in meaningful learning that resonates with the innate human capacities to puzzle, probe, discover and reach solutions. This process of learning is, in itself, social, dynamic and not confined by artificial subject barriers and boundaries. The autonomy, social interaction, and sense of shared concern and purpose that typify this conception of learning lead not only to more fruitful learning, but nurture the very democracy in which the institution is situated.

The idea of learning how to live for individual and social betterment in a context of meaningful, shared learning experiences motivated Dewey in advocating considerable reform of the schooling of his day. In traditional schools, there was an over-reliance on the transmission of what he regarded as inert knowledge in classrooms characterised by passivity, and there was little or no input by the learner. In Dewey's mind, this represented a gross misunderstanding of knowledge and a denial of the full realm of human capacity, and only induced passivity and lack of criticality in alienated learners.

By broadening the focus of education to take in wider social and political contexts, Dewey asserts that education and schooling are deeply influential in creating social change and transformation. The basis of his criticism of the traditional schooling of his time, as found in *The School and Society* (1900) and *Democracy and Education* (1916), is the view that, instead of preparing children for sharing in society, it only induced submissiveness to the status quo in learners, the result of the consumption of facts and unjustified immobility. Dewey believed that the development of socially responsible, communally aware individuals with a strong sense of the value of shared learning in a shared society ought to be the desired pathway for education.

---

### TASK 5.1: ENGAGING WITH DEWEY'S VIEWS ON SCHOOLING

Read the following from Dewey's 1897 article 'My Pedagogic Creed' and discuss the questions that follow:

> I believe that the school is primarily a social institution. Education being a social process, the school is simply that form of community life in which all those agencies are concentrated that will be most effective in bringing the child to share in the inherited resources of the race, and to use his own powers for social ends. I believe that education, therefore, is a process of living and not a preparation for future living.
>
> I believe that the school must represent present life-life as real and vital to the child as that which he carries on in the home, in the neighborhood, or on the playground. I believe that education which does not occur through forms of life, forms that are worth living for their own sake, is always a poor substitute for the genuine reality and tends to cramp and to deaden. (1897: 78–9)

- How do Dewey's views on the school concur with your perspective?
- In what ways do your views diverge from those of Dewey?
- What changes in schooling are implied by Dewey's viewpoint?

The Constructivist Classroom: Designing a City

In *The Child and the Curriculum* (1902), Dewey focussed on the traditional prevailing view of the curriculum and the learner. Traditional education, in his opinion, functioned with the perspective that 'the child is simply the immature being who is to be matured; he is the superficial being who is to be deepened' (1902: 13). Subject matter or content presented in this manner denies the origins of human knowledge by positing it as inert rather than vibrant and organic. It also denies the learner the experience of striving, evaluating, hypothesising and solving in a manner that reflects the discovery-led basis of all knowledge. Equally, Dewey was sceptical of educational theories that advocated some form of end point to be achieved and he argued that the end of education lay within itself, in the prospect of ongoing and continual growth, and the reconstruction of experience (Dewey, 1938: 27–30).

Importantly, Dewey saw the school as a context in which the child and the teacher acted together in a vibrant partnership in pursuit of meaningful learning for the real world of life, relationships, community and participation in democratic decision-making. He did not view school as a place where children were often abandoned without structures and appropriate teacher intervention. Some advocates of radical child-centred views on education had, in his opinion, gone to extremes in both rhetoric and practices in order to 'liberate' the child, and placed too much onus on the child as an individual learner without sufficient guidance (Dewey 1938: 17).

Dewey promoted classrooms that maintained equilibrium between the demands of subject matter and the experiences, interests and capacities of learners. He argued that 'the child and the curriculum are simply two limits which define a single process' (Dewey 1902: 16). By doing so, he sought to mend the artificial divide between the immense human capacities of the child and the historical human strivings that are inherent in gaining knowledge. In viewing the child and human knowledge as part of the same continuum, good schooling should see both child and knowledge not as opposites but as fellow passengers in the continual process of human growth. Schools should, therefore, strive to have learners collaboratively examine real-life situations, dilemmas and queries drawn from the learners' own interests, with subject matter and teachers serving the needs of the situation as valued resources rather than dominating and commandeering the entire process. By virtue of these and other arguments, Dewey gained considerable prestige as an advocate of child-centred education and continues to influence thinking in the sphere.

---

### TASK 5.2: THE CHILD AND THE CURRICULUM

In a group, discuss the following point of view expressed by Dewey. What implications derive from this viewpoint for teachers, learners, subjects, schools and methods?

> [T]he child and the curriculum are simply two limits which define a single process. Just as two points define a straight line, so the present standpoint of the child and the facts and truths of studies define instruction. It is continuous reconstruction, moving from the child's present experience out into that represented by the organised bodies of truth that we call studies.... To oppose one to the other is to oppose the infancy and maturity of the same growing life...it is to hold that the nature and destiny of the child war with each other. (Dewey 1902: 16)

---

### M-LEVEL TASK 5.1: DEWEY AND THE PRIMARY SCHOOL CURRICULUM

Discuss the following extract from the *Primary School Curriculum Introduction* (NCCA 1999) with reference to Dewey's insights on society and schooling. For a fruitful discussion, you may wish to refer to one or a number of the following works by Dewey: 'My Pedagogic Creed' (1897), *The School and Society* (1900), *The Child and the Curriculum* (1902), *Democracy and Education* (1916) and *Experience and Education* (1938).

> The relationship between education and society is dynamic and interactive. Education not only reflects a society but is an influence in shaping its development. It helps to equip children to share in the benefits of the society in which they live and to contribute effectively to that society's sustenance and evolution. The curriculum reflects the educational, cultural, social and economic aspirations and concerns of Irish society. It also takes cognisance of the changing nature of knowledge and society and caters for the needs of individual children in adjusting to such change. (NCCA 1999: 6)

## JEROME BRUNER: LEARNERS ACTIVELY CONSTRUCT KNOWLEDGE

Jerome Bruner has contributed significantly to the spectrum of learner-centred education, particularly with the perspectives he offers on thinking, learning, readiness and curriculum. Some of his views have found practical manifestation in curricula in recent years (NCCA 1999). In the first instance, he argues that the mind creates from experience a set of 'generic coding systems that permit one to go beyond the data to new and possibly fruitful predictions' (Bruner 1957: 234).

Consequently, for Bruner, significant outcomes of learning include not just the concepts and problem-solving procedures utilised previously within a culture and passed on by adults, including teachers, but also the learner's capacity to create their own procedures and processes. The aim of education should, therefore, be about the development of autonomous learners working with their own authentic problem-solving procedures.

Bruner (1966) argues that children display the following stages of representation (i.e. ways in which information and knowledge are stored and encoded) in the course of their cognitive development:

1. Enactive (action-based) representation
2. Iconic (image-based) representation
3. Symbolic (language-based) representation

Briefly, the *enactive representative stage* (0–1 year) involves a degree of coding and storage within memory of action-based information. Often described as the concrete stage, this first stage involves a physical process of learning. Bruner believes that initial learning begins with an action involving touching, feeling and manipulating. Here, the child manipulates objects directly without having any internal representation of the objects.

For example, an infant shakes a rattle and immediately hears a rattling sound. The infant has manipulated the rattle and the result is a sound that gives her a sense of pleasure. The infant may shake her hand in future, even if there is no rattle, and she may expect her hand to produce the sound. Clearly the infant has not formed an internal representation of the rattle and, consequently, does not comprehend that the rattle is necessary for producing the sound.

The second or *iconic representation stage* (often called the pictorial stage) (1–6 years) involves the use of images or other visuals to symbolise the concrete situation enacted in the first stage. This stage comprises an internal depiction of external objects visually on the part of the child and in the form of a mental image or representation. For example, a child drawing an image of a boat or thinking of an image of a boat would be descriptive of this stage.

The *symbolic representation stage* (sometimes called the abstract stage) (7+ years) involves the learner representing images using words and symbols. Words and symbols are abstract. They do not always have a direct connection to the concrete reality they represent. A number, for example, is a symbol used to describe how many of something there are. However, the number in itself has little meaning without the understanding that it stands for that number of items. Other examples include variables such as x or y, or mathematical symbols such as +, -, etc.

The symbolic stage is typified by the storage of information in the form of codes or symbols, very typically as language. Each symbol has a fixed connection to some thing or idea which it represents. For example, the word 'cat' is a symbolic depiction of a solitary class of animal. Symbols, quite unlike mental pictures or remembered actions, can be categorised and organised. At this point, most knowledge may be stored in the form of words and mathematical symbols, or by employing other symbolic systems. This use of words and symbols 'allows a student to organize information in the mind by relating concepts together' (Brahier 2009: 53). Similar to Piaget's stages, outlined in Chapter 4, Bruner's stages should not be viewed as rigidly divided stages but rather as incrementally linked modes of experiencing and representation. However, symbolic representation remains the eventual and desired mode.

Bruner's ideas impacted strongly on education, particularly as he went on to make significant arguments in respect of curriculum. Bruner (1961) argues that the aim of education is not the transmission of knowledge, but might best be conceived as the facilitation of a child's thinking and problem-solving skills, which can occur in a wide range of situations, not least in the context of an information age culture that will continue to influence enormously children's engagement with learning. Ultimately, education should lead to the development of symbolic thinking in children. At the heart of his theory lies the argument that children should be viewed primarily as active learners who construct their own knowledge and understandings.

Interestingly, Bruner (1960) displays considerable difficulty with Piaget's concept of readiness. Teachers under Piaget's influence, in Bruner's view, often unjustifiably devote significant time and effort to equating levels of difficulty within subject content to a child's cognitive stage. Material and content are often deemed inappropriate cognitively, or too advanced, and on occasion Bruner sees such avoidance as perhaps detrimental to children's progress and to the meaningful inclusion of all children. Bruner argues that a child (of any stage) has the capacity to understand intricate content: 'begin with the hypothesis that any subject can be taught effectively in some intellectually honest form to any child at any stage of development' (1960: 33).

## The Spiral Curriculum

This argument was to lead Bruner (1960) to develop his well-known intervention in curriculum planning and teaching – the concept of the spiral curriculum. This view of curriculum is premised on the argument that subjects have certain organisational elements – central ideas, key methodologies and well-established approaches to knowledge and understanding. These key understandings should, therefore, direct curriculum planning in a way that parallels the cognitive development of the child. This involves content being organised in a manner whereby intricate concepts can be initially taught at a basic level and then re-engaged with at more difficult levels later on. Consequently, disciplines would be taught at levels of progressively increasing complexity, as symbolised by a spiral pattern. Teaching conducted in this manner, Bruner argues, ought, therefore, to facilitate children in the acquisition of ever more complex problem-solving attributes.

Figure 5.1: The Spiral Curriculum

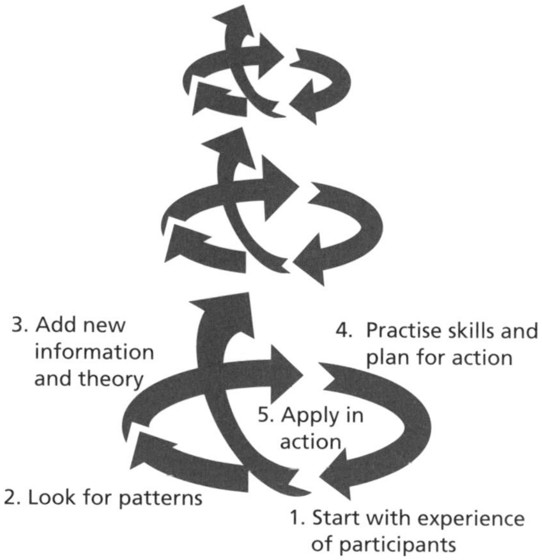

3. Add new information and theory

4. Practise skills and plan for action

5. Apply in action

2. Look for patterns

1. Start with experience of participants

Source: Adapted from http://vocalability.com/uncategorized/spiral-learning-and-voice/

Based on his advocacy of a spiral approach to content and his understandings in respect of cognitive growth, Bruner (1961) maintains that learners actually construct their own knowledge by classifying and sorting information using their innate coding systems, as touched upon above. The most effective manner of internal coding on the part of the learner, Bruner believes, does not rely on the imposition of rigid structures on the part of the teacher but on the process of discovery by the child. A teacher of this view avoids imparting content by means of rote learning and seeks to facilitate learning based on discovery, returning to topics with increasing levels of complexity while avoiding the imposition of overly rigid and external structures. At the heart of the process lies discovery learning and, like Vygotsky, Bruner also stresses the importance of the learner's milieu, especially the social environment, arguing that adults and peers play a vital role in facilitating the child's progression along innovative and unique learning pathways. In this manner, both Vygotsky and Bruner share a trust in the processes of scaffolding (Bruner *et al.* 1976). The scaffolding of learning, the spiral curriculum and Vygotsky's zone of proximal development share some commonalities and continue to exert considerable influence on curriculum design, organisation and planning, and on classroom and school practices.

---

### TASK 5.3: BRUNER'S INFLUENCE ON THE PRIMARY SCHOOL CURRICULUM

In writing about the spiral curriculum, Bruner argues that the teaching of content should focus on ideas that are inseparable from the understanding of the curricular area and that 'a curriculum as it develops should revisit these basic ideas repeatedly, building upon them until the student has grasped the full formal apparatus that goes with them' (Bruner 1960: 13). The *Primary School Curriculum Introduction* acknowledges Bruner's influence by supporting the view that 'by revisiting knowledge and ideas already acquired, as the starting point for new learning, it allows for the coherent expansion of knowledge and the gradual refinement of concepts' (NCCA 1999: 11).

Choose a topic, issue or subject and develop a plan as to how you might teach it to a particular age group. In doing so, try to apply Bruner's spiral approach. Evaluate the approach as you progress.

---

### M-LEVEL TASK 5.2: BRUNER'S INFLUENCE ON THE PRIMARY SCHOOL CURRICULUM 1999

Read through the *Primary School Curriculum Introduction* (NCCA 1999) and identify aspects of Bruner's ideas that have been incorporated into the text.

## CONSTRUCTIVISM, CHILD-CENTRED EDUCATION AND TEACHING

By bringing together the insights and views of Piaget, Dewey, Vygotsky and Bruner, we can now position them as providing a basis for constructivism in that all four theorists broadly take the view that the learners constructs their own unique sense of meaning and understanding of their environment by encountering and reflecting on ranges of experiences. Encountering something new presses us, the learners, to assimilate and accommodate and to alter our previous viewpoints as learners, and so the cycle continues in a continual process of construction and reconstruction, as we are active inventors of our own knowledge. The implications of constructivism and child-centred education and teaching are multi-faceted and can only be introduced here with the perspective that each facet eventually requires further elaboration and development.

It is feasible that many of you have experienced some characteristics of a constructivist classroom at various stages in your schooling. One clear indicator involves a distinct shift in priority within the classroom from the actions of the teacher to those of the learners. Learners are not perceived, either implicitly or explicitly, as deficient or lacking in knowledge, but rather as vibrant beings with a rich capacity for exploration, reflection, adjustment, reassessment and revision of previous understandings. Consequently, as argued by Dewey and outlined above, knowledge and understanding are seen as primarily dynamic and organic, with rich potential for the emergence of diverse and varied possibilities, rather than as inert, fixed and unchanging entities.

Significant features of a constructivist classroom environment are outlined in Task 5.4 below.

---

### Task 5.4: Degrees of Child-Centredness

Discuss the features of a constructivist classroom environment listed below. On a scale of one to seven, to what extent have you, at any stage in your formal learning, experienced each?

1. The current understandings, beliefs and insights of the learners, accurate or otherwise, are significant.
2. Understandings, insights and beliefs are attained by learners based on their own ways of deriving personal meaning from their environment, though all learners may undergo an ostensibly similar learning experience.
3. The means of reaching understandings, of making sense of or taking meaning from the environment, is an unceasing process of active exploration.
4. Real learning involves a degree of conceptual modification and change.

5. When learners create or reach a new insight or understanding, such meanings are accepted by them in a tentative manner rather than cemented in perpetuity without the possibility of review.
6. A climate in which learners take considerable responsibility for their own ongoing, active learning is visibly evident.

It may be beneficial to examine some distinctive attributes of a constructivist classroom in the context of contrasting them with those of a traditional or didactic setting (see the table in Task 5.5), though it is worth bearing in mind that there are many very complex situations where an amalgam of approaches may be in use by teachers. The constructivist setting, as opposed to the traditional one, involves very different understandings in respect of learners and their capacities, the role of the teacher, the processes of learning and the nature of knowledge itself. The key assumption of constructivist thinking is that the learner is the active agent in the process of gaining and accommodating new understandings, insights and knowledge, a view that has considerable impact on the organisational, relational and pedagogical features of the classroom.

## TASK 5.5: DIDACTIC VS. CONSTRUCTIVIST CLASSROOM

In reviewing the table below, adopt the position of a primary teacher who considers that her learners are ready to study the concept of weight. She can attempt to undertake the teaching of this concept either in a didactic or constructivist manner. Explore the possible implications of each approach in terms of methods to be employed, the role of the teacher, how knowledge is presented or reached, issues that might be encountered, resources required and the discussions that might emerge with the class.

| Traditional or Didactic Classroom | Constructivist Classroom |
| --- | --- |
| Curriculum demands have considerable imperative and progress through the curriculum is ordained by a progression of externally authorised steps. | The curriculum is viewed as an indispensable resource, but primary emphasis is placed on the issues, problems, questions and interests of the learners, as encountered in the classroom. |
| A stringent observance of fixed curriculum stages is generally maintained. | The exploration of learners' questions and interests is valued. |

| Traditional or Didactic Classroom | Constructivist Classroom |
|---|---|
| Prescribed texts and workbooks are to the fore in terms of classroom materials, and are generally used in a chronological manner. | A diverse range of materials is encouraged, is often sourced by learners, and includes primary concrete materials, artefacts and resources from a multiplicity of locations in each learner's environment. |
| A considerable emphasis is placed on the memorisation of key ideas. | The learner's prior knowledge is deemed valuable, and learning is seen as a process of developing interactively from that initial point. |
| The teacher's role, implicitly or explicitly, is one of distributing key insights, knowledge and information. Learners are often viewed as passive receivers. | Engagement between teacher and learners is exemplified by considerable dialogue, along with significant knowledge of the individual learners, an appreciation of individual learning styles and a willingness to assist learners in constructing their own meaning, on the part of the teacher. |
| The teacher's role may be based on a traditional understanding of authority and quite directive in nature. | The teacher's role is interactive, participative, exploratory and typified by a strong sense of negotiated authority. |
| Assessment is regular, is systematic, is often based on external norms and claims an objective basis with an emphasis on pre-defined criteria. | Assessment is multi-faceted and includes self-assessment and reflection, portfolios and ongoing observation, and is more formative than cumulative. |
| Knowledge may be perceived as static or fixed. | Knowledge is seen as organic, constantly in flux and interpretative in nature. |
| Learners are very often encouraged to adopt an individual attitude to their work and generally undertake their learning alone. | Group and pair work are encouraged, with considerable emphasis on sharing insights, ways of thinking and solving, and constructing meaning through engagement with peers. |

## PROBLEM-BASED LEARNING

As constructivism has developed and gained a great deal of attention within educational debate, various related attempts to locate it firmly within classrooms have also come to the fore. One of the most prominent constructivist-inspired approaches to teaching and learning is problem-based learning (PLB). PLB attempts to draw considerably on the insights offered by Vygotsky, Bruner and Dewey, and provides teachers with tangible and practical ways to develop a constructivist classroom where engaging and participative learning is to the fore. The principal basis of PBL is to initiate learners into modes of self-directed learning through solving problems, applying solutions to other problems, absorbing facts meaningfully rather than by rote memorisation and more didactic approaches.

It is argued that PBL has a number of unique features that enhance the quality of learning, for example:

- PBL seeks to engage with problems that are significant to, and very often generated by, the learners themselves. By engaging with these real issues, the learners not only encounter content meaningfully but also develop a strong sense of critical analysis.
- As a constructivist approach, PBL strives to support learners in becoming independent learners, and so responsibility for learning moves from teacher to learners in a planned and incremental way.
- The problems addressed are deliberately ones that allow for a variety of outcomes and possibilities, with many opportunities to revisit and review. This revisiting allows for new perspectives and an appreciation of knowledge as evolving rather than inert and fixed.
- The chosen problem provides the primary focal point for engagement with the curriculum.
- An aspiration towards developing life-long learners is embedded in PBL, with a strong emphasis on learners developing lasting curiosity, applicable learning attributes, and durable qualities of evaluation, review and reconsideration.

(Adapted from Stepien and Gallagher 1993)

Young learners will very often ask questions such as, 'Why are my eyes brown?' or 'Why is the grass green?' or 'Why is the sky blue?' and very often the rigours of curriculum transmission prompt teachers not to engage in addressing these concerns. In a classroom where PBL is to the fore, the learning opportunities these questions present are recognised and pursued. Beginning with a problem of considerable interest to the learner, and a belief that the learner has some prior but incomplete knowledge, the teacher strives to build a worthwhile structure for exploration of the problem. In many cases, the answers to these questions are multi-faceted and complex, and require an investigation that covers several aspects of a broad curriculum.

Very often, discussion among learners in groups with the purpose of sharing prior knowledge is the first stage. Ideas emerge. Further questions are structured. Some are set aside; others are given precedence but with the view that these questions may be revisited as the process evolves. Eventually, some hypotheses are formed and these working speculations are taken forward for further investigation. Very often, teachers introduce a structure of questioning along the following lines:

- What do I know about the question already?
- What do I want and need to know?
- How and where will I find the information?

As learners engage further, the questions above provide a degree of structure and direction for inquiry. By garnering information, insights and perspectives from ever-increasing sources, learners begin to develop skills of discernment, prioritisation of need and knowledge, and evaluation of materials and sources. This is particularly relevant when engaging in internet searching, but also has relevance to more traditional forms of inquiry through encyclopaedia, texts, magazines and reference material.

## The Teacher and Problem-Based Learning

The position given to problem-solving within the Primary School Curriculum 1999 is evident in the following aspiration:

> The curriculum envisages a particular relationship between the acquisition of knowledge and the development of concepts and skills.... Strong emphasis is placed on developing the ability to question, to analyse, to investigate, to think critically, to solve problems, and to interact effectively with others. (NCCA 1999: 11)

Adopting a problem-based learning approach further stresses such an orientation. It is clear that the traditional role of the teacher is quite fundamentally challenged by PBL. At the heart of problem-based learning is giving the learners a problem that really connects with their environment, empowering them to develop possible solutions and facilitating processes for the learning that ensues. Savoie and Hughes suggest the following set of steps in undertaking PBL:

1. Begin with a problem.
2. Ensure that the problem connects with the students' world.
3. Organise the subject matter around the problem, not around the disciplines.
4. Give students the major responsibility for shaping and directing their own learning.
5. Use small teams as the context for most learning.
6. Require students to demonstrate what they have learned through a product or a performance.

(1994: 54–7)

Although teacher involvement throughout the PBL process is essential, its nature changes substantially as learners move through the stages. In the initial stages – when you introduce PBL to your learners and initiate the challenge or problem – you are making decisions, giving information, providing insights, and responding to questions about how the process works and what is expected of your learners. As matters progress, learners take on more responsibility for their work, their planning and their research, and your role as teacher becomes more facilitative – you offer advice and work in tandem with them as they encounter difficulties. In the final stages, learners, hopefully, are engrossed in their own projects, while you provide support, additional advice, feedback and both formative and summative assessment of the work in progress.

What are some of the implications of PBL for our teaching and our conception of the role of the teacher? Kemp (2011) argues that if teaching were to be approached from a constructivist point of view, such as when PBL is adopted, teachers would:

- Make the social context of the classroom a central concern.
- Accept that the teacher is part of the equation and not all of the equation.
- Value learner understanding more than transmitting information.

(Adapted from Kemp 2011)

The issues raised by Kemp may provoke further questions, such as when to intervene, how much assistance is required, what kinds of expectations do we have of our learners, should we as teachers exemplify good research practices, how should we undertake that modelling, how ought we delegate more and more responsibility for learning to learners, and indeed many other questions. Addressing these questions and drawing on our observations and experience of learning may assist us in developing a perspective on PBL, one that offers balanced insight on claims such as that of Savery, who argues:

> [I]t is vitally important that current and future generations of students experience a problem-based learning approach and engage in constructive solution-seeking activities. The bar has been raised as the 21st century gathers momentum and, more than ever, higher-order thinking skills, self-regulated learning habits, and problem-solving skills are necessary for all students. Providing students with opportunities to develop and refine these skills will take the efforts of many individuals. (2006: 18)

---

### TASK 5.6: DEVISING QUESTIONS THAT IGNITE IMAGINATIONS

We are advised that in PBL the best projects always contain an 'essential question' that both inspires and requires students to conduct serious research. However, the essential question will probably change as you design your project. The following criteria should be borne in mind when devising a compelling question:

- It should be a question that relates to the 'real world'.
- It should be a question that is not easy to answer and stretches learners' intellectual muscles.
- It should be a question that ignites learners' imaginations.

For example:

- How have past inventions helped to create the complex life of today?
- How can we design homes that have a minimal ecological footprint?

Choose one of these age groups – 5–6 years, 7–8 years, 10–12 years. Devise three questions for your chosen age group that you think would meet the above criteria.

---

## COLLABORATIVE LEARNING

The emphasis placed by the Primary School Curriculum 1999 on the issue of collaborative learning in schools is noteworthy. The *Primary School Curriculum Introduction* elaborates in the following terms:

> While it is important that children experience a variety of classroom organisational frameworks, working collaboratively provides learning opportunities that have particular advantages. Children are stimulated by hearing the ideas and opinions of others, and by having the opportunity to react to them. Collaborative work exposes children to the individual perceptions that others may have of a problem or a situation. These will reflect the different personalities and particular abilities of other members of the group and make for an interactive exchange that will help to broaden and deepen individual children's understanding. Moreover, the experience of collaborative learning facilitates the child's social and personal development, and the practice of working with others brings children to an early appreciation of the benefits to be gained from co-operative effort. (NCCA 1999: 17)

Advocates of collaborative learning have argued that learners' critical abilities are strengthened when working together, learners' interest is heightened, responsibility for learning shifts in a beneficial way to the learners, and learners grasp and engage with concepts, ideas and facts more satisfactorily than in cases of solitary learning (Dooly 2008).

## What Is Collaborative Learning?

Collaborative learning is a broad term for a spectrum of methods all of which involve the combined efforts of learners working together. Activities may be very broad in scope, though generally the issues are related to exploring aspects of the curriculum directly. However, as outlined above, collaborative learning can also be built around questions that are raised by learners and the curriculum provides one of many resources. The teacher in this situation strives to build an environment in which learners are motivated and enabled to work together in a conducive and stimulating atmosphere, where ideas, thoughts and emerging understandings can be shared.

The teacher's role is to create an environment where young people are willing and able to work collaboratively, where there are plenty of opportunities and stimulating contexts for learners to work with others, and where learners feel safe to share their emerging ideas and understandings. However, it is well to note that merely putting learners in groups does not automatically ensure the success of collaborative learning, as Johnson and Johnson argue:

> (T)here is nothing magical about putting students in groups. Students can compete with groupmates, students can work individualistically while ignoring groupmates, or students can work cooperatively with groupmates. In order to structure cooperative learning effectively, teachers need to understand how to structure positive interdependence, individual accountability, promotive interaction, appropriate use of social skills, and group processing into learning situations. (Johnson and Johnson, 1998: 328)

From our own experience, we know that not all groups are automatically cooperative in their workings (Johnson and Johnson 2009). The arbitrary designation of groups based on size, location in the classroom or previous customs does not ensure worthwhile collaboration. To ensure meaningful collaboration and collaborative learning, and to attain the full possibilities of the group, a number of crucial rudiments need to be carefully designed into the classroom site. In Johnson and Johnson's view, these may be described as 'positive interdependence, individual and group accountability, promotive interaction, appropriate use of social skills, and group processing' (Johnson and Johnson 1998: 332). Johnson and Johnson's conditions for successful collaborative learning are outlined in Figure 5.2 and are described as follows:

1.  To the fore is positive interdependence whereby learners and teachers create an atmosphere of strong reliance on each other for the success of the learning process.

2. The second key aspect of collaborative learning focuses on individual and group accountability: while the group as a whole is responsible for achieving its goals, every individual must also be responsible for undertaking his or her part of the process.

3. As a third requirement, Johnson and Johnson emphasise what is termed 'promotive interaction' as indispensable. An atmosphere of mutuality, support, sharing and commitment to others is intrinsic to any worthwhile context of learners co-teaching each other, and discussing, offering and seeking explanations, direction and insight collaboratively.

4. The fourth element involves teachers teaching the rudiments of group work skills, such as listening, communication skills, leadership approaches, decision-making skills, how to build trust and resolve disputes, and other desirable capabilities required in undertaking a collaborative learning process.

5. As a final element, Johnson and Johnson focus on group processing, which might also be described as active reflection. The ability to reflect on individual and group progress, the sense of positive relationships within the group, how work is undertaken and the many other aspects of the collaborative process are viewed as central to enhancing and developing the process.

Figure 5.2: Conditions for Successful Collaborative Learning

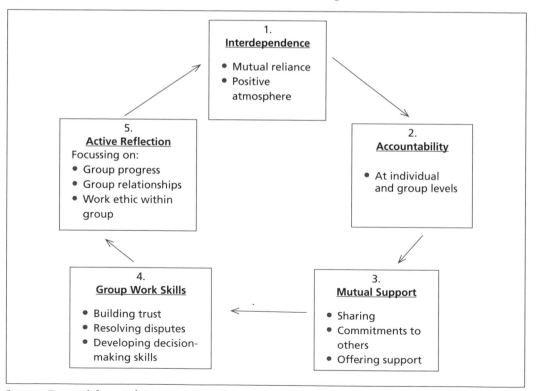

Source: Derived from Johnson, D.W. and Johnson, F.P. (2009), *Joining Together: Group Theory and Group Skills*, Boston: Allyn & Bacon: 332.

---

### TASK 5.7: WHY DOES WHOLE-CLASS TEACHING REMAIN THE DOMINANT APPROACH?

A recent review – *The Primary Classroom: Insights from the Growing Up in Ireland Study* – makes the following comments on group work and collaborative learning in Irish primary schools:

> The Primary School Curriculum (Government of Ireland, 1999) presented a strong vision of child-centred education, with children viewed as active agents in their own learning. To what extent is this vision matched by the reality? Findings in this report provide systematic evidence that whole-class teaching continues to be the dominant approach used in primary education, with much less use of active learning methods (such as group-work) than had been envisaged in the original curriculum document. (McCoy *et al.* 2012: ii)

Speculate as to why whole-class teaching continues to dominate in schooling, drawing on your own experiences as a learner.

---

### M-LEVEL TASK 5.3: PROMOTING COLLABORATIVE LEARNING

Read McCoy, S. *et al.* (2012), *The Primary Classroom: Insights from the Growing Up in Ireland Study*, Chapter 3, available from: http://www.ncca.ie/en/The_Primary_Classroom_ESRI_January_18_2012.pdf.

Suggest two strategies to advance the use of collaborative group approaches in primary schools.

---

Based on the insights we have gained into the work of Dewey, Vygotsky and Bruner above, we can reasonably speculate that these educators would locate such approaches as problem-based learning and collaborative learning within a constructivist framework. With these approaches, learners are viewed as active social agents undertaking meaningful and authentic tasks, addressing real issues, and creating knowledge and learning skills in active engagement with their physical and social environments. In this way, they create meaning for themselves about their surrounding world. The above theorists would all recognise, however, that the constructivist approach must be tempered by well-structured teaching and conscientious preparation. According to Dewey (1938), it is the educator's duty to guarantee that the following two features are present: initially, it is vital that the problem originates from the conditions of an experience that is within the capacity of learners; moreover, the problem ought to be sufficiently motivating so that learners will be moved to ascertain more insight and to stimulate the generation of fresh insights. These two features form the basis for the exploration of further ongoing experiences where new problems are encountered, and the process takes the form of a regenerating spiral of learning. Dewey also focuses on the responsibility schools have for building on learners' natural curiosity in their social environment, and on the need to do so by encouraging interpersonal communication and group engagement. When collaborating with others, learners experience the richness of others' insights, they absorb socially appropriate behaviours, and they come to appreciate the value of cooperating and working together. Dewey's approach to collaborative learning is not just an additional option that might or might not be employed. Instead, cooperative, collaborative learning emerges as a key aspect within his philosophy of education. According to Dewey, central to the work of schools is the creation of classroom environments in which learners have bountiful opportunities to explore their experiences, to enquire, to create, to experiment, to plan and to undertake activities cooperatively, and to learn for themselves but under the leadership of the teacher. Such environments, in Dewey's view, serve a broader societal set of values, namely to build

> A society of free individuals in which all, through their own work, contribute to the liberation and enrichment of the lives of others. [It] is the only environment in which any individual can really grow normally to his full stature. (1934: 12)

## PLAY-BASED LEARNING

Play is the means by which young learners explore and engage with the world, develop a sense of self and learn how to interact with others (Sanderson 2010). Article 31 of the 1989 United Nations Convention on the Rights of the Child recognises the need for learners to engage in age-appropriate 'play and recreational activities'.

Our understanding of the concept of play in early learning has evolved through the centuries and has embraced various definitions and perspectives formulated by theorists from a number of disciplines. This continuum spans the work of philosophers such as the Classical Greek philosopher Plato, John Amos Comenius (1592–1670) and John Locke (1632–1704), and educationalists such as Jean-Jacques Rousseau (1712–78), Johann Pestalozzi (1746–1827), Friedrich Fröbel (1782–1852), Maria Montessori (1870–1952), Rudolf Steiner (1861–1925), John Dewey (1859–1952), Jean Piaget (1896–1980), Lev Vygotsky (1896–1934), Jerome Bruner (1915–) and Loris Malaguzzi (1920–94). Montessori regarded play as 'the child's work' (1967: 180) and Dewey believed it was important to provide many different experiences to enable learning through play 'as a lifelong process in which children grew and learned along the way' (Platz and Arellano 2011: 56). More recently, Piaget and Bruner have highlighted play as a means of cognitive development. Vygotsky regarded play as 'an adaptive mechanism promoting cognitive growth' (Rubin *et al.* 1983: 709). In Italy, Loris Malaguzzi and the Reggio Emilia movement popularised the notion of young learners having agency and being 'architects of their own learning' (Dodd-Nufrio 2011: 236).

Much recent research has highlighted that play facilitates learners' self-regulation, literacy development and school readiness. Learners are more competent and creative across a range of cognitive areas when they are given the choice to engage in different well-organised and age-appropriate activities (CCL 2006). Playfulness, according to Sanderson (2010), is the expression of the learner's drive to freely and pleasurably engage with, connect with and explore the surrounding world. The capacity within each learner to fully and freely engage in play is represented in the following four domains:

- **Active engagement** – where the learner is intrinsically motivated to participate in the given activity.
- **Internal control** – refers to the learner's sense of safety, balance and competence that allow for comfortable engagement with the surrounding world. Internal control also refers to the learner's ability to self-regulate.
- **Social connection** – refers to the learner's cooperative interaction with others and the surrounding world. It is through play that learners connect with peers in complex ways and learn more about themselves and the world.
- **Joyfulness** – refers to the learner's sense of love, fulfillment and hope that are expressed with displays of pleasure and exuberance. Joyfulness is a necessary and universal component of the definition of play and is characterised by the learner's uninhibited abandon while engaged in the play activity.

(Adapted from Sanderson 2010)

*Aistear: The Early Childhood Curriculum Framework* (NCCA 2009) prioritises play as a pedagogy and endorses the centrality of play in early learning, as set out in 'Principles and Themes':

Much of children's early learning and development takes place through play and hands-on experiences. Through these, children explore social, physical and imaginary worlds. These experiences help them to manage their feelings, develop as thinkers and language users, develop socially, be creative and imaginative, and lay the foundations for becoming effective communicators and learners. (NCCA 2009: 11)

Throughout *Aistear*, examples are provided of learning experiences that promote the use of a variety of types of play to support learning across the four themes: *Well-being, Identity and Belonging, Communicating,* and *Exploring and Thinking.*

The *Primary School Curriculum Introduction* also espouses learning by doing and states that the learner should be an active agent in his or her own learning (NCCA 1999). It highlights the importance of play as a means of enabling young learners to be active in their learning:

> The curriculum for infants … is, in the first place, based on the uniqueness of the child and the particular needs of individual children at this stage of development. The informality of the learning experience inherent in it, and the emphasis it gives to the element of play, are particularly suited to the learning needs of young children. (NCCA 1999: 30)

## A SUMMARY OF KEY POINTS

- The basic tenets of child-centred education have been developed on the basis of many insights, not least those of John Dewy and Jerome Bruner.
- Some substantial and significant differences exist between a didactic and constructivist classroom.
- Problem-based learning, collaborative learning and play-based learning draw considerably on constructivist influences on learning. In such learning environments, learners have agency and are viewed as active social agents undertaking meaningful and authentic tasks, addressing real problems, and creating knowledge and learning skills in active engagement with their physical and social environment.

# CHAPTER SIX

# Research and a Research-led Profession of Teaching

*Why should I engage in research?*

*Are there different types of research?*

*What kinds of questions about education interest me?*

**When you have worked through this chapter you will have:**

- Gained an introduction to the importance of research in developing teaching as a research-led profession.
- Become familiar with existing paradigms within educational research.
- Developed an appreciation of a broad range of methodologies and approaches available to the researcher in education.
- Given consideration to initiating your own research inquiry in an aspect of education.

## INTRODUCTION

D eveloping as a student teacher requires the development of research skills. This requirement is based on evidence that teachers who actively engage in research and inquiry meet the challenges of teaching in a more thoughtful, informed and responsive manner.

---

### TASK 6.1: BENEFITS OF RESEARCH

Outline five benefits that might accrue to a teacher who undertakes regular research into his or her professional work.

---

Engaging with research as an intrinsic aspect of your scholarly work as a student teacher develops your awareness of emerging perspectives, approaches and findings within the field of educational theory. Undertaking your own research, which involves learning to analyse data and distill judgements, helps you to develop ownership of the research process.

Good research practice requires openness to many strands of research. When you engage meaningfully with the research process, you will become exposed to a multiplicity of insights. Educational research, since it principally involves the spectrum of human learning, is multi-faceted, complex and challenging. Often it raises contradictions, anomalies, dilemmas and questions which, in turn, stimulate further questioning and the application of different approaches and methods.

A key concept in teacher education nowadays is the development of an inquiry mindset and this idea underpins the prominent place of research. The importance of the teacher creating meaning within their own contexts, informed by their own scholarship, perceptions, reflections and the knowledge of their own particular challenges has been very widely recognised. This view of teaching has been recently endorsed by *Codes of Professional Conduct for Teachers* (Teaching Council 2007), which stresses that teachers, by '(d)rawing on practitioner-based research...plan for teaching and learning through continuous reflection on their own current practice' (17).

This term 'practitioner-based research' owes its origins to a wide range of scholars. A great deal can be derived from arguments advanced by Stenhouse (1975), Elliott (1991), Cochran-Smith and Lytle (1993), McNiff (2001), and Ziechner and Noffke (2001). In broad terms, these scholars argue for the necessity of considerable curriculum reform, with teachers taking central roles as researchers into both curriculum innovation and the practices of teaching. The following concerns are paramount within a practitioner-based research perspective:

- Teachers' own work, and their insights, motivations and interest should act a basis for research.
- Critical reflection and a systematic study of practice should be a key aspect.
- A sense of practitioner ownership and decision-making about research is of central importance. Undertaking the research is therefore perceived as an act of self-empowerment.
- The continual improvement of practice (McNiff 2001) is a key and unavoidable motivation for practitioner-based research.
- Very often the research is open-ended, ongoing and without fixed hypotheses.
- In many cases, it embodies a great deal of self-evaluation, but very often it is undertaken in a participatory climate with fellow professionals and learners, and in an environment of openness, democratic practice and mutuality.
- Typically, practitioner-based research maintains a healthy dynamic between diagnosis, action and reflection, thereby enhancing the quality of all learners' experiences of learning (McNiff 2001).
- Practitioner research is generally undertaken on a small scale and allows for the reality of practitioners' busy schedules.

You will engage with these concerns within your teacher education programme when you begin to prepare your dissertation in educational research.

---

### TASK 6.2: FORMULATING RESEARCH QUESTIONS

Think of an inquiry, an intervention or change you would like to undertake in your classroom work. Write a few notes about the intervention or change that you seek to initiate and formulate it as a question, for example:

- 'Will shared reading approaches give learners in Third Class more confidence in reading and tangibly impact their reading scores?'
- 'Does group work have a positive impact on some children's sense of confidence?'

Share your question with a peer and have them assess its clarity. Is the research question sufficiently directed and clear? Perhaps they might advise you on different means of gathering data. Rework your question with greater focus and clarity in mind, and consider different ways of deriving the data. This task can be undertaken in tandem with reading this chapter and coming to terms with the various research approaches outlined.

**M-LEVEL TASK 6.1: CONSIDERING PRACTITIONER RESEARCH**

Read and review the following article. In your review outline some key points of agreement and some key points of dispute with arguments advanced in the article.

Bartlett, S. and Burton, D. (2006), 'Practitioner research or descriptions of classroom practice? A discussion of teachers investigating their classrooms,' *Educational Action Research*, 14(3): 395–405.

## PARADIGMS IN EDUCATIONAL RESEARCH

The new researcher in education is faced with an array of ways to undertake research. Each approach or methodology is typified by different conceptual understandings, philosophies, methods and understandings. These methodologies and approaches are often controversial and disputed within this broad field. In this introductory chapter, we hope to come to terms with some key concepts, map out a broad set of understandings within the sphere and create a platform for your further study in the area.

Hammersley (2012) outlines many of the persistent controversies that surround educational research. Some of the disputes he cites have developed along the following lines:

> Should [educational research] be neutral in political orientation or should it be, for example, committed to challenging inequalities (in relation to social class, gender, sexual orientation, disability, ethnicity or race, religion, etc)?…Should the process and product of all research be under the control of specially trained researchers, or should it be pursued in partnership with participants in the setting being studied? More radically, should the latter be in control of research? Is qualitative evidence superior to quantitative evidence, or vice versa? Can and should these different methods be 'combined' or 'mixed'? Should there be criteria by which the quality of research is judged? If so, what are these? (Hammersley 2012:1)

The issues of research neutrality or objectivity, ethics, the control of research, the degree of partnership and participation within the research process, the nature of evidence and whether it is qualitatively or quantitatively derived, and the use of mixed approaches and methods are all issues of concern.

The terms 'quantitative' and 'qualitative' research are often used to designate a broad division as two distinct paradigms. A paradigm is a worldview, a framework of values, beliefs and methods; in this context, a paradigm is a worldview within which research takes place and researchers work.

## A Quantitative Approach within a Positivist Paradigm

The term 'quantitative research' is very often associated with a positivist paradigm. In the broadest terms, in research, a positivist paradigm exhibits several of the following understandings of knowledge, knowing and the nature of reality:

- There is an assumption that an objective and measurable world exists and can be known and explained by the inquirer. This is sometimes referred to as a realist ontology or realist sense of being (see Glossary).
- This reality can be examined, represented in an objective manner and compared with the findings and explanations of other inquirers or researchers. You could, for instance, identify, synthesise, analyse and compare a wide range of studies on the techniques employed in the use of paired reading.
- The positivist paradigm broadly holds that objective reality or objective knowledge is achievable and that its claims on truth can be compared with similar research or updated as further quantitative research occurs. Equally, the paradigm generally claims that more and more accurate degrees of prediction are possible, particularly as we undertake more and better quantitative research.
- Research within the positivist paradigm is typically undertaken by means of empirical, scientific or semi-scientific strategies with a heavy reliance on observation, quantification and statistical analysis.
- The positivist paradigm places faith in its capacity to be value free, particularly if strict methodological processes are followed. Belief in the emergence of objective knowledge from the research process is allied with the view that bias or subjectivity can be counteracted or minimalised. There is also an assertion that replication of one's findings by others is possible, as long as strict quantitative procedures are maintained.
- The process of research within the positivist paradigm usually begins with the generation of ideas, leading to the formulation of hypotheses. Certain hypotheses are then prioritised for further study and testing. For instance, a researcher may seek to pose the following hypotheses for testing, namely that 'teachers who are in receipt of higher remuneration for their work will have more positive attitudes toward learners than teachers who are given lower pay.' Testing such a hypothesis can take many forms, with tests and trials, experiments, and various forms of intervention. Broadly, however, most testing within a positivist paradigm is undertaken within a quantifiable framework that is reliant upon mathematical analysis. Researchers within the positivist framework and paradigm also tend to evaluate research in terms of the following criteria: validity, reliability and generalisability.

Joppe explains the concept of *validity* in quantitative research as follows:

> Validity determines whether the research truly measures that which it was intended to measure or how truthful the research results are. In other words, does the research instrument allow you to hit 'the bull's eye' of your research object? (cited in Golafshani 2003: 599)

*Reliability* can be described as the extent to which outcomes remain consistent. Findings are said to be reliable if other researchers can replicate the results of a study by using the same methods (Blaxter *et al.*, 1996: 200). Reliability, within the positivist paradigm, necessitates a choice of approaches and quantitative methods that clearly demonstrate 'consistency and replicability over time, over instruments and over groups of respondents' (Cohen *et al.*, 2000: 117).

*Generalisability* refers to the extent to which the findings of a study can be applied externally or more broadly outside of the study's context. A research finding may be entirely valid in one setting but not in another. However, generalisability depicts the extent to which research findings can be applied to surroundings other than those in which they were initially measured.

### The Possibilities and Limitations of Positivist Research

Positivism has played a significant role in educational research. Clearly, the positivist tradition has led to advances in our knowledge of children and learning. We need only to view the area of reading skills and related research to appreciate such developments. Before beginning a review of some alternative models, we can conclude this section by drawing together some of the important potentialities and, indeed, limitations of the positivist paradigm and its attendant quantitative methodological approaches:

- It displays a capacity to specify the research problem in exact and rigorous language (Frankfort-Nachmias and Nachmias 1992).
- It may have the ability to identify and recognise clearly all variables under investigation.
- It allows researchers to pursue research objectives rigorously, and to reach very objective findings while keeping a high level of reliability due to the use of controlled observations, laboratory experiments, mass surveys or other forms of research intervention (Balsley 1970).
- It is argued that adherence to the paradigm serves to eliminate or render impotent the qualities of subjectivity and personal judgement (Kealey and Protheroe 1996).
- Adherents of quantitative research argue that the researcher can maintain a

dispassionate interest in the outcomes, and, if the processes within the paradigm are properly applied, a strong degree of objectivity is established and sustained (Gall *et al.* 2003).

- Finally, the universality and consistency of quantitative methods are often advanced as a major advantage by proponents. Previously generated data, templates, methods, techniques, rules, rubrics and processes offer social scientists, including educational researchers, a wealth of replicable ways in which to undertake research in different contexts (Creswell 2003).

A great deal of criticism has also been generated in respect of the positivist paradigm in educational research and its reliance on quantitative methodologies. A substantial degree of this criticism focuses on the inextricable engagement of human subjects and human inquirers within the research process. The argument often takes the form that, because of the strict requirement to control variables, quantitative research on learners is often undertaken with little understanding of context. The emotional and tacit qualities that attend every human engagement are dismissed or sidelined, and the truly holistic nature of learners and learning may be ignored. Artificial environments may be constructed in which to undertake research. These settings may serve to alter behaviours, engagement and a myriad of other factors attending meaningful learning.

The apparent objectivity claimed by the positivist tradition has been regularly queried, with claims that in reality such objectivity is an illusion and that it is not feasible to negate the impact, biases and predilections of the researcher within the research process when encountering aspects of the human condition (Coffey 1999). In addition, reservations have been expressed regarding a tendency to isolate human capacities for the purposes of research. The scrutiny of singular aspects of human behaviour – for example, concepts such as recall, attention and perception – is criticised as it may be undertaken in a disembodied manner contrary to the ways in which these attributes are integrated in full human experiencing. Human experiencing, it is claimed, is far more complex and richer than the positivist paradigm accepts and some critics would even endorse Mack's assertion that

it is impossible for any theory in social science to be simple and precise because the world we live in and peoples' multiple perspectives and interpretations of events make theories complex and chaotic. So many variables affect different events and people's actions that it is impossible to determine an absolute truth. (Mack 2010: 7)

---

### TASK 6.3: EXPLORING QUANTITATIVE RESEARCH

Read the following paper and critique the benefits and limitations of the approach taken in the study described.

Spor, M.W. and Kane Schneider, B. (2001), 'A Quantitative Description of the Content Reading Practices of Beginning Teachers,' *Reading Horizons*, 41(4): 257–73.

---

## A Qualitative Paradigm

The following description by Johnson and Onwuegbuzie might serve to outline some of the key philosophical and methodological differences that separate the positivist paradigm from qualitatively inspired research.

> Qualitative purists (also called constructivists and interpretivists) reject what they call positivism….These purists contend that multiple-constructed realities abound, that time- and context-free generalizations are neither desirable nor possible, that research is value-bound, that it is impossible to differentiate fully causes and effects, that logic flows from specific to general (e.g., explanations are generated inductively from the data), and that knower and known cannot be separated because the subjective knower is the only source of reality (Guba, 1990). Qualitative purists also are characterized by a dislike of a detached and passive style of writing, preferring, instead, detailed, rich, and thick (empathic) description, written directly and somewhat informally. (2004: 14)

This description identifies some key characteristics of qualitative research. A key element of the qualitative approach is concerned with how we view reality. Is reality something from which we can be detached and separated? Indeed, is reality singular or multiple in nature? Is anything close to a value-free interpretation of reality even possible?

---

### M-LEVEL TASK 6.2: REVIEWING RESEARCH PARADIGMS

Read and review the following article. In your review make an evaluation of the authors' categorisation of research typologies and paradigms.

Johnson, R.B. and Onwuegbuzie, A.J. (2004), 'Mixed Methods Research: A Research Paradigm Whose Time Has Come,' *Educational Researcher*, 33(7): 14–26, available from: http://www.jstor.org/stable/3700093.

Some prominent methodologies have been developed within the qualitative paradigm, and a brief introduction to these is provided below. In your ongoing engagement with educational research, you will encounter more comprehensive and in-depth descriptions of these methodologies and perhaps be in a position to engage with some through your own research.

## Phenomenological Research

Phenomenological research involves the inquirer seeking to understand how individuals actually experience a particular phenomenon in their lives. An example might be a phenomenological study of a young learner who has recently arrived from another society so that we might better understand how children deal with emigration and resettlement. Central to such a phenomenological study is the researcher's effort to comprehend how the phenomenon of emigration and resettlement is experienced from the perspective of the person undergoing the experience. The goal is to understand the perspectives and experiences of each participant by entering their inner world. Some significant phenomenological studies have been undertaken in recent years. Clearly related to the topic just cited is Anna Kirova and Michael Emme's study entitled 'Immigrant Children's Bodily Engagement in Accessing Their Lived Experiences of Immigration' (2009). Such research seeks to illustrate the complexities of the motivations and often elusive emotional experiencing at play in such a complex context.

## Ethnographic Research

Ethnography is a form of qualitative research used by anthropologists to study human culture and society, and the actions of people within the labyrinths of culture and society. Significantly, most ethnographers hold a broad view of culture that encompasses the attitudes, beliefs, actions and values that impact on behaviour patterns within a group of people. While some disputes exist about the nature of ethnography, we might proceed, albeit in a tentative manner, with the following definition of the field:

> Ethnography refers primarily to a particular method or set of methods. In its most characteristic form it involves the ethnographer participating overtly or covertly in people's daily lives for an extended period of time, watching what happens, listening to what is said, asking questions – in fact collecting whatever data are available to throw light on the issues that are the focus of research. (Hammersley and Atkinson 2007: 1)

Ethnographers in educational research undertake a sustained examination of the dynamics involved in a particular social setting, such as a classroom, playground, parents' group or staff room. These settings can be complicated, with many influences on learning, interaction, relationships, group dynamics, etc., and ethnographers seek to come to understand these and other less discernible factors. In doing so, they employ 'ethnographic approaches'. Highly detailed participant observation, observation and recording in 'naturally occurring settings', interviews with groups and individuals, the study of photos, audio and video recordings, the collection and examination of the significance of artefacts within the location, assiduous note-taking, the collection of cultural stories, and examining informal and formal written and spoken documents generated within the social group under examination are some of the most commonly applied methods within the ethnographic approach.

Advocates of ethnographic research claim that it can unearth many hidden influences at work in a setting in a manner often not available to other forms of research. Immersion in the situation, it is claimed, allows a more comprehensive picture of the situation to emerge, be that interaction in the playground, learners' behaviour in the corridors or teachers' views on individual learners, as expressed in the staff room or elsewhere.

This process is not without issues of concern. Very significantly, similarities and differences in understanding between the researcher and members of the group being researched often emerge as very pertinent and can prompt questions about the influence of subjectivity in the generation of insight and knowledge. The ethnographic approach involves moving from description to explanation, and in that shift lie many troubling dilemmas for the researcher as they must come to terms with their own biases, personal beliefs, cultural understandings and unconscious acceptance of established institutional arrangements (Tedlock 2001).

## Case Studies

It is claimed that case study research has the particular benefits of assisting our understanding of quite complex situations, broadening our experience of these complexities and connecting our new insights with what is already known through previous research. More specifically, a case study is a methodological approach centred on unearthing a thorough depiction of a particular situation, process or activity at a precise time. Willig (2008) argues that case studies 'are not characterized by the methods used to collect and analyze data, but rather [their] focus on a particular unit of analysis: a case' (74).

Defining what constitutes a case can, however, require considerable reflection. Case studies tend to be limited in specific ways and involve the scrutiny of an individual or a number of individuals, an organisation or sub-unit of an organisation, a school or small number of schools, a class or number of classes within a school, or, indeed, an event within any of these organisations. In general terms, case studies derive and present information or data that is usually gleaned through a multiplicity of means, including, but not confined to, observations, interviews, audio and video recordings, and relevant documents. Typically, however, many case studies employ a number of approaches drawn from the following: direct observation of human actions within a particular environment; the use of interviews (often open-ended and undertaken with significant participants within the setting); the scrutiny of archival records (roll books, attendance sheets, results); the examination of relevant documents (circulars, letters and policy statements); varying degrees of participant observation (perhaps sometimes with the researcher fulfilling a dual role as both researcher and participant within the situation under scrutiny); and the examination of artefacts within the setting, such as artwork, computer records, etc. The purpose of collecting data through a diversity of approaches is to enrich the theory-generating abilities of the case and to examine the validity or otherwise of points of view advanced by the researcher or by the human subjects or actors within the case itself.

Many highly renowned case study researchers such as Stake (2008) and Yin (2005) have explored a variety of approaches to undertaking case studies. Some of their common operational suggestions for conducting successful case study research may be set out in the following six stages, about which some level of agreement exists in the field of case study research:

1. The determination and definition of the research questions
2. The selection of cases and determination of the data gathering and analysis techniques
3. Preparation for the collection of data
4. Collection of data in the field
5. Evaluation and analysis of the data
6. Preparation of the report

Undoubtedly, case studies are multi-faceted, complex and dependent on several sources of information or data. Several occurrences and events may merit attention within one case study in order to construct as vivid a picture as possible. Consequently, large amounts of data may be generated, posing a considerable issue for analysis and processing. Researchers from many areas of study employ case studies in order to explain a situation or phenomenon, to augment or dispute an existing theory or set of theories, to discern solutions to a persistent problem, to generate new theoretical perspectives and, often, to give much greater access to readers in terms of comprehending tangible real-life and contemporary situations and problems.

Some critics of the case study maintain that the very particularity of the method and its application to very specific situations undermines its ability to offer reliable and generalisable explanations and insight. Others argue that the very immersion of the researcher in the process can prejudice the findings. However, case study research continues to be well represented in social science and advocates abound, not least

Stoecker, who argues that the case study is intensive research in which interpretations are given 'based on observable concrete interconnections between actual properties and people within an actual concrete setting' (1991: 95). Stoecker also contends that a 'case study is the best way by which we can refine general theory and apply effective interventions in complex situations' (109). In other words, case studies allow researchers to explore the different outcomes of general processes suggested by theories in different contexts, which may suit educational settings where the application of theories to actual practice is pertinent.

---

### TASK 6.4: REVIEWING CASE STUDIES

Green-Schools Ireland (http://www.greenschoolsireland.org/case-studies.146.html) has conducted a number of case studies in respect of environmental awareness in the education sector. Choose one such study and review it in terms of approaches adopted, data generated, findings outlined and recommendations offered.

---

### M-LEVEL TASK 6.3: FORMULATING CASE STUDY RESEARCH QUESTIONS

In a group of four, choose a topic for a case study you would like to undertake. Identify some simple questions to be addressed by your case study and then think about them in the context of the following:

- Does the naming of these questions also set the boundaries of your case, with regard to the appropriate duration of time within which evidence is to be amassed?
- Do the questions set boundaries for the organisation or geographic area to be explored?
- Do the questions you have set assist you in recognising the nature of the data that should be collected?

Having examined them in terms of the above points, perhaps you need to redefine your set of questions that will form the basis for your study.

---

The spectrum of qualitative research in education is broad and continues to develop. Any summary of approaches would be incomplete without mention of a number of outstanding research processes, including grounded theory, historical research and philosophical research. As your engagement with research in education continues, these approaches will inevitably emerge as significant aspects of the qualitative paradigm.

## Grounded Theory

Grounded theory is largely a qualitative research method devised by Glaser and Strauss (1967). It offers a general methodology for devising theory that is founded or grounded in data that is assiduously collected and scrutinised (Strauss and Corbin 1994). Theory emerges and develops during the research processes because of the interaction between the collection of data and the processes of analysis. An essential aspect of grounded theory is the generation of a theory based on possible and probable connections between data, concepts and the researcher. As such, grounded theory may be said to be characterised by flux, evolution, and considerable analysis and revision on the part of the researcher.

Grounded theory is a systematic method of qualitative data analysis leading to the discovery of theory from data. In this method, data collection, analysis and eventual theory stand in close relationship with one another. A researcher does not begin with pre-conceived notions but lets the theory emerge as the study progresses and the data are analysed. Grounded theory aims to organise the many ideas that emerge from systematic data analysis and to generate theory that is tested through further recursive analysis. The activities of collecting data, analysing data and writing up the research often occur simultaneously.

Typically, researchers in grounded theory employ some of the following techniques:

- **Participant observation:** this requires the researchers to immerse themselves in the daily routines of those being examined. This fieldwork necessitates considerable work in the chosen setting.
- **Interviewing:** a researcher can learn a great deal by using formal, informal, structured and semi-structured interviews when studying a particular group of teachers, parents, students, etc.
- **Artefacts and documentation:** researchers using a grounded theory approach can also gain considerable insight into a situation, subculture or group by studying artefacts (e.g. policy documents, rules, textbooks, handouts, etc.).

Central to grounded theory is a process of constant comparative analysis, necessitating the inquirer to move between the processes of data collection and analysis. This leads gradually to the creation of iterations, which are further refined and revised as the process continues, leading to newer theories that again are reviewed. The process is undertaken until the researcher reaches a point of saturation – the point at which very few new insights emerge from the data. Moreover, at this stage the researcher may notice evidence of repetition in the themes he or she has already observed and highlighted. In developing outcomes at this point, the researcher normally employs a complex coding process, which, it is claimed, assists in displaying the criteria of fit, understanding, generality and control in findings (Strauss and Corbin 1990).

As with all methodological frameworks within research, criticisms of grounded theory exist. Detractors often point to the very sizeable level of data, unmanageable levels according to some, which can be generated. It is also argued that researchers require considerable skill when employing grounded theory methods. Equally, some argue that the sphere of inquiry lacks standard rules to follow for the identification of categories. Perhaps most important is the argument that grounded theory fails to note the extent to which the researcher can become embedded within the situation, culture or sub-group and lose focus and agency as a result (Bryant and Charmaz, 2007).

## Historical Research in Education

Historical research has a long tradition in the education of student teachers and is often used within History of Education modules. Its spectrum is broad and it may involve different interpretations within its remit. The word 'historiography' is used by historians to describe the spectrum of approaches and methods employed in historical research.

While quantitative approaches may sometimes be employed in dealing with statistical and factual data, a great amount of interpretation is also undertaken. The evolution of systems of education, the influence of broader political concerns, philosophies and movements on education policy formulation, the origins of practices, and organisational features and structures in education have been of considerable interest to historians of education. The availability of education, or otherwise, to different social groups, classes and races in the past has also prompted much research. The historic marginalisation of women in many societies by means of various types of educational provision has proved revealing. In recent times, renewed interest in the history of education has been linked with the evaluation of new policy initiatives in attempts to offer perspective on change and the impact of changes, or, as argued by McCulloch and Richardson, the study of the history of education allows us to 'ponder the nature of continuity and change in education and the societies with which it interacts' (2000: 125).

Indeed, the sphere of education abounds with issues and topics of interest to historians of education, not least the origins of institutions, the impact of political ideologies on educational provision, the evolution of policy in respect of education, comparative studies of curricular developments in different societies, the influence of court decisions on education policies, the scrutiny of different incidences of curriculum reform in previous times and so on.

Often historians of education speak of primary and secondary sources. A primary source is a first-hand account of an event or period in history, which is open to interpretation. Primary sources include diaries, journals, letters, interviews, speeches, memos, manuscripts, official records, memoirs, autobiographies, minutes, reports, photos, sketches and films, as well as other first-hand data. Secondary sources can be described as accounts that are based on primary sources but seek to interpret and analyse those primary sources. Secondary sources are some steps removed from the historical event. They often include pictures, quotes or graphics from primary sources. Secondary sources include publications such as textbooks, magazine articles, histories, criticisms, commentaries and encyclopaedias.

Many historians of education would argue that their research often follows the familiar pattern of identifying a researchable phenomenon, developing a hypothesis, collecting data, checking and verifying outcomes, and writing a report, academic essay, paper or book in order to disseminate their findings. It is important to note that other evolving forms of historical research have emerged within the sphere, not least of which is narrative research. Some interesting insights into the wide spectrum of Irish education history can be gleaned by reading Coolahan, J. and O'Donovan, P.F. (2009), *A History of Ireland's School Inspectorate 1831–2008*, or Glendenning, D. (1999), *Education and the Law*.

---

### TASK 6.5: EVALUATING THE BENEFITS OF HISTORICAL RESEARCH

The following are some claims commonly made about the apparent benefits of studying the history of education and undertaking historical research in the field. Working within a group, discuss these claims. Agree on a rank order for them and offer a justification for your preferences.

Studying the history of education and undertaking historical research:

- Helps student teachers to appreciate the various aspects of past educational processes so as to link them to the present.
- Enables student teachers to understand the type of education we had in the past and the purposes it served.
- Gives student teachers the opportunity to know the past mistakes in our education system with the view to making necessary amendments.
- Gives student teachers the opportunity to study other people's educational ideas and programmes with the aim of developing ours.
- Provides student teachers with a solid foundation to plan for our present and future educational development.
- Helps student teachers to understand some major trends and developments in our educational system.
- Helps student teachers to formulate and implement better philosophies of education.

Developing the Skill of Research

## *Philosophical Research in Education*

Philosophical research in education focuses on the critique, interpretation and reconstruction of educational ideas and arguments. Often, philosophers of education pose questions that may seem initially to be either self-explanatory or tangential to the daily pressures on teachers, such as what does it mean to be educated, what are the purposes of education, how can we define indoctrination and what purposes should schools seek to fulfil in democratic societies. However, a closer look and some reflection on these questions often reveal the significance of such routes of inquiry.

It is often obvious that answering many such questions cannot be facilitated by pursuing a quantitative mode of research. Within the research spectrum of the philosophy of education, such questions can evoke matters of value, meaning and ethical judgement, and can elude the application of positivist research approaches. Recurring research issues within the philosophy of education include the nature of knowledge, the significance of culture, gender and exclusion in schooling, the precarious place of love, care and empathy in education, the nature of learning, the role of imagination in schooling, questions around denominational, secular and inter-denominational education, and building justice in schools and the community. Equally, considerable focus is placed on language usage and the nature and power of discourse in education, how education and democracy can interact, and the role of the teacher as either a curriculum transmitter or as an agent of change. Many other issues also undergo regular scrutiny within the sphere. Clearly, these questions have considerable influence on the eternal interplay in education between schools, community, knowledge, learners and educators. Moreover, the wealth of insight advanced by philosophers in the past about the sphere of education, the practices of teaching, and the role of education in society and communities continues to inform present-day readers and offer many ideas for ongoing discussion, dispute and exploration.

The key research approaches of philosophy often involve the use of interpretative strategies such as the close reading of texts, the undertaking of logical and ethical scrutiny, and the contextualisation of ideas within their historical evolution. Philosophical inquiry in the sphere of education often seeks to undertake questioning by means of measured reasoning, vigilant argument and analysis, and the creation of distinctions in fact and language. Sometimes a substantive position is argued and defended, and yet very often the key characteristics of philosophical research are the pursuit of clarification and differentiation between ideas, concepts, ideologies, and linguistic constructs.

As with many disciplines, a wide spectrum of approaches, schools of thought and interpretations have developed within philosophy over several centuries, and these varying traditions have influenced the manner in which research is perceived and undertaken. Indeed, in the debates over the nature of educational research there are even some philosophers of education who agree with Carr that 'the forms of human association characteristic of educational engagement are not really apt for scientific or empirical study at all,' but are fundamentally philosophical issues (Carr 2003: 54–5). It is not our intention in this context to explore the rifts and cleavages within and between the different perspectives on philosophical research in the sphere of education. You will encounter some of these traditions, schools and controversies as your engagement with the philosophy of education develops. However, the processes of analysis, clarification, comparison and critique may emerge as broad commonalities within and between various interpretations of philosophy and its role in educational research. Dewey, who is recognised as a towering figure in the field of philosophy of education, makes a broad claim for the importance of philosophical examination and research:

> If we are willing to conceive of education as the process of forming fundamental dispositions, intellectual and emotional, toward nature and fellow men, philosophy may even be defined as the general theory of education. (1916: 328)

## Task 6.6: Exploring What the term 'Education' Means to Us

In small groups discuss what we mean by the term 'education'. You might initally respond by seeing the definition of the concept as obvious. You might equate it with schooling. You might assert that it is the process you have been experiencing in institutions dedicated to education throughout your life. However, you might pursue the discussion with some recognition that differences may exist between education, training, schooling, learning, indoctrination and instruction.

Bear in mind the following indicators as your discussion develops:

- Please define! Offer your understanding of what education is.
- Discuss
- Compare
- Argue a case.
- Give reasons.
- Evaluate your reasons.
- Evaluate others' reasons.

Would you describe this discussion as philosophical in nature? Why?

## M-Level Task 6.4: Exploring Dewey's View of Education

How do you regard Dewey's philosophical conception of education as cited above (p. 121)? What issues does it raise? Does his view still have relevance to your conception of education? If not, attempt to elaborate on your critique.

## Mixed Methods Research

In mixed methods research, the inquirer employs a combination of quantitative and qualitative methods and approaches within a research study. This combined approach has gained considerable currency in educational research in recent times. The qualitative and quantitative elements of the research project may be undertaken either simultaneously or consecutively. The use of multiple research methods is widely viewed as advantageous to educational research. The weaknesses of one method may be counteracted by the strengths of another. In this way, and in certain studies, quantitative and qualitative research methods can be seen as highly complementary (Creswell 2009, 2013).

Johnson and Onwuegbuzie (2004) cite both weaknesses and strengths in a review of the mixed methods approach to educational research. Among its strengths is an acknowledgement of the manner in which it can compensate for 'the weaknesses in another method'. Equally, a mixed methods approach 'can provide stronger evidence for a conclusion through convergence and corroboration of findings'. Indeed, Johnson and Onwuegbuzie (2004) claim that a mixed methods approach 'can be used to increase the generalizability of the results [and] qualitative and quantitative research used together produce more complete knowledge necessary to inform theory and practice' (21).

Among the weaknesses of a mixed methods approach we find not only logistical problems relating to time and expense but also the requirement that researchers be adept in a wide variety of approaches and have considerable ability in the analysis of both qualitative and quantitative data. Johnson and Onwuegbuzie (2004: 23–4), in reviewing many perspectives on the issue, argue for the overall benefits of a mixed methods approach. They base their endorsement on the argument that investigators who conduct mixed methods research are more likely to select approaches with respect to their underlying research questions rather than with regard to some preconceived biases about which research paradigm should have hegemony in social science research. By narrowing the divide between quantitative and qualitative researchers, mixed methods research has the potential to promote shared responsibility in the quest for accountability with regard to educational quality.

## ETHICS AND RESEARCH

All research work that involves humans interacting raises ethical questions and dilemmas. Such human interaction is at the very heart of educational research. Ethical dilemmas, problems and queries can arise in a wide variety of ways. Some may be predictable; others will be unforeseen. Indeed, at times, some dilemmas may threaten to throw a research project off course. At one level, researchers primarily need to be familiar with some broad, agreed guidelines that determine how the research is to be conducted. At a second level, researchers have a duty to ensure the integrity of the research process itself. This will require adherence to reliable practices in the identification of data, the allocation of adequate resources, appropriate and fair referencing of sources, etc. Each of the research approaches that we have examined above will raise different demands in terms of ensuring the integrity of research undertaken within its strictures.

A familiarity with the broad principles of ethical research should alert us to the complexities involved and prepare us for engaging with more specific research dilemmas when we encounter and undertake detailed research projects as reflective practitioners.

Hammersley and Trainanou (2012) outline five commonly recognised principles that may serve as a useful introduction to ethical research:

- Minimising harm
- Respecting autonomy

- Protecting privacy
- Offering reciprocity
- Treating people equitably

In the case of minimising harm, questions about reputational damage, neglecting a learner's learning progress, undermining the work of a school or a teacher and similar issues may all come to mind. In the case of respecting autonomy, the issue of whether or not participation in the research project is in fact voluntary is raised, particularly in the case of younger learners. Many interesting ethical questions are raised in respect of protecting privacy. As research has a duty to inform the debate, and to explain and improve practice and insight, we are faced with questions about what aspects of the research data ought to be confidential or not. How much anonymity should be afforded to the participants? This is of particular significance in small-scale research projects in an easily identifiable setting such as a classroom. The question of reciprocity is one that seeks to address the troubling issue of infringing on people's time and work. Being interviewed, being observed or answering questionnaires is very often an imposition on a person's time and whether some reciprocity should be afforded raises some ethical dilemmas:

- Does the receipt of payment by the subject change the dynamic of the research?
- Do subjects behave or answer differently when reciprocity is involved?
- Are there more preferable and ethical ways of ensuring and maintaining participation in the research process?

Finally, the question of treating people equitably requires us as researchers to interact justly and impartially with all individuals and groups we encounter as part of our research work. This can be of particular pertinence when we encounter contexts where organisational structures or styles of learning and engagement are not of our choosing.

Quite clearly the issue of undertaking research specifically with children requires even more stringent ethical guidelines. A publication by the Department of Children and Youth Affairs entitled *Guidance for Developing Ethical Research Projects Involving Children* (2012) offers insight into many of the issues.

The publication endorses research with children as highly beneficial and forefronts certain broad ethical issues that would arise from this and would need attention. The broad issues are very much in line with those outlined by Hammersley and Trainanou (2012) above. However, undertaking research work specifically with children makes more particular demands on us as researchers and is outlined as follows:

In addition to core ethical principles, research with children requires that legal and policy commitments in relation to children, especially national and international child protection policies and guidelines, are adhered to and that a child-centred, inclusive approach to research is adopted. Parental/guardian consent is required for a child to participate in research, but good practice also requires the child's agreement or assent. Confidentiality is key to research practice, but a limitation exists in child-related research if a child protection issue arises and this restriction in relation to confidentiality must be explained when obtaining consent.... Every effort should be made to actively involve children as participants in the research process and care must be taken to protect the rights of all children, as well as specific groups of children, in research activity. (Department of Children and Youth Affairs 2012: 8)

Another initial source of guidance for all researchers conducting research with children in the Irish context would be the key principles enunciated in *Children First: National Guidance for the Protection and Welfare of Children* (Department of Children and Youth Affairs, 2011).

---

### TASK 6.7: ETHICAL RESEARCH

Read, analyse and discuss the document Department of Children and Youth Affairs (2012), *Guidance for Developing Ethical Research Projects Involving Children*, available from: http://www.dcya.gov.ie/documents/Publications/Ethics_Guidance.pdf, with a particular emphasis on the concluding points outlined on page 8.

---

## CONCLUSION

From the outset, our concern in this chapter has been to introduce a spectrum of research approaches relevant to student teachers. However, it is important to appreciate that, though undertaking research makes many demands on our expertise, our time and our analytic abilities, the implications are quite profound. Reconceptualising the teacher as a researcher and the profession as research-based does much more than add extra duties to the role of the teacher. It is a reconceptualisation that challenges embedded and older conceptions of teaching. Stenhouse (1984) attempts to tease out some of the implications that ought to emerge when we conceive of teaching as a research-led profession:

Good teachers are necessarily autonomous in professional judgement. They do not need to be told what to do. They are not professionally the dependents of researchers or superintendents, of innovators or supervisors. This does not mean that they do not welcome access to ideas created by other people at other places or in other times.... But they do know that ideas are not of much real use until they are subject to the teacher's own judgement. In short, it is the task of all educationalists outside the classroom to serve the teachers; for only teachers are in the position to create good teaching. (69)

## A SUMMARY OF KEY POINTS

- Teachers' own reflections on their practices provide a basis for empowering the profession as a research-led occupation.
- Schools, classrooms and the school community provide situations meriting many and varied forms of research.
- Research undertaken within education settings may be quantitative, qualitative or in a tradition of mixed methods, and the opportunity to engage with a variety of approaches may well be central to your dissertation.
- A wide variety of methodologies may be drawn upon in undertaking meaningful and worthwhile research in the education spectrum.
- The continual improvement of practice is a key motivation for practitioner-based research.
- A practitioner-led research culture involves self-evaluation on the part of the individual teacher, and often involves participation with fellow professionals and learners in a spirit of openness and mutuality.

# CHAPTER SEVEN

# Observing in Classrooms

What can I learn from observing in classrooms?

Are there different ways of observing?

How can I ensure that my observations are valid?

**Once you have worked through this chapter, you will have learned about the**

- Purposes and value of observation.
- Principles of observation.
- Considerations required prior to observing.
- Processes involved in observation.

## INTRODUCTION

Observation is a way in which we find out about the world around us. Classroom observation is a core feature of your initial teacher education experience. It is likely that you will have a number of different opportunities to observe your cooperating teachers and your peers teaching in classroom or microteaching contexts. Observation is a skill we use every day and in many different contexts, so a chapter on classroom observation may seem unnecessary. However, classrooms are dynamic and fast-moving environments involving hundreds of daily interactions, many of them occurring simultaneously. Classroom observation requires skill and awareness in order to understand and interpret what is transpiring moment by moment. To maximise the rich potential for learning from your classroom observations, it is important to consider issues of purpose, focus and method, as well as the assumptions and expectations that inform the particular orientation of your observational lens.

## BEING AWARE OF YOUR ASSUMPTIONS

You may have begun your teacher education programme with some experience of teaching or of assisting in classrooms. Or perhaps you have never set foot in a classroom as an adult. Whatever your prior experience, you certainly will have ideas about how classrooms work and what constitutes effective learning and teaching. These ideas or personal theories may be conscious or subconscious (tacit). Whether they fill you with enthusiasm or dread about school placement experiences, they are sure to influence how you view your classroom observations and teaching encounters.

Let's begin with a simple exercise. Read each italicised sentence below separately (adapted from a study by Sanford and Garrod 1981: 114) and create a mental picture from the words.

> *Jack was on the bus to school.*

> What picture formed in your mind as you read this sentence? What time of day is it? Who is Jack? How old is he? What is he wearing? What can he see from the window of the bus?
> Remember your images and read on.

> *He was feeling really anxious.*

> Describe the image you see now. Has it changed from your previous one? Why do you think Jack is feeling anxious?
> Keep reading.

> *They were doing gymnastics in PE again today.*

> Has anything in your mental picture changed? What? Why?
> Now keep reading.

> *Being solely responsible for first aid was a lot to expect of a student teacher.*

> What do you see now in your mental picture? How old is Jack? What does he look like? Were you surprised at the information in the last sentence? Why?

The exercise above demonstrates that we are constantly creating images and forming hypotheses about the world. We only notice this when someone plays a trick on us like in the story of Jack. Then our mental scenarios are dismantled only to be reformulated into new ones. Our images and perspectives are influenced by the experiences we have and by our interpretations of these experiences. Bartlett and Burton (2012) state:

> Our knowledge of the world is the product of a complex network of factors: family background, formative experiences, cultural identity, social class, gender and language are all contributory to our sense of who we are but also our sense of what the world is like and what constitutes significant knowledge. Different ways of life and belief systems will inevitably produce different knowledge and different orientations towards it. (78)

Recording and verbalising your observations will help to make more explicit your assumptions and expectations. Therefore, as you prepare to observe in classrooms, it is important to consider what sort of 'lens' you will observe through.

---

### TASK 7.1: THROUGH THE WINDOW OF PERCEPTION

What are the characteristics of your worldview? How might your worldview affect the way you 'see' particular teachers or classrooms?

Let's consider our latent gender biases. Which, if any, of the following statements feel intuitively true for you?

- Boys are naturally boisterous, active and unruly.
- Boys are more rational.
- Boys are socially uncommunicative.
- Boys are academically able.
- Boys are better at science and maths than girls.
- Girls are quiet and polite.
- Girls are studious.
- Girls have better social skills than boys.
- Girls are better at languages than boys.

Discuss with a peer how society reinforces some of these biases.

---

Teachers have the capacity to challenge bias, but they can also inadvertently contribute to it through their practices, curriculum choices and assessment strategies (Corra 2007; Nosek *et al.* 2009). Teachers' unconscious biases can result in limiting expectations regarding the success and participation of certain learners. Research has shown that teachers make assumptions regarding behaviours and abilities of learners based on their gender, colour, language, social class and ethnicity. Tobin and Gallagher (1987), for example, found that male, white learners were afforded more teachers' time and classroom resources. This cohort asked and was invited to answer most of the questions in the classroom. More recently, Shumow and Schmidt (2013) found that, despite denying that they held beliefs about gender differences in science performance, high school science teachers spent on average 39 per cent more time addressing male learners than female learners. Teachers addressed males more often than females about content knowledge, course content and classroom management. Horner *et al.* (2010) found that in US schools, although learner aggression and poor behaviour were important factors in discipline decisions, a learner's race was the most important factor. They found that the probability of being disciplined compared to the probability of not being disciplined was multiplied by nearly seven for African Americans, relative to learners of other races, holding all other variables constant.

Classroom Observation

## WHY ENGAGE IN CLASSROOM OBSERVATION?

Classroom observation provides:

- Rich insights into classroom life.
- Opportunities to experience how teachers and learners interact.
- Access to the classroom routines and organisational methods of experienced teachers.

- Insights into the interests and ability levels of learners.
- Exposure to different pedagogical approaches.

Classroom observation provides a valuable opportunity to explore processes of teaching that can stimulate your professional growth (Wajnryb 1992). The process of observation and subsequent reflection deliver rich possibilities to link your experiences of classroom practice with your emerging ideas about educational theory and pedagogy. It also encourages the development of a language for discussing and reflecting on learning and teaching. However, learning how to observe requires time, sensitivity and careful reflection. The range of roles one may play as observer – complete observer, observer-as-participant, participant-as-observer and complete participant – have been described by many researchers (see Gold 1958; Spradley 1980; Adler and Adler 1994; McKechnie 2000; Labaree 2002; Baker 2006). Irrespective of which role you adopt, it is important to remember philosopher Karl Popper's advice that 'all possible forms of observation presuppose a point of view, a perspective, an expectation, a theory from which such an observation becomes possible' (Popper 1963: 46). According to Popper, statements about observations are therefore always interpretations of facts in the light of either consciously acknowledged or subconsciously unacknowledged theories. Hence, although we constantly need to use our personal theories to construct our worlds, making judgements without interrogating them for bias is one of the main characteristics of poor observation.

## Observing in the Early Primary Years

As part of the ongoing recording and monitoring of young learners, observation can provide evidence leading to more informed planning, a greater understanding of individual learners' current competence and developmental levels, information for sharing with parents as well as information on the appropriateness of the learning environment for young learners. *Aistear: The Early Childhood Curriculum Framework* (2009) highlights the value of observation for young learners:

> Observation involves watching and listening to children and using the information gathered through this to enhance their learning and development. The adult may use different types of observations depending on what he/she wants to find out. (NCCA, 2009: 87)

*Síolta: The National Quality Framework* also highlights the importance of documenting young learners' experiences and stresses the importance of systematic observation and Assessment for Learning:

Planning for curriculum or programme implementation is based on the child's individual profile, which is established through systematic observation and assessment for learning. (CECDE 2006: 50)

### Points to Remember When Observing:

- You are a guest in the classroom.
- Your purpose is to learn through observing, not to evaluate the teacher or the class.
- The presence of a visitor affects classroom dynamics – be aware that your presence may affect what you observe in the classroom.
- When noting your observations, try to be as unobtrusive as possible.
- Invite direction from the teacher regarding where to sit and how to participate.
- References to individuals should be written in a manner that ensures anonymity.
- Field notes should be shared with your cooperating teacher on request.
- Avoid making sweeping generalisations and be aware that what you observe is only a sample of classroom life.
- Perspectives, feelings and motivations are difficult to observe. This is true in the case of both learners and teachers.
- Describe what you observed in a particular lesson or period and refrain from assuming that is typical of all lessons or periods.
- Be aware that what you observe is filtered through the lens of your own experiences, assumptions and beliefs. Be open to challenging these beliefs.

## The Initial Classroom Visit

Before you begin your observations, you will usually have a pre-observation meeting with your cooperating teacher. This initial visit presents an opportunity for you to obtain valuable contextual information about your designated class to assist you in planning your observations. Your cooperating teacher may suggest things to look for during an observation. We recommend that you focus on just one or two aspects of each lesson/session to avoid attempting to explore too many events at the same time. You may find certain aspects relatively easy to observe (such as the kinds of questions learners ask), whereas other aspects may not be observable and may have to be inferred (such as levels of learner contentment or motivation, teacher decisions or subtle classroom dynamics). You may indicate to your cooperating teacher that there are particular areas that you would like to focus on, such as the organisation of groups or dealing with classroom management challenges.

Draw a detailed sketch of the classroom, indicating the location of furniture, windows, doors and other structural aspects of the room. Visual maps use pictures instead of words to portray the spatial relationships among physical objects. Include any resources and materials that are present, for example, computers, white/blackboards, noticeboards, displays, any special curricular areas within the classroom, for example, play area, library, discovery zone, etc. Note the seating of learners within the class. Request a copy of the timetable.

## OBSERVATION AS A REFLECTIVE PROCESS

In Chapter 2 we explored different levels of reflective thinking and reflective writing, and proposed a framework for reflective writing that embraces descriptive, comparative and critical reflection. We also explored the critical lenses proposed by Brookfield (1998) as well as a range of different models for engaging in structured reflection.

To maximise the potential of your reflective observations, it is important to ensure that your attention is directed not only at questions and experiences that stimulate descriptive or technical reflection (i.e. 'how things work' questions), but also that you expand your perceptual lens to embrace critical reflection (i.e. asking 'why', 'why not' and 'what if' questions).

Let's look at how you might engage in reflection at the different levels.

At the level of **descriptive reflection**, you could focus on what works to gain and maintain attention, to explain and question, or to manage behaviour. It could involve reflecting on patterns of response or reaction from individuals or groups within the class. Fundamentally, descriptive reflection involves answering the question, 'How can I make sense of what I have observed?' It entails more than just reporting the facts. It involves finding significance in an experience so that you can recognise the salient features, become aware of causes and consequences, and inform your understanding.

The level of **comparative reflection** involves comparing different interpretations of the same event. In Chapter 2, we explored Brookfield's (1998) critical lenses, which seek lines of inquiry and insight from varying perspectives: our perspectives, the learners' eyes, the perspectives of peers and the theoretical literature. When we consider alternative perspectives or varying ways to interpret an event, we discover meaning we might otherwise miss. Questions to consider here include:

- What are the alternative views of what happened?
- How do other people who were directly or indirectly involved describe and explain what happened?
- What does research contribute to an understanding of this matter?

At the level of **critical reflection**, you might observe differences between the ways in which boys and girls or members of different ethnic or ability groups communicate and behave in the classroom. You might observe various interests and ability levels amongst groups, or study learner responses to particular teaching strategies, or analyse the question-and-answer patterns in class discussions. You might observe if all learners are included and treated fairly and wonder about the implicit and explicit power structures in the classroom or school. Throughout the observational process, you would draw insight from the application of educational theory to these enduring questions.

## APPROACHES TO OBSERVATION

A range of methods can be used to conduct classroom observation, ranging from qualitative methods, which are mostly narrative or descriptive, to quantitative methods, which focus on gathering quantifiable data that can be counted and analysed statistically. Many observers employ a mixed methods focus that embraces a combination of both approaches (see Chapter 6).

In this section, we summarise briefly some of the more frequently used methods of recording classroom observations.

## Qualitative Approaches

### Descriptive Accounts

Descriptive accounts constitute the least structured method of recording classroom observations. Descriptive accounts are open-ended and give you the freedom to describe events, in written form, as they occur. You can choose what aspects to include and what to exclude from the observations. Once written, the account can subsequently be used as a basis for reflective writing and interrogated from different standpoints to extract maximum potential for your professional learning.

### Critical Incident Reports

Brookfield describes a critical incident in teaching as any 'vividly remembered event' (1990: 84). A critical incident is not necessarily a dramatic event; rather, it is an event that you deem significant, that made you stop and think or that raised questions for you. It may have made you question an aspect of your beliefs, values, attitudes or behaviours. By reflecting on these incidents, we can uncover new understandings or challenge some of our taken-for-granted perceptions of learning and teaching (Richards and Farrell 2005). Reflecting on critical incidents involves describing and explaining what has transpired (Tripp 1993). In the description phase, a specific event or incident is observed and documented. The incident is then explained and given meaning, or interpreted. Even though an incident may appear typical rather than critical at first, through analysis you may observe that it interrupts (or highlights) taken-for-granted ways of thinking about teaching.

## Ethnographic Records

Ethnography is the observation and study of particular cultures (see Chapter 6). Educational ethnography often focusses on the culture of the school. This embraces the common habits, customs, traditions, histories and geographies of the school community. Should you adopt an ethnographic approach while observing in the classroom, you could keep a journal in which you record double-entry field notes. It is usual to divide the recording page into two columns. In one column, record your observations about the classroom and in the other column record your reflections, explanations and questions. Include any metacognitive reflections to document what you observe about yourself as a learner during your observations.

---

**M-LEVEL TASK 7.1: ETHNOGRAPHY FOR TEACHER EDUCATION**

Read and discuss the following article:

Frank, C.R. and Uy, F.L. (2004), 'Ethnography for teacher education,' *Journal of Teacher Education*, 55(3): 269–83.

This research used observation methods from ethnography and sociolinguistics to help pre-service teachers to refrain from making critical evaluations based on too little evidence. The authors developed a very interesting study in which 42 pre-service teachers learned how to observe through this approach.

---

# Quantitative Approaches
## Classroom Coding Systems

Observation systems that help you record the frequency with which various teacher and learner behaviours occur are called classroom coding systems. Interactive coding systems are often used to record the behaviours of learners and teachers during intervals of time. An advantage of coding systems is that they typically do not require you to interpret what is being observed as the observation is taking place. The most well-known coding system is the Flanders Interaction Analysis system (Flanders 1968), which consists of 10 categories of communication. Seven categories relate to levels of teacher talk, two relate to levels of learner talk and one category refers to periods of silence or confusion.

If using this system, you will make timed observations, usually every three seconds, and categorise the behaviour you observe into one of the 10 categories.

Figure 7.1: Categories of the Flanders Interaction Analysis System

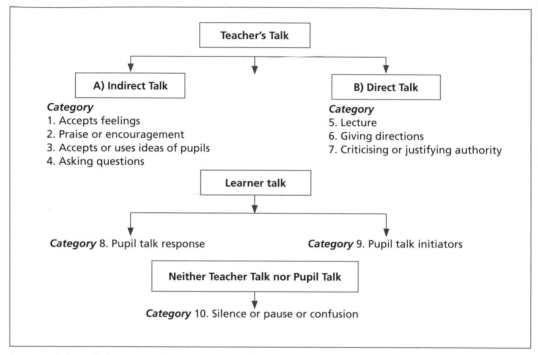

Source: Adapted from Arockiasamy, S., 'Educational Technology: BEd Notes', available from: http://stxaviersbedcollege.org/sim/technology_arock.pdf: 7.

## Target Child Observations

Target child observations are frequently used in early years settings and are also useful when observing learners with special learning needs. They provide a detailed record of a learner's activities during a period of time, which can highlight:

- Activities the learner has selected.
- Preferred areas within the room.
- Patterns of interaction.
- Patterns of language.

While observing a learner in this way, it is useful to have a watch nearby to record the time at intervals, specifying the time spent on each activity.

Codes can be used to facilitate recording, such as:

| | | | |
|---|---|---|---|
| TC | = target child | A1, A2, A3, etc. | = adults |
| B1, B2, B3, etc. | = other boys | AA | = art area |
| G1, G2, G3, etc. | = other girls | HC | = home corner |
| ST | = sand tray | P | = cooperative play |
| BP | = brick play | SP | = solitary play |
| L | = library | PP | = parallel play |
| MA | = maths area | | |

## Checklists

Checklists consist of a list of the behaviours to be observed alongside response boxes labelled 'yes/no' or 'present/absent'. This allows an observer to note the presence or absence of a particular behaviour during an observation, for example:

Teacher asked higher order questions:  Yes  ✔  No  ☐

Simple checklists of this sort are most useful when you are observing behaviours that are difficult to evaluate in degree, but that can be identified as either occurring or not occurring.

## Seating Chart Observation Records (SCORE)

SCORE charts (Acheson and Gall 1987) provide quantifiable data on patterns of interaction between teachers and learners, which may yield insights into how frequently the teacher interacts with certain individual learners or groups of learners within the class and the nature of those interactions. SCORE can provide details of the teacher's questioning, such as:

- The number of whole-class questions asked.
- The number of learners who answer these questions.
- The number of individual questions asked.
- The number of learners who answered these individual questions.
- Which learners are asked the most questions.
- Which gender receives most questions, etc.

This data can form the basis for further interrogation.

Because of the variety of seating patterns that can occur in classrooms, we suggest that you create a seating chart for your particular class on a blank sheet of paper. Use a box to represent each learner. You can put the first names of the learners in the appropriate boxes. Arrows are used to indicate the flow of verbal interaction. The base of the arrow indicates who initiated the conversation, and the arrowhead indicates the person to whom the conversation is directed (see Figure 7.2).

Figure 7.2: The Score Chart

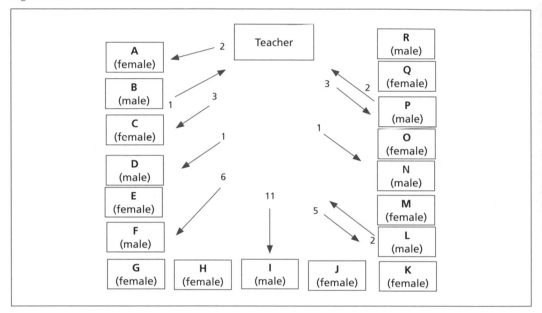

### TASK 7.2: WHAT'S THE SCORE?

Refer to Figure 7.2 when answering the following questions:

- How many questions in total were asked by the teacher?
- Out of the total class of 18 learners, how many individuals were asked questions by the teacher?
- How many learners asked a question or initiated talk?
- What observations can you make about the patterns of interaction in the classroom?
- What do you observe about gender involvement?

## Task 7.3: Keeping SCORE

Read the following article:

Farrell, Thomas S.C. (2011), '"Keeping SCORE": Reflective Practice Through Classroom Observations,' *RELC Journal*, 42(3): 265–72.

This paper reports on a case study of a short series of classroom observations in which the author mentored a novice teacher. The classroom observation process included the use of a seating or SCORE chart to help the teacher become more aware of her classroom practices and improve her instruction.

- While reading the article, compare Figure 1: Score I with Figure 2: Score II.
- Comment on the reasons for the differences between the two observations.

## FOCUS OF OBSERVATIONS

Observations are more meaningful when they are focussed and conducted with a clear purpose in mind. The following are examples of areas of potential focus for your classroom observations:

- Beginnings and endings, lesson structure, lesson activities, links between activities and transitions
- Strategies for classroom management, how groups are set up, time management
- Seating arrangements, special groupings within the class
- Levels of attentiveness, levels of participation, quiet/vocal learners
- Styles of learning
- Ability to listen
- Response to teacher's praise
- Willingness to participate
- Types of questions asked, resources used, pace of instruction

## The Learning Climate

The classroom climate encompasses the physical, social and emotional environment in which learning takes place and exerts a significant influence on learners' attitudes and motivations towards learning. As such, the skills involved in establishing a positive classroom climate are of immense importance. Research indicates that the type of climate generally considered to best facilitate learning is one that can be described as task-oriented, warm, supportive, relaxed, purposeful and possessing a sense of order. In such an atmosphere, learning is promoted by establishing and maintaining positive attitudes by learners towards the lesson. As you observe the learning climate of a classroom, you may note how learners feel about themselves, about one another and about learning, and the experiences and activities that promote feelings most conducive to learning.

## Learner Motivation

Motivation energises, directs and sustains learning. We often observe learner motivation through cognitive, emotional and behavioural engagement in certain activities. As you observe, note the ways that learners are motivated intrinsically (from within) and extrinsically (from factors outside themselves). When observing learner motivation, you may consider the following questions.

- What interests learners at the age in question?
- Which activities give them a sense of pride?
- When do they seem to lack interest?
- What topics do they talk about with enthusiasm?
- What do they find humorous?
- How do they respond to being given a choice in assignments?
- How do teachers show their approval to learners?
- How do teachers give praise or affirmation?
- What types of rewards do teachers give?
- What warnings do teachers give?
- What sanctions are given?
- What forms of peer pressure do you observe?
- How do teachers promote enthusiasm for an assignment?

## Classroom Management

Classroom management involves how teachers organise the classroom, and anticipate and respond to learner behaviour so as to provide an environment that is conducive to learning. Because many student teachers encounter classroom management challenges, it will be important to pay close attention to how your cooperating teachers orchestrate and facilitate learning through effective classroom management. Observable features of classroom management include:

- How the physical environment of the classroom is organised.
- How classroom expectations and rules are communicated.
- Behavioural incentives and consequences.
- Level and type of academic engagement by learners.
- Behaviour during transition periods within and between lessons.

## Lesson Clarity

An effective lesson has clarity and uses simple, accessible language to present concepts. Lesson clarity refers to the ability of the teacher to speak clearly and directly while structuring and organising content to be appropriate to learners' understanding. Features of lesson clarity that are observable include sharing learning expectations with learners; explicitly relating lesson content to prior learning; recalling and summarising; and using analogies, illustrations, demonstrations and appropriate resources to clarify lesson content.

## Learning Skills

Learners experience most success when they are actively engaged in the learning process. Active engagement can be observed when learners:

- Can explain what they are doing.
- Are able to work collaboratively.
- Can relate learning to their lives.
- Are able to find things out and solve problems for themselves.
- Make connections between their learning in different parts of the curriculum.
- Can use technology for independent learning.

## SUGGESTED SEQUENCE FOR PLANNING YOUR OBSERVATIONS

1. Prepare a checklist of questions to ask your cooperating teacher during the initial visit.
2. Schedule the initial visit.
3. Meet with the cooperating teacher to discuss questions and plan observations.
4. Find out about classroom rules and procedures.
5. Draw a detailed sketch of the classroom, noting seating arrangements.
6. Obtain a copy of the timetable and familiarise yourself with the daily schedule and classroom routine.
7. Plan the focus of your observations and the methods you intend to use (quantitative, qualitative or mixed methods). The focus of your observation will influence your choice of observation methods.
8. Prepare observation materials, e.g. schedules, checklists, coding charts, ethnographic journal, etc.
9. Finalise with your cooperating teacher the time, focus and method(s) of observation, in addition to the type of role that you will play as observer.

## A SUMMARY OF KEY POINTS

- Classroom observation requires skill and awareness in order to understand and interpret what is transpiring.
- It is important to consider issues of purpose, focus and method, as well as the assumptions and expectations you bring to the process.
- Reflecting on your classroom observations provide rich opportunities to link your experiences of classroom practice with your emerging ideas about educational theory and pedagogy.
- A range of methods can be used to conduct classroom observations.
- Qualitative methods are mostly narrative or descriptive in focus.
- Quantitative methods are used to gather quantifiable data that can be counted and analysed statistically.

# CHAPTER EIGHT

# Lesson Planning

What do I need to consider when planning and preparing?

How can I plan to include learners of different abilities?

How detailed should my planning be?

**When you have worked through this chapter you will be able to:**

- Outline and develop the basics of lesson planning.
- Appreciate the significance of objectives.
- Differentiate between learning objectives.
- Understand the need for integration within lesson planning.
- Acknowledge the importance of developing a pedagogical frame of mind based on critical reflection.

## INTRODUCTION

Effective planning is at the core of successful teaching. Good planning has the potential to build your confidence and make you feel more secure in your competence as a teacher.

In many respects, a lesson is like a journey of exploration and a lesson plan takes on some of the features of a map. In a lesson plan, not only are the beginning, middle and end of the journey outlined, but the very steps, ways of working, strategies and points of interest that exist throughout the journey are also set out. In this sense, a lesson plan resembles a guidebook as well as a map, as we and our learners explore and are enriched by the learning within the journey.

As student teachers, you will engage initially with short-term planning. Gradually you will develop the ability to plan educational experiences for your learners for periods of longer duration. This chapter commences with an examination of short-term planning, and an exploration of perspectives on this significant aspect of teaching.

---

**TASK 8.1: ANTICIPATING PLANNING**

Consider the following questions:

- What do I anticipate as being involved in planning?
- How might planning benefit my teaching?
- How might planning contribute to my development as a reflective practitioner?

---

In answering the questions in Task 8.1, you may have mentioned dimensions of planning such as selecting different methodologies, setting objectives, dealing with issues of timing, taking into account different styles of learning, consolidation of learning, assessment and many other matters. All these factors and others are involved in this complex process of planning for learning and teaching.

## WHAT IS A LESSON PLAN?

Lesson plans are the outcome of a teacher's visualisation about his or her lessons; as Scrivener argues, 'it's important to realise that planning is essentially a thinking skill' (2005: 109). As a thinking skill involving visualisation, what are some of the key elements of lesson planning? Many factors are intrinsic, including your prior knowledge of the learners; their varying levels of prior knowledge; the ethnic, linguistic, social and cultural differences between learners; the appropriateness of content; and many acts of predicting, imagining, anticipating and sequencing. This complex thinking process – this act of visualisation – relies heavily on well-honed reflection, which allows you to use previous experiences in a new, unique situation of learning. It may assist us to see planning as 'the ability to visualise before class how things might look, feel and sound when they are done in class' (Scrivener 2005: 109).

## LESSON PLANNING FOR TEACHING ON SCHOOL PLACEMENT

For student teachers, lesson planning is usually undertaken in the form of written notes for each lesson. As you gain more experience of the process of planned visualisation based on reflective thinking, your ability to plan should deepen. At the outset it is beneficial to plan in considerable detail by describing each and every phase of a lesson, outlining your objectives, questions and instructions, and detailing where, when and how different methodological approaches are introduced. You should also note any classroom organisational changes to be undertaken in accordance with lesson objectives and how you intend to incorporate your strategies in respect of consolidating and assessing learning. This tradition of structured planning is firmly embedded in teacher preparation and is supported within the current Primary School Curriculum, which notes:

> [I]t is the responsibility of the teacher to ensure that the complexity of children's learning needs is served by a learning process that is rich and varied. This involves the teacher in classroom planning and in the wider process of school planning, making judgements and decisions about the choice of content, the way different elements of content are combined, and the sequence in which these are introduced. (NCCA 1999: 21)

While variations occur, many commonalities exist between different traditions in lesson planning. The National Induction Programme for Teachers (NIPT) cites the following aspects as intrinsic to the short-term planning process:

For each subject area the short-term plan should contain:

- Date, subject, class level
- Strand, Strand Unit
- Content Objectives and Skills (where appropriate)
- Learning Objectives
- Learning Activities
- Resources
- Differentiation
- Assessment
- Linkage and integration
- Reflection

(NIPT 2013: 16)

We will look at these elements in more detail below. However, it is worthwhile noting that they are not meant to signal an unthinking and formulaic form of lesson planning, but one that is underpinned by a disposition of informed reflection and visualisation, which is distinctive to each teacher and may vary from day to day or from lesson to lesson.

TASK 8.2: REFLECTING ON YOUR ATTITUDE TO PLANNING

One of the most important [principles of good teaching] is the need for planning. Far from compromising spontaneity, planning provides a structure and context for both teacher and students, as well as a framework for reflection and evaluation.

(Spencer 2003: 25)

Planning is an essential aspect of teaching and vital in many aspects of life. You might reflect initially on planning in general and assess its importance. Second, attempt to self-evaluate your approach to planning in the broader sphere of your life.

Many of your strengths and perhaps some weaknesses may become clear to you in the course of this reflection.

How might you employ, address, adjust and engage with your own planning profile as you begin to plan for teaching?

M-LEVEL TASK 8.1: COLLABORATIVE LESSON PLANNING

In a small group of peers, choose a topic from the History Curriculum (NCCA 1999c) for a class level of your choice. Reflect collaboratively on how a lesson on the topic might be planned using the headings pertaining to short-term planning listed above (NCCA 2013).

## Important Considerations in Lesson Planning

Prior to planning any lesson, think about your learners and answer the following questions:

- Who are they and what motivates them?
- What do they know from previous learning?
- What is the relevance of this lesson/topic/theme?
- How does it relate to and build on the learners' interests?
- How does it relate to the curriculum for this level?
- How can I plan for the learners to engage actively with their learning?
- How can I plan for learners to exercise choice in their learning?
- How will they demonstrate their learning?

Can you think of other appropriate and necessary questions?

## Lesson Planning Templates

In terms of day-to-day planning for teaching on school placement, the following considerations should always be taken into account:

- Devising lesson objectives in a structured and systematic manner
- Sharing the learning intentions and success criteria
- Context of the lesson within the strand unit
- Developing learner motivation
- Building on the relevant prior knowledge and experiences of learners
- Research-based instructional strategies highlighting learner-centred instruction
- Assessment, including self-assessment by learners
- Feedback
- Differentiation
- Scaffolding
- Closure

Figure 8.1: Short-term Planning Template

| ■ Date: | Class level: | | Subject: |
|---|---|---|---|
| ■ Strand: | Strand unit: | | |
| ■ Content objective/s:<br>■ Skills *(where appropriate):* | | | |
| ■ Learning objectives:<br>*(Informed by strand, strand unit, content objectives, the skills and concepts to be developed)* | ■ Learning activities:<br>*(Informed by approaches and methodologies in long-term plan)* | | |
| | ■ Resources: | | |
| ■ Differentiation: | | | |
| ■ Assessment: | | | |
| ■ Linkage and integration: | | | |
| ■ Reflection: *Refer to Teacher Reflection document to support your short-term planning.* | | | |

Source: Adapted from http://www.teacherinduction.ie.

Lesson plans may adhere to different formats and your teacher education programme is likely to make particular recommendations in this regard during your various school placement experiences. The National Induction Programme for primary teachers recommends a template along the lines of Figure 8.1 for beginning teachers.

In your initial experience of teaching within a teacher education programme, you will encounter other variations on these recommendations, and two other examples of lesson planning templates used in initial teacher education are displayed in Figures 8.2 and 8.3.

Figure 8.2 is an example of the typical structure of a lesson plan using the content/methods delineation.

Figure 8.2: Lesson Planning Template: Content/Methods Delineation

---

**Subject:**
**Strand:**
**Strand unit:**
**Lesson:**
**Class:**
**Date:**
**Time:**
**Objectives:** State what you expect the learners to have achieved by the end of the lesson as a result of your instruction. You may preface your objectives with the following phrase:

At the end of the lesson learners will....

**Teaching resources:**
* Materials required by the teacher:
* Materials required by the learners:

**Introduction:**
Specify the approaches used to
* Introduce learners to the lesson,
* Elicit their prior knowledge regarding the lesson topic and
* Motivate them to become involved fully in the lesson development.

Specify also the learning intention and success criteria for the lesson and how they will be shared with the learners (see 'Sharing the Learning Intentions and Success Criteria' on pages 221–3).

**Development:**

| Lesson Content | Methods |
|---|---|
| Briefly outline the content/knowledge/ concepts/skills to be taught. | Provide a detailed account of the instructional approaches to be used during each stage of the lesson, indicating: |
| Ensure the content and skills are appropriate to the lesson objectives and the abilities of the learners. | • Activities to be undertaken by the teacher, including detail of the questions to be asked at different levels of cognitive challenge. |
| Outline diagrammatically a summary of the IWB or whiteboard layout, indicating the relevant points for noting on the board. | • Activities to be undertaken by the learners, specifying your planning for differentiation. |
| | • Classroom organisation – individual/ pairs/groups/whole class |

| Lesson Content | Methods |
|---|---|
|  | Where appropriate, divide the lesson development into stages, checking for learning after each stage before progressing to the next.

Use action verbs (e.g. compare, contrast, analyse, explain, discuss) to indicate how learners will be engaged during the various lesson stages. |

**Lesson conclusion:** Indicate clearly how you will conclude the lesson and check that learning intentions for the lesson have been achieved by learners.

**Differentiation:** Outline in detail how differentiation is pursued.

**Assessment:** Outline specific assessment strategies that you intend to use.

**Linkage and integration:** Indicate how aspects of this lesson are linked thematically with other strands.

**Reflection:** Allow space for your retrospective reflection, which is completed after the lesson has been taught and will inform your planning of future lessons.

Figure 8.3 is an example of the typical structure of a lesson plan using the lesson steps format.

Figure 8.3: Lesson Planning Template: Step Format

**Subject:**
**Strand:**
**Lesson:**
**Class:**
**Date:**
**Time:**
**Objectives:** State what you expect the learners to have achieved by the end of the lesson as a result of your instruction. You may preface your objectives with the phrase:

At the end of the lesson learners will....
*Ensure coherence between the lesson objectives, teaching methods, content and assessment.*

**Teaching resources:**
* Materials required by the teacher:
* Materials required by the learners:

**Introduction:**

Specify the approaches used to

- Introduce learners to the lesson,
- Elicit their prior knowledge regarding the lesson topic and
- Motivate them to become involved fully in the lesson development.

Specify also the learning intention and success criteria for the lesson and how they will be shared with the learners (see 'Sharing the Learning Intentions and Success Criteria' on pages 221–3).

**Development:**

### Step 1: Heading Outlining Content Area to Be Covered during this Step of the Lesson

1. Provide a detailed account of the instructional approaches, specifying the
   - **Activities to be undertaken by the teacher,** including detail of the questions to be asked at different levels of cognitive challenge.
   - **Activities to be undertaken by the learners,** specifying planning for differentiation.
   - **Classroom organisation** – individual/pairs/groups/whole class.

2. Use action verbs (e.g. compare, tell, explain, discuss, elicit) to indicate clearly how the material will be presented during this stage of the lesson.

3. Revise each lesson step briefly before proceeding to the next step, outlining sample questions that you intend to use.

### Step 2 and Step 3: Heading Outlining Content Area to Be Covered during this Step of the Lesson

Follow the same format outlined in Step 1 (i.e. repeat stages 1, 2 and 3 above).

**Lesson conclusion:** Indicate clearly how you will conclude the lesson and check that learning intentions for the lesson have been achieved by learners.

**Differentiation:** Outline in detail how differentiation is pursued.

**Assessment:** Outline specific assessment strategies that you intend to use.

**Linkage and integration:** Indicate how aspects of this lesson are linked thematically with other strands.

**Reflection:** Allow space for your retrospective reflection, which is completed after the lesson has been taught and will inform your planning of future lessons.

We will now give further consideration to some key aspects of all the templates outlined above, specifically: devising objectives, understanding the need for differentiation, building thematic links, choosing learning activities and undertaking reflection. Other fields within the templates, such as questioning and assessment, will be discussed in Chapters 9 and 11 respectively.

## Lesson Objectives

Well-formulated objectives are a crucial aspect of effective lesson plans as, in the absence of stated objectives, there is no measure against which to evaluate success. Therefore, initially, you should spend time thinking about the purpose of your lesson plan and the desired learning outcomes. Consider the following questions in order to help you clarify your thinking regarding your desired learning outcomes for all your learners. This will assist you in devising your lesson objectives.

- Who are the learners?
- What is the primary focus of my lesson?
- What do I want different learners to know, experience or be able to do as a result of the lesson? Under what conditions? How well?
- How will I share my lesson objective(s) or learning intention(s) with my learners?

Lesson Planning

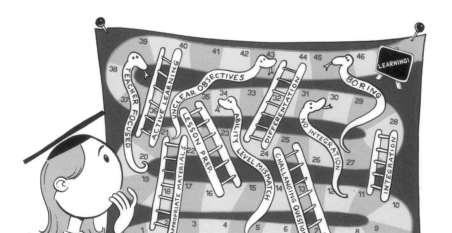

Well-constructed lesson objectives point to discernible and often measurable gains in learners' behaviour, attitudes, knowledge base, level of appreciation and understanding. For this reason, it is important to formulate specific objectives employing verbs that point to a tangible sense of achievement. For instance, in the case of a lesson about a local castle or building of interest, the teacher might intend that by the end of this lesson learners will be in a position to demonstrate learning that can be described by the following verbs:

> **Discover – Use – Identify – Perform – Describe – Devise – Construct – Reason – Apply – Recall – Answer – Discuss – Explore – Recognise – Distinguish – Select – Invent**

It is essential that objectives are clear and describe the intended learning outcomes, as well as communicating the learning expectations to the learners in an accessible and age-appropriate manner.

Heinich *et al.* (2001) present worthwhile guidance for the writing of instructional objectives and suggest that consideration needs to be given to audience, behaviour, condition and degree (ABCD) when writing objectives:

- **Audience** – the profile of the learners for whom the objectives are written
- **Behaviour** – inclusion of the verbs that describe what the learners will be able to do as a result of the lesson (e.g. discover, use, identify, perform, describe, devise, synthesise, argue, communicate, etc.)
- **Condition** – the context(s) in which the learners will perform the behaviours
- **Degree** – the expected level of competence in the behaviour (i.e. how well the learner performs the behaviour)

### Deriving Assessment from the Learning Objectives

Based on the principles of backward design developed by Wiggins and McTighe (1998), instructors identify the lesson objectives or desired results and then decide what they will accept as evidence of learners' knowledge and skills. The concept of backward design holds that you must begin with the end in mind (i.e. what the learner should be able to know, understand or do at the end of a lesson) and then map backward from the desired result to the current context and the learner's current ability/skill levels to determine the best way to reach the performance goal.

**TASK 8.3: THE ABCD OF INSTRUCTIONAL OBJECTIVES**

Evaluate the following objectives against the ABCD approach. Discuss and rewrite if necessary.

- At the conclusion of the class, learners should be able to read the map.
- At the end of the class, the learners will have learned how to read weather charts.
- At the end of the lesson, the learners will be able to appreciate the benefits and risks of wind power in our community.
- At the end of the lesson, learners will know the story of Brian Boru.

## Blooms' Taxonomy of Educational Objectives

Objectives may be classified according to a number of models. One such classification model has gained considerable currency in the discourse of education. It is attributable to Bloom *et al.* (1956) and seeks to delineate a stratum of capacities for educators to draw on when establishing learning objectives for their learners. In the first instance, there is the cognitive domain, which seeks to depict and outline cognition skills and is usually connected to the realm of knowledge and understanding. Second, the affective domain is intended to depict a spectrum of emotional areas open to growth and development. Third, the psychomotor domain delineates the potential for development of physical and motor skills and attributes.

The cognitive domain of Bloom's Taxonomy of Educational Objectives can be portrayed as shown in Figure 8.4.

Figure 8.4: Bloom's Taxonomy of Educational Objectives – Cognitive Domain

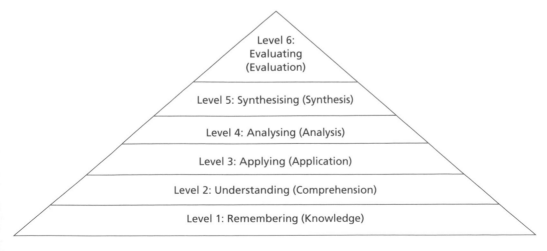

Source: Adapted from Bloom *et al.* (1956), *Taxonomy of Educational Objectives: The Classification of Educational Goals. Handbook I: Cognitive Domain*, New York: David McKay Company: 62–162.

## TASK 8.4: REVIEWING BLOOM'S COGNITIVE DOMAIN

The table below outlines the thinking attributes related to the cognitive domain (see Figure 8.4) and a range of suggested verbs for each. Choose one of the thinking attributes and assess the suggested verbs in terms of nurturing this thinking skill. Show your understanding using examples drawn from a chosen topic – you can identify the topic of your choice from the Primary School Curriculum 1999. Are these verbs of assistance in identifying the direction of the learning you plan within the topic chosen? Are they restrictive, enabling, thought-provoking or unduly inflexible? Are attempts to describe human thinking worthwhile, futile, beneficial or misguided? Make an overall assessment of the usefulness of the cognitive domain in terms of devising objectives.

Cognitive Domain: Useful Verbs in Devising Learning Objectives

| 1. Knowledge | 2. Comprehension | 3. Application | 4. Analysis | 5. Synthesis | 6. Evaluation |
|---|---|---|---|---|---|
| List, Name, Identify Show, Define Recognise Recall, State Visualise | Summarise, Explain, Interpret, Describe, Compare Paraphrase Differentiate Demonstrate Classify | Solve, Illustrate Calculate, Use, Interpret, Relate Manipulate Apply, Modify | Analyse Organise Deduce Contrast Compare Distinguish Discuss, Plan Devise | Design Hypothesise Support Schematise Write, Report Justify | Evaluate Choose Estimate Judge Defend Criticise |

In Figure 8.4, we can see that progressing upwards from Level 1 to Level 6 involves higher levels of demand and capability. At level 1 the emphasis is clearly on the recall of ideas, facts, information and sequence. Each subsequent level is typified by incrementally more demanding cognitive processes. To give some concrete expression to each sphere, the verbs employed in the table in Task 8.4 in respect of each level may be beneficial. However, language and terminology often fall short in terms of describing the complexities of human understanding. It might be worth noting this appraisal of Bloom's Taxonomy:

> [A]s anyone who has worked with a group of educators to classify a group of questions and learning activities according to the Taxonomy can attest, there is little consensus about what seemingly self-evident terms like 'analysis' or 'evaluation' mean. In addition, so many worthwhile activities, such as authentic problems and projects, cannot be mapped to the Taxonomy, and trying to do that would diminish their potential as learning opportunities. (Intel® Teach Program 2007: 1–2)

Critics of Bloom's Taxonomy have queried whether human understanding can be separated into these unique, sequential and hierarchical categories. Others welcome the categorisation for its usefulness, while acknowledging that it does not depict the fullness and richness of human learning. Some criticisms focus on the manner in which it may often be employed, involving an over-rigid and linear adherence to the hierarchical structure with educators becoming fixed on one stage rather than addressing several stages within a lesson. Consequently, some educators advise that Bloom's Taxonomy should be seen as a group of non-hierarchical ranges in which no one form of understanding is more or less important than others (Abbott, 2014).

---

**M-LEVEL TASK 8.2: REVISING BLOOM**

Attempts have been made to revise Bloom's Taxonomy. One of the more notable attempts was undertaken by Anderson and Krathwohl *et al.* (2001), which the following article summarises:

Wilson, L.O. (2013), 'A succinct discussion of the revisions to Bloom's classic cognitive taxonomy by Anderson and Krathwohl and how to use them effectively,' available from: http://thesecondprinciple.com/teaching-essentials/beyond-bloom-cognitive-taxonomy-revised/.

Read Wilson's article and identify and articulate six significant revisions of Bloom's original work as advanced by Anderson and Krathwohl (2001).

---

**TASK 8.5: DIFFERENTIATING YOUR OBJECTIVES**

Imagine a class with a very wide range of learning abilities. You wish to introduce them to a new topic in a subject of your choice. Devise five objectives that might be relevant and attainable within the class, but take account of the range of learning abilities in the group.

---

## Differentiation

As we saw in Chapter 4, considerable variations exist in the ways human learn, as influenced by different styles, abilities, pace and interests. Observation in classrooms and your own reflections will have informed you that not all learners possess the same capacities, or, indeed, prior experience, sense of interest, motivation, etc., and as a teacher you must identify different pathways in the learning journey by which different learners can reach broadly agreed outcomes. Indeed, the meaningful inclusion of all learners in the learning process requires teachers to give the utmost importance to differentiated teaching and learning. Heacox describes differentiation as 'changing the pace, level, or kind of instruction you provide in response to individual learners' needs, styles or interests' (2002: 5).

Consequently, in planning a lesson or a group of lessons, the teacher must decide on core learning outcomes for each learner and how these might be best reached. In the context of many classes, several learners will often share common abilities, capacities, interests and learning approaches, and these commonalities can be taken into account by the teacher while planning.

In most situations, however, it will be necessary to create specific outcomes for learners with learning difficulties and for those whose abilities exceed those of most others. This is at the heart of differentiation, and it revolves around a critical reflective ability to devise varying learning expectations for learners of differing abilities. At times and in different ways, it implies and demands employing different teaching methodologies and strategies, or, indeed, deploying various levels of support, as required.

Quite simply, differentiation is the set of approaches by which we try to make sure that all learners have the necessary levels of relevant assistance, coupled with an appropriate set of challenges to their capacities, so that all make viable advances in their learning. Teachers have developed several ways of undertaking differentiation and continue to do so based on reflection, observation and experience.

The NCCA (2007a) outlines some approaches in the context of gifted learners and our need to differentiate for their learning needs. However, their applicability to all learners should seem obvious to any teacher. Seven strategies are cited by which differentiation can be applied. These are listed as:

- Tasks
- Outcomes
- Resources
- Dialogue
- Support
- Pace
- Choice

In elaborating on these strategies, the NCCA advocates that 'a variety of tasks are set which relate to the same activity', and by which learners of differing abilities can proceed. Results can also differ so that 'the outcome of the work is not prescribed,' and so flexibility for a broad range of learners is inherent. In terms of resources, a variety of materials is employed with different learners, even though as a whole the class may be pursuing similar learning objectives, and 'the resources used will be matched to ability' (NCCA 2007a: 62). Dialogue is cited as a key factor in that it refers to our verbal engagement with learners, an engagement that is informed by observation and reflection. Differentiated language in addressing the needs of different learners appears vital. In some cases, a brief explanation will suffice, while in other situations a detailed exposition with multiple examples will be necessary. Employing questioning as a key teaching skill is also vital, as setting appropriate questions can have a significant impact on gaining and sustaining motivation.

## *Support*

In terms of support, the reflective teacher with considerable knowledge of his or her learners realises that the nature of support varies. Support intervention may be needed from the outset by some learners, rarely by others, and the support itself should be enabling to the process rather than fixated on the outcomes. An understanding of varying levels of pace on the part of learners also seems very significant. A slow pace of working may indicate great conscientiousness rather than difficulty, and a hurried pace may indicate either considerable ability or sometimes even a lack of engagement. Other underlying issues may be there that will require thought by any teacher as he or she comes to know a class of learners.

Finally, creating and encouraging choice for learners is cited as the key to differentiation. Given the opportunity to select work for themselves, learners can choose activities that they find more interesting and in line with their abilities (NCCA 2007a).

Glazzard *et al.* (2014) see differentiation as being facilitated in three ways: by task, by support, and by differentiated questioning, feedback and targets. It is important to note that differentiating your teaching does not amount to imposing prescribed approaches and strategies. Indeed, new and different strategies continue to emerge. The *Primary Curriculum Review*, published in 2008, found that a wide variety of approaches were in use, including pair and group work, varying content, varying pace, and employing circle time for greater access to discussion for all learners. However, it is pertinent to note that the report found little evidence of

> differentiation by structure (for example, planning small steps of learning for some children while other children are learning whole units of integrated material), and in particular the specification of different levels of achievement for curriculum objectives for different children. (NCCA 2008: 161)

It seems, therefore, that in our short-term planning, differentiation strategies will be developed incrementally and with greater effectiveness as a result of our ongoing reflection on classroom dynamics, our learners' needs and capacities, and our devising and revising appropriate and achievable learning objectives.

---

### TASK 8.6: STRATEGIES FOR DIFFERENTIATION

Review SESS, 'Differentiation in the Classroom for Children with Special Education Needs,' Cork: Special Education Support Service, PowerPoint presentation, available from: http://www.sess.ie/resources/teaching-methods-and-organisation. In doing so, offer critique, suggestions and amendments in terms of making the strategies proposed appropriate to a group of your choosing.

---

## Building Thematic Links

The Primary School Curriculum (PSC) 1999 advances the following view in respect of the integration of learning and the child's engagement with subjects, content knowledge and the environment:

> For the young child, the distinctions between subjects are not relevant; what is more important is that he or she experiences a coherent learning process that accommodates a variety of elements. It is important, therefore, to make connections between learning in different subjects. As they mature, integration gives children's learning a broader and richer perspective, emphasises the interconnectedness of knowledge and ideas, and reinforces the learning process (NCCA 1999: 16).

The theme of integration lies at the heart of child-centred education and is endorsed by the PSC 1999. Consequently, a significant aspect of your short- and long-term planning is to identify, create and facilitate opportunities and situations where meaningful linkages between knowledge, ideas, concepts and themes can be pursued by learners.

In your short-term planning, two questions will remain a constant focus of your thoughts:

- How can I build links with other knowledge within the subject area?
- How can I build links with knowledge in subject areas other than the one I am engaging with at present?

Clearly, engaging with these questions requires you to go beyond the demands of short-term planning and maintain a keen awareness of a broad range of possibilities. A wide and in-depth knowledge of the curriculum, its subject areas and strands is required if you are to be alert and amenable to making such internal subject and cross-subject linkages. Of equal importance is an awareness of your learners' prior knowledge, their interests, predispositions and sources of motivation. Importantly, a view of learning that sees rich possibilities for integration and linkage within and between subjects is congruent with a constructivist view of learning. It adheres to the viewpoint that 'deep, meaningful understanding occurs when children participate fully in their own learning with previous knowledge and experiences as the starting point for new learning. Active learning and full participation lead to deeper and richer understanding and use of knowledge....' (Harris and Alexander 1998: 116).

---

### Task 8.7: Planning for Integration

Below is an excerpt from NCCA (1999a), *Primary School Curriculum: Geography – Social, Environmental and Scientific Education*: 56. In a group of three, choose one bullet point and develop a set of possibilities around linkage and integration in relation to it. Speculate on learners' prior knowledge, interests, previous encounters in the curriculum with related areas and any other relevant ideas. Design a visual depiction of the possibilities for linkage and integration. It is important to note that integration and linkage should arise naturally rather than be artificially contrived. However, within your group you should notice how different members of the group create linkages in knowledge, concepts and ideas in ways that differ from you. A small number of subjects are cited below as relevant, but the possibilities are undoubtedly greater.

**Strand Unit: People and Other Lands**

*The child should be enabled to:*

- Study some aspects of the environments and lives of people in *one* location in Europe and *one* location in another part of the world.
  *location of these areas; peoples and communities that live there; language(s); myths and stories, art and culture; clothes; play and pastimes; features of the natural environment; interrelationships of the lives of people and these features; settlements: homes and other buildings; common building materials and features; foods and farming; work and work-places; similarities to and contrasts with Ireland*
- Develop an awareness of the interdependence of these people and people in Ireland.
- Begin to develop a sense of belonging to local, county, national, European and global communities.

*Integration*

History: Story; Early people and ancient societies.

Science: Designing and making

## Learning Activities, Strategies and Pedagogies

As we begin our experience of teaching, we see that our planning must include a range of strategies appropriate to the lesson objectives we have set out for the lesson. This puts extra onus on the goals we devise to be achievable, and also in some ways on the outcomes to be demonstrable. This brings us to the sphere of pedagogical approaches, and why and how we choose certain approaches to lesson planning over others. What is pedagogy? Although pedagogy has sometimes been seen as a set of skills for the transmission of knowledge, more recent reviews posit it as a complex array of insights, positions, observations, reflections, knowledge and skills necessary for effective teaching. Arguments have arisen as to whether it should be solely scientific in its orientation, or wholly artistic, or based entirely on personal insight. However, we view pedagogy as a rich field incorporating insights from research, observation, and teacher experience and understanding of the multi-faceted nature of learning and learners. It is 'a highly complex blend of theoretical understanding and practical skill' (Lovat 2003: 11). Developing pedagogical perspectives would seem therefore to lie at the heart of teacher education. Asking oneself questions along the following lines emerges as crucial:

- How am I going to assist learners in achieving the learning objectives?
- From the wide range of strategies available, which ones are most suitable for the learners in the context of this place, time and set of learning outcomes?
- Are the strategies I choose congruent with the outcomes sought or is there an inherent contradiction?
- What kind of classroom management strategies should I arrange for the most effective teaching at this time?
- What types of teacher–learner and learner–learner interactions should I initiate (individual, pair work, group work, circle time, type of group work, etc.)?
- How best might I arrange and plan the introduction of resources in terms of time, distribution, impact and intention?

A serious engagement with these questions and others should give credence to Lovat's view that a teacher is 'a highly developed autonomous professional, with a requisite professional knowledge base and practitioner skills', with much of that expertise resting on his or her initiation into an ever-developing pedagogical frame of reflective thought (Lovat 2003: 11).

High-quality pedagogy demands a broad range of strategies and approaches based on sustained reflection, research and experimentation. All these aspects focus on both conceptualising and employing strategies that facilitate learners to learn in a particular context, and allow for individual learning differences.

Clearly, teachers need to be informed by quality educational research in choosing from the vast array of pedagogical models and strategies. Equally, teachers must also refine the art and science of teaching themselves, adapting it as they proceed in line with their own needs, strengths, observations, reflections and resources, and the particular contexts of their learners.

---

### M-LEVEL TASK 8.3: PEDAGOGICALLY SPEAKING!

Research the pedagogical approaches most suitable for learners in the early primary years. In doing so, assess the importance of cultivating a pedagogical frame of thinking in your development as a teacher.

---

Recent research (Husbands and Pearce 2012) outlines the following principles, which should guide any teacher in choosing a range of pedagogical approaches:

*   Effective pedagogies give serious consideration to learner voice.
*   Effective pedagogies depend on behaviour (what teachers do), knowledge and understanding (what teachers know), and beliefs (why teachers act as they do).
*   Effective pedagogies involve clear thinking about longer-term learning outcomes as well as short-term goals.
*   Effective pedagogies build on learners' prior learning and experience.
*   Effective pedagogies involve the scaffolding of learning.
*   Effective pedagogies involve a range of techniques, including whole-class and structured group work, guided learning and individual activity.
*   Effective pedagogies focus on developing higher order thinking…and make good use of dialogue and questioning in order to do so.
*   Effective pedagogies embed Assessment for Learning.
*   Effective pedagogies are inclusive and take the diverse needs of a range of learners, as well as matters of student equity, into account.

---

### M-LEVEL TASK 8.4: EFFECTIVE PEDAGOGIES

Review the above principles and assess how they might assist you in choosing a set of strategies for any topic outlined for Third/Fourth Class in NCCA (1999b), *Primary School Curriculum: Social, Personal and Health Education*, Dublin: National Council for Curriculum Assessment, available from: http://www.ncca.ie/uploadedfiles/Curriculum/SPHE_Curr.pdf.

The range of pedagogical strategies available to teachers is immense and continues to expand. Some are generic to many subjects, while others have been developed within the context of specific disciplines. As you progress in your education as a student teacher, you will encounter many of these strategies within specific pedagogical areas. Some you may have experienced as a learner in your own schooling. Others will be novel and perhaps perplexing at the outset. Commonly used strategies include the following:

- Talk and discussion
- Improvisational drama
- Paired reading/buddy reading/peer reading
- Play and games
- Mime
- Drawing concept maps
- Outdoor trails (for maths, geography, history, science, etc.)
- Guided discovery activities
- Use of artefacts
- Exploration of pictures and photographs
- Use of oral evidence
- Fieldwork
- Patch studies
- Brainstorming
- Thinking time
- Circle time
- Structured interviews
- Co-operative games
- Simulations
- Group decision-making
- Collaborative problem-solving
- Designing and conducting surveys and questionnaires
- Maintaining a portfolio or journal

Choosing a pedagogical approach, from the above list or elsewhere, and employing it depends to a large extent upon our understanding of the learning context in which we find ourselves. It seems clear that developing a pedagogical frame of thinking is akin to developing a reflective spirit and that 'a shared understanding of the "why", "what", "how", "when", "where" and "who" of pedagogy allows us to continue to challenge, to question, and to review our practice' (Education Scotland 2005: 13).

---

### Task 8.8: Pedagogies in the SPHE Curriculum

The below pedagogical strategies (NIPT 2013) have been highlighted by the NCCA as ones regularly used in the teaching of Social, Personal and Health Education (SPHE) at primary level.

Consult NCCA (1999b), *Primary School Curriculum: Social, Personal and Health Education*, Dublin: National Council for Curriculum Assessment, available from: http://www.ncca.ie/uploadedfiles/Curriculum/SPHE_Curr.pdf. Identify a SPHE topic for any class level of your choice and then select at least three of these approaches for your teaching plan. In researching the approaches that you have chosen in more detail, you will develop a justification for your choice.

Circle time, thinking time, brainstorming, structured interviews, co-operative games, simulations, photo language, role play/drama activities, agree/disagree, diamond nine/ranking, group decision-making, collaborative problem-solving, designing and conducting surveys and questionnaires, free writing, reflective writing, maintaining a portfolio. (NIPT 2013: 13)

## Assessment as, for and of Learning

See Chapter 11 for a detailed explication of assessment and its role and function in lesson planning.

## Reflecting on Planning and Teaching

Reflection is a key and recurring aspect of each teaching encounter, and student teachers are asked to review lessons taught as soon as possible after teaching has ended. This is based on the view that 'teaching is a complex and highly skilled activity which, above all, requires classroom teachers to exercise judgement in deciding how to act' (Pollard *et al.* 2008: 5). This requirement for reflection is based on the belief that it will serve to enrich your understanding of the intricacies of teaching, inform future and subsequent lessons, and contribute to the nature of the dialogue to be undertaken with your mentor and co-operating teacher.

A key argument for regular and worthwhile reflection is that it maintains your focus on the quality of learning in the classroom. Since the quality of learning is of paramount importance in education, the requirement to reflect, make judgements, adapt and innovate in respect of learning is inescapable. Danielson describes highly reflective teachers as possessing 'an intentional competence that enables them to identify and replicate best practice, refine serendipitous practice, and avoid inferior practice. Because of their ability to reflect, great teachers know not only what to do, but also why' (2009: 8).

As beginning teachers, it is worth seeing your initial steps in reflection as part of a longer journey towards a deeper engagement with the complexities of teaching as your confidence, experiences and observational skills develop. That realm of advanced reflection has been adverted to by Pollard *et al.*, who posit that high-quality reflective teaching:

- implies an active concern with aims and consequences, as well as means and technical efficiency.
- is applied in a cyclical or spiralling process.
- requires competencies in methods of evidence-based classroom enquiry.
- requires attitudes of open-mindedness, responsibility and wholeheartedness.
- is based on teacher judgement, informed by evidence-based enquiry and insights from other research.
- along with professional learning and personal fulfilment, is enhanced through collaboration and dialogue with colleagues.
- enables teachers creatively to mediate externally developed frameworks for teaching and learning.

(2008: 14)

These concerns receive attention in other sections of this book (see Chapter 2 in particular), with emphasis placed on the significance of research-based evidence, collaboration in the process of reflection, and a sense of criticality and open-mindedness. Consequently, the process of reflection may be seen as one that synthesises many themes and characteristics that underpin high-quality teaching and learning.

### Reviewing My Planning and Preparation

As noted earlier (see Chapter 2), Schön has identified two distinct forms of reflection. The initial form, reflection-in-action, is concerned with the immediate judgements that we make in response to issues that arise in the lesson. Our responses are often based on our evolving experience, some theoretical insights and our general practice-based knowledge or repertoire of successful approaches from prior teaching. Schön has called this form of reflection 'knowledge-in-action', and it is undertaken often with great alacrity, involving a matrix of judgement, timing and implementation.

In a different manner, Schön's second form of reflection, reflection-on-action, takes place in the aftermath of teaching and is characterised by a systematic inquiry, profound consideration of the experience, an exploration of the active influences present, and an evaluation of outcomes in terms of learning, behaviour and organisation within the lesson or period of teaching and learning. Pollard *et al.*'s characteristics of reflection, outlined above, become more relevant as teachers develop and employ a broad range of approaches to enhance their reflection-on-action. Among these approaches, teachers have often seen merit in the use of portfolios, reflective journals, field notes and a variety of other aids.

Student teachers, however, might pose questions of the following nature when commencing to reflect on their recent teaching encounters:

- Can I identify a number of positive teaching qualities and attributes that I developed during the teaching experience?
- What features of my teaching still require cultivation during the teaching experience?
- What inferences can I now glean from my teaching experience to inform my next experience of teaching?

These opening questions, when addressed with open-mindedness and criticality, allow you to unravel some of the complexities of any teaching experience at an initial level. As experience in teaching and reflection is enhanced, more complex and concrete questions will begin to emerge. Some of these questions might take the following direction:

- What aspects of the lesson went well (or not) and why?
- What unexpected things occurred, and how did I deal with the emerging situation?
- What did the learners achieve from the lesson and how do I know they have achieved it?
- How would I adjust the progression, pace and teaching methods in order to augment learning, particularly for learners who have learning difficulties?
- What was the most difficult moment in my teaching?
- If I could change one aspect of my approach in order to augment learning, what would it be?
- Were the learning outcomes sufficiently clear in advance of the lesson?
- Did I provide sufficiently for differentiation in content and methods within the lesson?
- How appropriate were my chosen assessment approaches in identifying what the learners had learned?
- How did I accommodate the varying learner needs and styles in the class?

And, in focussing on one learner and his or her progress throughout the lesson:

- Did I give due attention to this learner's learning style, and social, emotional and behavioural needs?
- How effective were the approaches I employed, the language register I used, and the classroom organisational strategies I planned in supporting this learner's engagement?

An inexhaustible range of questions can be raised and probed. It is important to bear in mind that the process of reflection begins simply and expands as our experiences and challenges multiply and deepen. Even at the initial stages of inquiry, it is a process that can nourish and enhance our teaching engagement, as long as we see reflection as a

form of mental processing that we use to fulfil a purpose or to achieve some anticipated outcome. It is applied to gain a better understanding of relatively complicated or unstructured ideas and is largely based on the reprocessing of knowledge, understanding and, possibly, emotions that we already possess. (Moon 2005: 1)

## A SUMMARY OF KEY POINTS

- Lesson planning is intrinsic to effective teaching and involves a multitude of factors: your prior knowledge of the learners, their varying levels of prior knowledge, the differences between learners, the appropriateness of content, and many acts of predicting, imagining, anticipating, and sequencing.
- Lesson planning is a complex act of visualisation that relies on well-focussed reflection by which previous experiences are brought into play in the new situation of learning.
- Effective planning involves an ability to clarify, construct and differentiate appropriate objectives.
- Differentiation is critical to ensure the meaningful inclusion of children with special educational needs.
- Effective planning necessitates an awareness of integration and the possibilities involved in creating linkages within learning.
- Developing a pedagogical frame of mind is inextricably connected with ongoing and sustained reflection on learning and the processes of learning.

# CHAPTER NINE

# Fostering Classroom Dialogue

How can I develop learners' talking and thinking?

How can I ask better questions?

What is dialogic teaching?

**When you have worked through this chapter you will:**

- Appreciate the importance of talk as a vehicle for learning.
- Understand the concepts of dialogic and exploratory talk.
- Be aware of how skilful questioning can be used to promote thinking and learning.

## TALKING ABOUT CLASSROOM TALK

We would like to begin this chapter by asking you to imagine that you are observing the following interaction in a classroom:

| Teacher: | Hands up, who can recall the story we were reading yesterday? Good. I see a lot of you have your hands up. Ruth, please stop fiddling with your pencil case. Who can remember what it was called? No shouting out. Let me see, who is sitting quietly? OK, Mark, can you tell us, please? |
|---|---|

| Mark: | *Charlotte's Web.* |
|---|---|
| Teacher: | Well done, that's correct; it was called *Charlotte's Web*, wasn't it? Can anyone remember who Charlotte is? Hannah, can you tell us? |
| Hannah: | A spider. |
| Teacher: | Very good, Charlotte is a spider. |

What do you notice about this example of classroom dialogue? Did you observe that it is the teacher who does most of the talking? The majority of the learners do not have an opportunity to speak and those who are selected respond with single words or short phrases. This traditional type of classroom discourse, where for the most part teachers talk and learners listen, is a one-way communication system (Galton *et al.*, 1999). Tharp and Gallimore (1988) describe this type of interaction as comprising three parts. First, the teacher Initiates (I) the interaction by asking a question. This prompts a Response (R) from the learner, and a Follow-up (F) comment from the teacher, which often initiates another cycle, and so the I-R-F pattern is repeated. While IRF exchanges can be useful to assess recall, maintain attention, and encourage listening and feedback on what learners have heard, IRF exchanges have been found to be limited as a means of promoting language development and higher order thinking skills. Smith *et al.* (2004) found that average learner response in IRF classrooms lasted only five seconds and was limited to three words or fewer in 70 per cent of answers. However, IRF sequences are frequently the default mode used by teachers to interact with learners, presenting few opportunities for learners to give expanded answers, initiate talk or ask questions (Resnick *et al.* 2010; Alexander 2001; Smith *et al.* 2004).

## DIALOGIC TEACHING

The 'Five Nations Study' investigated teacher talk in primary classrooms in five countries – England, the US, France, India and Russia – and found that the IRF sequence was observed most frequently in schools in the UK and the US (Alexander 2001). In contrast, dialogic teaching methods featured most strongly in French and Russian classrooms and the children in these classrooms were found to have benefited in terms of classroom behaviour, learning and social development. Alexander (2001) found that variation between dialogic and IRF approaches arose from the more subtle aspects of teacher–learner interaction, such as the extent to which teachers elicited learners' own ideas about their work, shared the nature and purposes of tasks, encouraged them to discuss errors and misunderstandings, and engaged them in extended sequences of dialogue.

Dialogic teaching has been defined as an approach where both learners and teachers make substantial contributions to classroom dialogue, through which learners' thinking on particular ideas and/or themes is advanced (Mercer and Littleton 2007). In order to promote dialogic talk, Alexander states that it is not sufficient simply to repeat or rephrase a learner's contribution, but rather 'what is said needs actually to be reflected upon, discussed, even argued about…' (2004: 20).

## Dialogic Talk Sequence: Fifth Class – The Action of Yeast in Bread Making

| | |
|---|---|
| **Teacher:** | OK, I'm just going to repeat what Mary said. Listening ears everyone for a minute. Mary said that we should use lukewarm water because the lukewarm water will make the flour softer and easier to knead. All right, that's one idea. Let's hold that idea in our heads. Mark? |
| **Mark:** | Um, I actually think it's different to what Mary said. I think the lukewarm water creates steam in the dough and that helps the dough to rise in the oven. |
| **Teacher:** | That's a good point, Mark. So you are both agreeing that the temperature of the water is important but for different reasons. Yes, Ruby? |
| **Ruby:** | I'm not sure if this is right but…um…but if yeast is a living thing and we want the yeast to work on the flour, maybe it works better if the dough is lukewarm. It's like the opposite of why we put stuff in the fridge. |
| **Teacher:** | OK. We are getting some really great ideas now. So, Ruby, you are suggesting that we use lukewarm water because it will speed up the action of the yeast. Who else? Sadhbh? |
| **Sadhbh:** | Once we made apple wine and we used yeast to start it off. The yeast made the apple juice fizzy. Mom said that the yeast eats the sugar in the apple juice and makes a gas. I think that is what causes the bubbles in the dough. |
| **Teacher:** | OK, so we have some excellent suggestions. Right, let's take some of those ideas and try and see if we can create a test to find out what is happening. |

## Characteristics of Dialogic Teaching

Dialogic teaching is indicated by certain features of classroom interaction:

- questions are structured so as to provoke thoughtful answers.
- answers provoke further questions and are seen as the building blocks of dialogue rather than its terminal point.
- individual teacher–learner and learner–learner exchanges are chained into coherent lines of enquiry rather than left stranded and disconnected.

(Alexander 2004: 32)

Hence, dialogic teaching is:

- **collective**

  *Participants address learning tasks together.*
- **reciprocal**

  *Participants listen to each other, share ideas and consider alternative viewpoints.*
- **supportive**

  *Pupils express their ideas freely, without fear of embarrassment over 'wrong' answers, and they help each other to reach common understandings.*
- **cumulative**

  *Participants build on answers and other oral contributions and chain them into coherent lines of thinking and understanding.*
- **purposeful**

  *Classroom talk, though open and dialogic, is also planned and structured with specific learning goals in view.*

(Alexander 2010: 3–4)

In terms of what the teacher actually does in classroom interaction, Mercer *et al.* describe 'dialogic teaching' as that which:

1. gives students opportunities and encouragement to question, state points of view, and comment on ideas and issues which arise in lessons;
2. engages in discussions with students, which explore and support the development of their understanding of content;
3. takes students' contributions into account in developing the subject theme of the lesson and in devising activities which enable students to pursue their understanding themselves, through talk and other activity;
4. uses talk to provide a cumulative, continuing, contextual frame to enable students' involvement with the new knowledge they are encountering;

5. encourages the children to recognise that talk is not merely the prosaic chat of everyday life but is a valuable tool for the joint construction of knowledge.

(2010: 369–70)

## Exploratory Talk

Exploratory talk (Barnes 1975, 2008; Mercer *et al.* 1999, 2000), wherein learners share ideas in order to explore meaning and develop and refine understandings, underpins the value of discussion as a vehicle for learning. When learners verbalise, explain and justify their decisions to each other, these processes lead to the development of higher-order thinking skills. As it involves experimentation with new ideas, by its nature exploratory talk tends to be hesitant and tentative, and involve incomplete sentences:

> Exploratory talk is hesitant and incomplete because it enables the speaker to try out ideas, to hear how they sound, to see what others make of them, to arrange information and ideas into different patterns.... (Barnes, cited in Mercer and Hodgkinson 2008: 4)

Exploratory talk requires the learner to be actively engaged and take responsibility for their learning by asking questions, making predictions and inferences, and generally being thoughtful and critical about their learning. It is through this crucial but constructive engagement that students are able to challenge and counter-challenge thinking and to make reasoning visible in the talk (Kerawalla *et al.* 2010).

Exploratory talk provides an important avenue for enhanced understanding, but, in order for it to be effective, learners must feel comfortable expressing their emerging ideas in the company of their peers without the fear of ridicule or undermining contradiction:

> In exploratory talk, then, a speaker 'thinks aloud', taking the risk that others can hear, and comment on, partly-formed ideas. Engaging in exploratory talk is therefore rather a brave thing to do, and tends not to happen unless there is a degree of trust within a discussion group. (Mercer and Dawes 2008: 67)

Mercer describes how exploratory talk proceeds:

> Exploratory talk is that in which partners engage critically but constructively with each other's ideas. Relevant information is offered for joint consideration. Proposals may be challenged and counter-challenged, but if so reasons are given and alternatives are offered. Agreement is sought as a basis for joint progress. Knowledge is made publicly accountable and reasoning is visible in the talk. (2000: 98)

The ground rules that enable exploratory talk should include the following:

- Partners engage critically but constructively with each other's ideas.
- Everyone participates.
- Tentative ideas are treated with respect.
- Ideas offered for joint consideration may be challenged.
- Challenges are justified and alternative ideas or understandings are offered.
- Opinions are sought and considered before decisions are jointly made.
- Knowledge is made publicly accountable (and so reasoning is visible in the talk).

(Mercer and Hodgkinson 2008: 66)

---

### TASK 9.1: PLANNING FOR THINKING TOGETHER

Read and review the findings of the 'Thinking Together' research project: CREET, *Thinking Together in the Primary Classroom*, Milton Keynes: Centre for Research in Education and Educational Technology and the Open University, available from: http://www.open.ac.uk/creet/main/sites/www.open.ac.uk.creet.main/files/08%20 Thinking%20Together.pdf.

How might the recommendations of the research impact your planning for talk promotion in your classroom?

Consider the following questions:

- At what points in a lesson might exploratory talk be most easily integrated?
- How can you gather information about the learners' talking and/or thinking skills? For example, what words do they use? How do they share their ideas with each other and with you?
- How could you further extend the learners' talking and thinking?

---

## Accountable Talk

Similar in focus to exploratory talk, accountable talk is a means of enhancing the quality of learner talk in classrooms. Accountable talk requires that learners provide evidence to support their statements (Michaels *et al.* 2002). When engaged in accountable talk, learners are interested in each other's thought processes. They seek elaborations and clarifications in order to extend their thinking and respond to each other's reasoning. Figure 9.1 is an example of a desk poster that can be used to scaffold accountable talk between learners.

Figure 9.1: Example of a Desk Poster that Can Be Used to Scaffold Accountable Talk between Learners

| Be sure to: | Some prompts to help you: |
|---|---|
| Explain why your idea is good. | I agree with _____ because _____ .<br>This reminds me of _____ because _____.<br>I believe this is true because _____. |
| Check by asking questions if you are not sure or don't understand. | Can you give me an example of what you mean?<br>Can you tell me more?<br>Can you give me another example so that it is more clear? |
| Ask for more detail if something sounds incorrect. | I disagree with that because _____ .<br>I still have questions about _____ .<br>I want to add to what [Name] said about_____.<br>Based on my evidence, I think _____ . |
| Give evidence to support your statements. | The big idea is _____ .<br>This is different because _____ .<br>This is the same because _____ . |
| Use ideas from others to add to your own. | I agree with [Name] because _____.<br>[Name]'s suggestion reminds me of _____.<br>How did you reach that conclusion?<br>What if we had started with ___ rather than ___?<br>Have we thought of all the possible solutions? |

## Talk in the Early Primary Years

Recent research conducted in Ireland reinforces the importance of developing children's language in the early years and the importance of language as a precursor to later literacy development (Ring and Mhic Mhathúna *et al.* 2015). Larson and Peterson suggest that 'early childhood educators should give children ample opportunities to participate in extended discourse forms, including narratives, explanations, pretend talk, and other forms of complex conversations, in order to achieve successful school-based outcomes' (2003: 309). The importance of conversations and interactions in the early years has been underpinned by findings from research (Sylva *et al.* 2004), which followed 3,000 learners as they moved from preschool to school. The research identified that the 'quality of adult–child verbal interactions is a critical component in effective early childhood programs' (5). Researchers used the term 'sustained shared thinking' to describe the kind of interactions that best support and extend learning. Sustained, shared thinking occurs 'when two or more individuals work together in an intellectual way to solve a problem, clarify a concept [or] evaluate an activity…. Both parties must contribute to the thinking and it must develop and extend the understanding' (Sylva *et al.* 2004: 6). Defined in this way, we can see that sustained shared thinking has a resonance with exploratory talk as outlined above.

Creating contexts where young learners can play together greatly enhances opportunities for talk and thinking. The NCCA suggests the following strategies for promoting sustained shared thinking among young learners:

- **Use open-ended comments**, for example:
  I wonder how the ice melted.
  I noticed sea shells just like that when I was at the beach last week.
  Hmmm, that is interesting how you mixed the colours together.
  I love the way the sun is making a rainbow on the frosted spider's web.

- **Use open-ended questions** to encourage explanations and predictions, for example:
  How did you manage to make a hill for the cars to roll down?
  What kind of clothes do we need to put on the teddies before we take them outside for a walk?
  Remember when we went on the trip to the farm, what did you like best?

- **Model thinking**
  I think we might need to plan how to make that magic potion.
  We might need to think about how we'll fix the problem of the fallen roof.

- **Recap**
  So you mixed the red and yellow paints to make orange.
  You made a ramp using the long piece of wood.

- **Draw on learners' own stories, interests and home lives**
  Can you tell me about your dog Rusty?
  I know very little about dinosaurs, can you tell me about them?

- **Offering your own experiences**
  Porridge is my favourite breakfast.
  I went to Italy for my holidays.
  I'm a bit scared of hospitals too.

- **Using specific feedback to encourage further thinking**
  You've worked hard to build the bridge.
  What can we do to make sure that lorry is going to fit under it?

(Adapted from NCCA (n.d.), 'Practitioners and children talking and thinking together')

## USING QUESTIONING TO PROMOTE THINKING AND TALKING AT ALL PRIMARY LEVELS

A five-year-old girl returned from her first day at school and announced that her teacher was no good because she didn't know anything. When asked why she thought that, she replied, 'The teacher just kept on asking us things...' (Brown and Wragg 1993: 3). It is a little ironic that teachers spend so much of the time asking questions, since it is teachers who often have the knowledge and expertise. However, there are many reasons why teachers should ask questions, for example:

- To establish what learners already know about a topic or what skills they already have.
- To promote learners' cognitive engagement with a topic.
- To check learning after a unit of work.
- To monitor the effectiveness of one's own teaching.

Good questions are:

- Purposeful, useful and relate to the objectives of the lesson.
- Distributed appropriately around the class, targeting learners of different abilities.
- Pitched appropriately in terms of cognitive challenge and language register.
- Focussed on the developmental needs of learners.
- Supportive in tone, encouraging learners to take risks.

---

**TASK 9.2: THINKING ABOUT QUESTIONS**

Think about and discuss the following questions:

- What types of question provide cognitive challenge?
- How might you encourage learners to express their perspectives, ideas, feelings and opinions?
- What approaches can you use to extend dialogue?
- How might you create an environment in your classroom where learners feel comfortable explaining their thinking, even when they give the wrong answer?

Co-constructing Meaning

## Questions and Levels of Thinking

Good teaching involves challenging learners in a variety of ways. By using a range of questions, we stimulate the learners to think at a variety of levels. Questions that provoke a depth of thinking are known as 'higher order' or 'open' questions. Questions that simply elicit the recall of knowledge or information are known as 'lower order' or 'closed' questions. A study by Smith *et al.* (2004), which investigated the discourse strategies used by a national sample of UK primary teachers during whole-class teaching, found that:

> Open questions made up 10% of the questioning exchanges and 15% of the sample did not ask any such questions. Probing by the teacher, where the teacher stayed with the same child to ask further questions to encourage sustained and extended dialogue, occurred in just over 11% of the questioning exchanges. . . . Only rarely were teachers' questions used to assist pupils to more complete or elaborated ideas. Most of the pupils' exchanges were very short, with answers lasting on average 5 seconds, and were limited to three words or fewer for 70% of the time. It was also very rare for pupils to initiate the questioning. (408)

## Improving Whole-Class Questioning

While priority should be given to the promotion of dialogic teaching methods, with an emphasis on exploratory talk involving sustained engagement between pairs and groups, whole-class teacher–learner exchanges also play a useful and important function as a form of classroom interaction. Familiarity with, and competence in, the strategies outlined below will significantly enhance your ability to question the whole class as well as groups and individual learners within the class.

### Strategies to Improve Whole-Class Questioning

*Pose the question to the whole group, <u>before</u> asking a learner to respond.*
When you call on a learner before asking the question, the rest of the class is less likely to listen to the question, much less to think about a response. Asking the question of the whole class indicates to learners that they should be prepared to answer *every* question.

*Allow sufficient 'thinking time' after asking a question of the whole group.*
Classroom discussion and the quality of learner thinking can be enhanced considerably by the appropriate use of wait time. This has been found particularly important for children with special educational needs.

   Pausing after the question has been asked allows you an opportunity to monitor the level of response and gives all learners a chance to process the question and formulate a thoughtful response. Ask learners to refrain from responding until you ask for a volunteer or invite someone to respond. Use the time to provide encouragement to those who are less confident. Those who are more eager can use the time to write down the responses they compose. Laminated A4 cardboard sheets make very useful individual whiteboards on which learners can quickly jot down their ideas.

The following are useful phrases that you can use to signal wait time:

- I'm going to give you time to think before I ask anyone to answer the next question.
- Now think for a minute before you raise your hand.
- Think carefully before you put up your hand.
- Take your time to think out your answer to this next question.

*Give all learners an opportunity to respond rather than relying on volunteers.*
Keep track of whom you invite to respond, so you can ensure that all learners have an equal chance to contribute. If you call on a learner who is not ready or does not know the answer, allow the learner to 'pass' and then give them another opportunity later.

*Expect and facilitate the participation and contribution of all learners.*
Do not answer your own questions! If you get an inadequate level of response, rephrase the question to ensure clarity or give a prompt to scaffold their answers.

*Differentiate questions to provide appropriate levels of challenge for all learners.*
Taking time to get to know your learners' abilities and interests will assist you in the formulation of questions at the appropriate level of challenge for each individual. This will help to ensure that all learners experience the satisfaction of being able to answer questions that are asked of them and gain self-confidence and motivation as a result.

*Establish a safe atmosphere for risk-taking by guiding learners in the process of learning from their mistakes.*
Always affirm the effort of the learner who gives an incorrect response. When learners make mistakes, build their confidence and trust by asking follow-up questions to help them self-correct and achieve success.

*Use individualised whiteboards.*
Providing each learner with a small whiteboard on which to formulate answers is a very effective means of maximising learner involvement while reducing their anxiety about making mistakes. All learners write the answer at the same time and hold it up for you to see.

### Using Prompting, Probing and Refocussing Questions

### Prompting

Prompting is effective when the learner's response is inadequate or not forthcoming. On these occasions, you may consider giving hints or asking a series of questions that may enable the learner to answer the question.

*Prompting: Example 1 – Teacher with Infant Class*
**Matching the numeral 2 with sets of 2 objects**

| | |
|---|---|
| Teacher: | Now, we are going to play a game. All eyes focussed this way. How many teddies do I have? [Teacher holds up two teddies and waits as children raise their hands.] |
| Teacher: | Yes, Cliona…. |
| Cliona: | Two, Miss. |
| Teacher: | Good girl, Cliona. |

|  | OK, who is going to pick out two cars from our object box? [Teacher points to flashcard of numeral 2.] Michael, I haven't asked you for a while, up you come! [Michael picks out and holds up three cars.] Can you count the cars you have for me, Michael? |
|---|---|
| Michael: | One, two, three. |
| Teacher: | Very good. Now, what number is this? [Teacher points to the numeral 2 on the flashcard.] |
| Michael: | Ahm…. |
| Teacher: | OK, Let's look at the number line. [Teacher points to numeral 2 on the number line and asks Michael to count the 2 oranges in the picture.] |
| Michael: | One, two. |
| Teacher: | Very good. What number is this? [Teacher points to the numeral 2 beside the set of 2 oranges on the number line.] |
| Michael: | Two. |
| Teacher: | Excellent. Now, what number is this? [Teacher holds up the flashcard of the numeral 2.] |
| Michael: | Two. |
| Teacher: | Very good. Now, Michael, I'm sure you can pick out two cars from the box for us now? [Michael duly selects two cars as requested.] |

### *Prompting: Example 2 – Teacher with First Class (Learning Support Group)*
### Matching picture to word activity

| Teacher: | I'm going to call different people up to the blackboard and when I point to one of the objects on the chart, I want you to be able to point out the word from our list that matches that object. OK, are we ready? Frank, will you come up, please? [Teacher points to a bus.] |
|---|---|
| Frank: | [Puts his finger on the word 'car' and looks at teacher.] |
| Teacher: | Are you sure? [Pause.] Don't mind the words for a minute. What am I pointing at? |
| Frank: | This one! [Extends his hand in the direction of the chart.] |

| | |
|---|---|
| Teacher: | Yes, and what do we call that? |
| Frank: | A bus. |
| Teacher: | Very good. Now, what sound does the word 'bus' begin with? |
| Frank: | Em…. |
| Teacher: | Listen to the word carefully: b—…b—…b— [the teacher makes the sound of the letter 'b'.]…bus? |
| Frank: | 'B', Teacher. |
| Teacher: | Now, show me the word over there that begins with the letter with the 'b' sound. Good, well done. |

### *Prompting: Example 3 – Teacher with Fifth Class*
### Commercial ports in Ireland

| | |
|---|---|
| Teacher: | Who can name some of the major commercial ports in Ireland? Let me see…Ellen, please? |
| Ellen: | Dingle. |
| Teacher: | OK, Ellen, I am looking for commercial ports, not fishing ports. Try again. |
| Ellen: | Waterford. |
| Teacher: | Good, any others? [Pause.] Yes, Olive? |

### *Prompting: Example 4 – Teacher with a learner with Autistic Spectrum Disorder*
### Irish legends

Prompting is a particularly important strategy in the context of working with learners with special educational needs, as it can encourage deeper levels of thinking and help learners to experience success in answering questions.

| | |
|---|---|
| Teacher: | What about a story. Is there any story that we did that you could tell someone and they'd know you were Irish? [Pause.] Do you remember the stories we did before our break, the Irish stories? [Pause.] Do you remember about the hurley and the sliotar and the dog? [Pause.] |
| Peter: | 'Setanta'. |
| Teacher: | Very good. 'Setanta'. Wouldn't that be a nice story to tell people, the story of Setanta? Because people in |

|  | different parts of the world, would they know that story? |
|---|---|
| **Peter:** | No. |
| **Teacher:** | And it's an Irish story. Is there any other story you could tell them? [Pause.] |
| **Peter:** | 'Finn MacCumhaill and the Salmon of Knowledge'. |
| **Teacher:** | Very good. 'Finn MacCumhaill and the Salmon of Knowledge'. Anyone else? I know you know. |
| **Roisín:** | 'Tír na nÓg'. |
| **Teacher:** | 'Tír na nÓg'. 'Tír na nÓg'. Excellent. |

(Adapted from Ring 2010)

Frequently, part of a response by a learner is correct and by varying the application of the prompting skill it is possible to focus on this and avoid being negative while correcting the response. When, having prompted the learner, the response is still not forthcoming, the following phrases may be used to move on sensitively and elicit a response from other members of the class:

'Think a little more and I'll come back to you later.'
or
'Listen to some of the other answers and I'm sure that you will come up with ideas yourself.'

An important consideration in all of the above approaches is to maintain a positive atmosphere in the class with due regard for and recognition of individual difference.

## Probing

There is a clear distinction between probing questions and prompting questions. Prompting questions involve a series of steps by which the learner is led to a more accurate response should the initial question prove to be unclear or too difficult. Probing questions do not involve the giving of additional information but rather seek clarification from a learner's response.

### Probing: Example 1 – Teacher with Fourth Class
#### Discussion on uses of boats

| **Teacher:** | I want you to think of the various ways in which boats are used. |
|---|---|

| John: | Sailing. |
| Teacher: | Good. Mary? |
| Mary: | Rescue. |
| Teacher: | Very good. Now, how might boats be used in a rescue? |
| Mary: | Well, lifeboats, Teacher. Those boats are specially made for rescuing people at sea. |
| Teacher: | Good, another use of boats please…. Joe? |
| Joe: | We went to France last Summer with our car on a boat. |
| Teacher: | Great, and what do we call that type of boat? |
| Joan: | A ship, Teacher. |
| Teacher: | Well, yes it is a ship, but a special type of ship. Anybody? |
| Jason: | A ferry, Teacher. |
| Teacher: | Very good. [The dialogue continues in this vein.] |

*Probing: Example 2 – Teacher with Third Class*
**Spring**

| Teacher: | What happens in the season of Spring? [Pause.] |
| John: | The lambs are born. |
| Teacher: | Is that the only kind of new life that we see? |
| John: | The leaves come on the trees and the flowers grow too. |
| Teacher: | Good. Any other changes? [Pause.] Helen? |

The above examples use probing to explore the depth of the learners' understanding and to maintain the flow of classroom dialogue. Can you identify the probing questions in the dialogue?

Probing may involve a number of learners in the unfolding dialogue. It is important that the teacher has a clear sense of the direction in which they wish the dialogue to go; on occasion, they may need to use a refocussing question to bring the lesson back on course.

## Refocussing

Refocussing questions are used to refocus the discussion on the main topic of the lesson. They serve as an appropriate intervention on the part of the teacher when he or she senses that the conversation has become tangential to the main focus of the lesson.

### Refocussing: Example 1 – Teacher with Fourth Class
**Astronomy**

| | |
|---|---|
| **Teacher:** | What stars do you recognise at night? [Pause.] Mary? |
| **Mary:** | I don't know any of their names. |
| **Teacher:** | One group has the same name as a piece of machinery a farmer uses in the field. [Pause.] Tony, do you know? |
| **Tony:** | A tractor? |
| **Teacher:** | Something used to break up the ground before the seeds are planted. |
| **Siobhán:** | A plough. |
| **Teacher:** | Excellent – that's the word I was looking for. The Plough is also the name given to a group of stars.... [Teacher shows the Plough constellation of stars on the interactive whiteboard and explains the origin of the name.] |
| **Noreen:** | My aunt is a farmer. She has a big Massey Ferguson, and I got a ride on it last summer when I was there on my holidays. |
| **Teacher:** | That must have been exciting. Now, when you were on holidays with you aunt, did you ever look up at the sky at night and see that shape? [Teacher points to the illustration of the Plough.] |

As you can see from the above dialogue, the skilled teacher can accept positively the tangential anecdotes of the learners and, through the use of appropriate refocussing questions, get the lesson back on track quickly.

---

#### TASK 9.3: REFORMULATING QUESTIONS

The following are questions that have been posed by student teachers. Comment on the clarity of each and reformulate in a more appropriate fashion. What issues arise when trying to reformulate the questions? What other information do you require?

1. The lion is known as the 'what' among the beasts?
2. Who is the Taoiseach? Do you know? Don't you know?
3. What do you think that gives us?
4. What about the Celts? What did they do a lot of?

5. What are some of the things we cut around the home?
6. What is one way you can tell time? How do you tell time? How many ways are there?
7. After you write the main paragraph, what do you write after this?
8. Tell me all you have learned.
9. Butter contains cream and salt. What does butter contain?

### Ineffective Questioning Styles

While all teachers have their own particular style of engaging with learners and of asking questions, some examples of less effective approaches are given below. Read and discuss the following. Can you identify why they might be problematic?

**Affirmation Seeker**: Now we all enjoyed that lovely song, didn't we, everyone?

This question will probably get exaggerated nods from some compliant learners keen to please the teacher, whereas other learners will probably respond with bored indifference and some even with subversive mutterings: 'No, it was a terrible song, the way you sang it anyway.' Here, the teacher seeks bland positive feedback from the entire class using a closed question to which there is really only one 'right' answer. It is also rhetorical in that it does not actually require an answer; in fact, it is barely a question at all, so it won't get much of a response.

**Provoker**: Who likes…?

Here the teacher chooses a sports team, pop group or personality, at which point a heated debate is provoked as the class immediately divides into 'They're rubbish' and 'They're the best' camps. The ensuing mayhem casts the teacher into the role of referee, with the lesson careening off track.

**Mind Boggler**: Would anyone – and I'm looking for answers from people who haven't put up their hands yet; Mary, I'm looking at you – be able to tell me in a few sentences about the Famine? Do you remember last week we talked about the Famine, and especially about the relationship between the potato crop and the Famine? So what I want now is a few ideas on where the Famine was worst felt by the people, that is, in what part of Ireland?

This type of questioning is likely to meet with silence or confused responses.

**Can You Read my Mind?:**    I'm thinking of something that lives in the country but sometimes can be found in cities also. It eats animals and is widespread throughout Ireland. What is it?

This question will likely receive a variety of answers of varying degrees of plausibility, including 'dog', 'owl', 'badger' and perhaps eventually the answer that the teacher was hoping for: 'fox'. Such a style of questioning may go nowhere and is likely to present an inadequate challenge for most learners.

The above examples may appear extreme. However, any experienced observer of teachers will testify to their existence and perhaps even be able to add a couple of others.

Other common examples of inadequate questioning include the following:

- **Closed questions that elicit simple 'yes' or 'no' responses**

  *e.g. Last time, did we discover that Scotland is bigger than Ireland?*

- **Echo questions**

  *e.g. Water contains hydrogen and oxygen. What does water contain?*

- **Poor word arrangement**

  *e.g. When Cromwell came to Ireland, what did he do when he came here?*

- **Repeating the question or repeating learners' responses**
  Habitually repeating the question or learners' responses causes learners to pay less attention because they know the question or response will be repeated. It is also wasteful of time.

- **Ambiguous Questions**

  *e.g. What happens when you walk out of school?*

## TASK 9.4: ASSESSING THE COGNITIVE CHALLENGE OF QUESTIONS

This task is based on the work of Anderson and Krathwohl *et al.* (2001), who revised Bloom's Taxonomy of Educational Objectives (Bloom *et al.* 1956) (see Chapter 8). The following table provides an overview of the question categories and the levels of thinking prompted by their associated questions. In the third column there is a list of randomly ordered questions, not associated with a category. Consider each of the questions listed in the third column and match it to what you consider to be the most appropriate question category.

| Question Category | Level of Thinking Prompted by Questions | Questions for matching to the correct category |
|---|---|---|
| REMEMBERING<br><br>Who? What? Where? When? Which?<br><br>List, describe, name, tell, label | Recalls information, observations or definitions | 'Compare life in the city with life in the country.'<br><br>'When was the Battle of the Boyne?'<br><br>If you believed that gods lived in every tree, how would you view the clearing of a forest?' |
| UNDERSTANDING<br><br>Compare, contrast, explain, rephrase, summarise, identify the main ideas | Understands the meaning of information by showing an interpretation of what has been learned | 'What formula would you use to find the size of this angle?'<br><br>'Why does the author choose to start the novel in that unusual way?' |
| APPLYING<br><br>Apply, solve, sort into groups, select, choose, use, calculate | Applies or uses information in a different situation or context | 'Explain, in your own words, what happened in the story.' |

| Question Category | Level of Thinking Prompted by Questions | Questions for matching to the correct category |
|---|---|---|
| ANALYSING<br><br>Identify cause or reason, conclude, infer, deduce, draw a conclusion, compare, categorise | Identifies motives or causes. Makes inferences. Finds evidence to support generalisations | 'What would happen if the world ran out of coal or oil?'<br><br>'What is the capital of France?'<br><br>'Why do you think hedgehogs have prickly spines?' |
| EVALUATING<br><br>Decide, judge, justify, choose, propose | Makes decisions based on detailed assessment, critique and reflection<br><br>Gives opinions on issues. Judges the validity of ideas. Judges the merit of a solution | 'What does this poem tell us about the poet's feelings?'<br><br>'If you were planning to sunbathe, what time of the day are you most likely to become sunburnt?'<br><br>'If the woodcutter had not been working that day, who else might have come to Granny's aid?' |
| CREATING<br><br>Invent, design, plan, imagine, predict | Creates new ideas and information based on previously learned material | 'Tell, in your own words, what happened in the story.' |

## A SUMMARY OF KEY POINTS

- When learners verbalise, explain and justify their decisions to each other, these processes lead to the development of higher-order thinking skills.
- Dialogic teaching involves both learners and teachers making substantial contributions to classroom dialogue.
- Exploratory talk is that in which learners engage critically but constructively with each other's ideas.
- Creating contexts where young learners can play together greatly enhances opportunities for talk and thinking.
- Questions that provoke a depth of thinking are known as 'higher order' or 'open' questions.
- Questions that simply elicit the recall of knowledge or information are known as 'lower order' or 'closed' questions.

# CHAPTER TEN

# Establishing a Positive Classroom Climate

What is my role in developing a positive classroom climate?

How does a positive classroom climate benefit learning?

Are there strategies that help?

Once you have worked through this chapter, you will have learned about the

- Significance of the teacher in creating and developing a positive classroom climate.
- Importance of reflection within the classroom as a key to building a positive atmosphere in any learning environment.
- Range of approaches available in respect of establishing a positive climate for learning.
- Importance of developing your own unique approach to developing classroom climate, informed by ongoing research.

## INTRODUCTION

The teacher is the pivotal agent in establishing a positive classroom climate. Such a climate generally has a major influence on learners' motivations and attitudes towards learning (Cullingford 2003; Pollard *et al.* 2000). Indeed, our core concern as teachers is to create an environment that fosters 'the desire to go on learning' (Dewey 1938: 48). Day *et al.* (2006, 2007) established that having the ability to create a positive classroom climate, and specifically to build a positive relationship with learners, was regarded by teachers as being at the very core of their own view of themselves as effective teachers.

Research indicates that the type of climate generally considered to facilitate optimal learning is one that can be described as being task oriented, warm, supportive, relaxed, purposeful and possessing a sense of order (Kyriacou 2007: 68 ). In such an atmosphere, learning is promoted by establishing and maintaining positive attitudes on the part of learners.

As we all have personal experiences of classrooms, it may be beneficial for us to reflect on a particular class in which we participated as learners, especially on the ethos or climate of that classroom (see Task 10.1).

---

### TASK 10.1: RECALLING THE CHARACTERISTICS OF A POSITIVE CLASSROOM CLIMATE

If you can recall a particularly positive classroom climate, consider to what extent the following aspects applied to that context. If other factors pertained, please also note these.

- The classroom was a happy place.
- I enjoyed coming to school.
- I did not miss many days from school.
- I was proud to be a learner in this school.
- I felt comfortable with the work I was expected to do.
- I was proud of my work.
- Learners in this class were encouraged to do their best in all their work.
- The teacher was sensitive to learners' problems.
- Learners in this class were encouraged to express their own opinions.
- We respected one another and listened to other people's points of view.
- We respected the property of others.
- The class, school and school grounds were attractive.

---

## CREATING A POSITIVE CLASSROOM CLIMATE

Creating a positive classroom climate is by no means accidental. It requires the engaged presence of a reflective teacher who consciously examines and reviews practices in the light of ongoing experience. A range of research has examined what learners value in a classroom environment. There appears to be a significant degree of consistency in the findings. Wei and Elias (2011), in an example of such research, find the quality of *affiliation* to be the most important dimension of learners' relationship to their classroom. Learners then rank rule clarity, teacher support, task orientation, involvement, and, lastly, the order and organisation of the classroom as the other most significant features in nurturing a positive and motivating classroom climate. Their findings are consistent with the findings of Levine and Donitsa-Schmidt (1996) and Cheng (1999), who also find that learners perceive affiliation most positively.

As 'affiliation' can be an elusive concept, another study may come closer to describing the texture of a positive classroom environment. Batten *et al.* (1993) reveal a range of teacher attributes that are most frequently approved by learners; qualities that are deemed ineluctable to a positive classroom climate. Specifically, students think that a good teacher should be a person who helps learners with their work; explains well so that they can understand; is friendly; is easy to get on with; doesn't yell; plans interesting and enjoyable lessons; exhibits care for learners; is always prepared to listen and understand; displays a sense of humour; and has good classroom control.

In a more recent study, Kington *et al.*'s findings in respect of learners and their views on a positive classroom climate indicate many of the same attributes. All told, considerable similarities exist across the research, and the teacher qualities that are found to be most conducive to building a positive classroom climate are firmly located in the realm of the personal. In Kington *et al.*'s study, learners give expression to their thoughts in the following manner:

- I have enjoyed being in my class.
- My teacher is friendly.
- My teacher makes me feel good about their teaching.
- My teacher helps me to see why what I am learning is important.
- This school is a friendly place.
- My teacher is easy to get to know.
- I feel safe in this school.
- I like most of the lesson.

(Kington *et al.* 2012: 10)

---

**TASK 10.2: HOW DO YOUR OWN LEARNING EXPERIENCES RELATE TO THE RESEARCH?**

Reflect on the lists of attributes relating to a positive classroom environment from Day *et al.* (1990) and Kington *et al.* (2012) above.

Based on your own experience, suggest any further factors that you consider important in establishing a positive classroom climate.

---

In line with the research above, it appears appropriate and beneficial to garner feedback from your learners as an important way of getting an insight into your teaching. This is wholly consistent with the view of student teachers as being actively engaged in reflection on their own practice (see Brookfield 1998). Much research, however, remains to be done on learners' perceptions of the learning context. One significant and major study that touched on the issue of a positive classroom climate was undertaken by Pollard *et al.* (2000). It offers a very significant set of insights into learners' perceptions of their teachers and, indeed, claims that the quality of relationships with their teachers is of paramount importance to learners (107). Pollard *et al.* conclude from the data that this focus on the quality of the relationship by learners is entirely

> consistent with [learners'] definitions of the ideal teacher where the personal qualities of kindness, cheerfulness and a sense of humour were given greater weight than qualities relating to teaching and learning. (2000: 130)

Developing a sense of positive relationship requires reflective experience gained over a period of time, involving a broad range of learners and learning situations. Situations, contexts, personalities and conditions vary immensely, and prescribing a single template for creating a positive classroom climate may not be wise. At the heart of reflective teaching, which is central to building a positive classroom climate, are the qualities of open-mindedness and flexibility, both of which can be vital in responding to the complexities of classroom life. In the words of Eisner (1994):

> Life in classrooms, like that outside them, is seldom neat or linear. Although it may be a shock to some, goals are not always clear. Purposes are not always precise. (116)

Evertson and Weinstein delineate what is required of teachers in creating positive classroom environments, stating that they must

1. develop caring, supportive relationships with and among students;
2. organise and implement instruction in ways that optimize students' access to learning;
3. use group management methods that encourage students' engagement in academic tasks;
4. promote the development of students' social skills and self-regulation; and
5. use appropriate interventions to assist students with behaviour problems.
   (2013: 6)

Clearly, classroom management is a multi-faceted endeavour that is far more complex than establishing rules, rewards and penalties to control students' behaviour.

In exploring the building of a positive classroom climate, we will progress gradually from broad principles to more specific ideas. In discussing principles, we may also begin to develop a range of very practical insights pertinent to our needs as teachers. Building a positive classroom climate is the result of a wide mixture of factors, influences, personalities and contexts, and is inextricably linked to effective class and lesson management. Initially, these broad principles for the cultivation of a positive classroom environment can be outlined in the following manner:

- Having stimulating, well-prepared and appropriately differentiated lesson content and activities
- Creating a safe environment for purposeful and motivated learning
- Developing skilful and sensitive management approaches for the class and groups within the class
- Providing clearly stated boundaries of acceptable behaviour and, indeed, responding appropriately in situations where boundaries are tested
- Employing appropriate incentives and keeping the importance of motivation to the fore
- Advancing the view that a positive classroom atmosphere is based on a sense of community and shared values
- Exemplifying a spectrum of positive standards, behaviours, approaches and values that are to be expected from learners
- Allowing learners a voice in respect of their learning, and the pace and direction of their learning
- Knowing how to identify and support learners whose progress and sense of well-being is affected by changing circumstances, and assisting them in accessing specialised support
- Building a relationship with learners based on fairness, trust and the availability of support

- Conveying high expectations to learners and a sense of caring about the achievement of their full potential

(Adapted from Training and Development Agency UK 2007)

---

### TASK 10.3: APPLYING THE PRINCIPLES

Choose any one the broad principles for building a positive classroom climate listed above and explore its implications for your relationship with a group of learners known to you. In doing so, compile some practical suggestions for the achievement of the principle. Share and discuss these suggestions within a peer-group setting.

---

### M-LEVEL TASK 10.1: EVALUATING RESEARCH ON CLASSROOM CLIMATE

Choose one of the broad principles for building a positive classroom climate outlined above. Identify one published research study that has explored this principle. Evaluate the findings and devise a summary report on the findings.

---

We may largely agree with the broad principles outlined above, and we may also have derived a broad spectrum of practical suggestions for pursuing each of them. But it is worth remembering that the contexts, circumstances and personalities involved are various and will offer different influences. It is interesting to note two significant sets of influences that undoubtedly affect the climate we wish to cultivate in classrooms: out-of-school and in-school influences on classroom behaviour.

## Out-of-School Influences on Classroom Behaviour

Regular reflection on your learners' in-class behaviour should indicate that they are influenced by circumstances inside and outside the classroom. Developing an awareness of these factors and engaging meaningfully with them can be of considerable benefit in responding to behavioural issues (Belvel 2010).

The Centre for Inclusive Child Care (2011) cites a range of external factors that can influence a child's behaviour, among them neglect, poverty and worry about finances in the home, inconsistencies in caring, exposure to media violence, substance abuse within the home, an environment of frequent argumentation, unmet emotional needs, infrequent opportunities to make choices, being rewarded for aggression, and witnessing or being a victim of abuse (sexual, physical or emotional).

## In-School Influences on Classroom Behaviour

Among the many in-school causes of classroom problems we find boredom, prolonged mental effort, emotional difficulties, an inability to do the work, a sense of low academic self-esteem, the social demands of school and the lack of negative consequences (Kyriacou 2007: 84–5). Interestingly, these factors echo some earlier research by Curwin and Mendler (1988), who argue that unclear limits within the classroom fail to foster a well-functioning climate, while learner boredom is often the result of over- or under-challenging material, leading to disengagement. Finally, a sense of failure among learners with unaddressed learning needs may prompt some to misbehave, simply because they feel they cannot be successful in school. Undoubtedly, this is a complex area, as learners' situations and personalities intertwine with different contexts and render accurate prediction or early judgement of problems very difficult.

---

### TASK 10.4: APPROACHES TO CLASSROOM MANAGEMENT

Discuss the approaches to dealing with classroom management difficulties that you had experience of as a learner in primary or post-primary school. Discuss these approaches in terms of their effectiveness. Ensure that your reflections are anonymised and do not identify any individual.

What do you consider to be the single greatest cause of classroom management problems in schools?

---

## Factors Associated with Positive Classroom Environments

It is our intention to emphasise a positive perspective in respect of classroom environments, and to progress on the understanding that building positive classroom environments is always desirable and feasible. In certain contexts, difficulties may arise, but the educational, social, personal and professional benefits of learning together as a class, in a welcoming and supportive environment, remain undisputed. By surveying some key research work in the area, we can begin to appraise a number of recurring factors that have either a positive or a negative influence. Researchers continue to explore these issues and will undoubtedly offer more insight as time progresses. The following summary of findings within relevant research is presented for reflection, analysis and further discussion:

- Considerable research insight supports the view that teachers who are well prepared and organised tend to experience fewer classroom management problems. Effective, organised teachers tend to build absorbing and supportive classrooms that are typified by high quality, worthwhile learning (Marzano *et al.* 2003; Shellard and Protheroe 2000). Typically, these teachers negotiate and devise rules and procedures with learners, seek to understand learners' needs, are prepared for the unforeseen and ensure that procedures are well known by all learners (McLeod *et al.* 2003). Interestingly, only a minimum amount of rules are employed, in the interests of safety and promoting worthwhile interaction in the classroom. Classroom routines are very well established from the outset, and teachers are purposeful and task oriented and exude a sense of order, all of which are seen as key to effective classroom management (McLeod *et al.* 2003).

- Research indicates that teachers who communicate a sense of caring about their learners tend to have higher levels of positive in-school behaviour, as well as accruing other benefits. Murdock and Miller (2003) find that learners' views on the nature and quality of their relationships with their teachers provide a significant predictor of their commitment to schooling. A much more positive commitment to learning exists, since learners internalise the values and standards of their teachers when the relationship is characterised by mutual respect and admiration (Battistich *et al.* 1997; Connell and Wellborn 1991). This may be shown in many ways, including giving praise and recognition for sincere effort, quality work and positive behaviour, and the extent to which learners are treated equally and justly by the teacher (Fraser 2002).

- A positive classroom climate can also be advanced by encouraging learners to take on greater responsibility for their own learning and the extent to which learners perceive themselves as having a considerable 'say' in respect of their own learning processes, assisted by a climate of support and affirmation (Johnson *et al.*, 2000). This sense of ownership on the part of learners can also be facilitated and developed in classrooms when learners are encouraged to undertake responsibility for the smooth running of classroom organisational affairs, and this has a positive effect on behaviour and the classroom climate. Indeed, a focus on learner input and sense of engagement is generally understood to be a primary approach that enables motivational processes to contribute to learning and general development (Furrer and Skinner 2003). Equally, a tangible sense of participation and voice is nurtured, both qualities of which are endorsed in such significant documents as the *UN Convention on the Rights of the Child* (1989, Art. 12) and Ireland's national children's strategy, *Our Children – Their Lives* (Government of Ireland 2000: 11).

- There has been increasing interest in learner self-regulation in recent years. Self-regulation theory is concerned with what learners do to create and maintain their own sense of participation. Self-regulation is premised on the view that learners are active constructivists of their own learning, and behaviour is an intrinsic part of learning and education. Zimmerman claims that 'self-regulated learners plan, set goals, organise, self-monitor, and self-evaluate at various points during the process' of learning (2000: 4–5). The very process itself encourages self-awareness and responsible decision-making as ongoing desirable educational goals (Zimmerman 2000).

- In a related way, research indicates that a positive, learner-centred climate is more likely to lead to the creation of 'a trusting classroom culture which promotes: (1) cooperative learning; (2) authentic learning; and (3) meaningful assessment of the learning process' (Abel and Campbell 2009: 6). Opdenakker and Van Damme's work (2006) managed to clarify a number of key characteristics within a learner-centred teaching style. This teaching approach is typified by the importance given to differentiated methods, expectations and activities; the inclusion of specific approaches to assist learners with problems; a focus on active learner engagement; an openness between colleagues in respect of one's teaching; a focus on the holistic development of the learner; and building a trusting relationship with the learner.

---

### TASK 10.5: OBSERVING CLASSROOMS OF EXPERIENCED TEACHERS

Wragg (2005) reported on research that compared the approaches of experienced teachers with those of student teachers when both groups encountered new classes.

In summary, Wragg found that teachers with experience exhibited more confidence and established a strong sense of presence. They exuded more warmth and were considerably friendlier. These experienced teachers appeared more business-like and gave a clear outline of classroom rules. They used the room space with greater mobility and employed much more eye contact, and their teaching was more stimulating, with humour as an important ingredient.

As you undertake some classroom observation and engagement, draw on Wragg's insights in the above summary to assist you in reflecting on your initial engagement with your learners.

---

## Classroom Relationships

Good classroom relationships are the result of the interplay between a great number of factors and influences, and are also inextricably linked to effective class and lesson management. In this way, the relationship between teacher and learners is not so much an imposed situation but an agreed one. Classroom management becomes an orderly set of behaviours agreed and intrinsically valued by everyone for the sake of achieving defined goals. Disruption is viewed negatively by the majority of the learners since it interferes with orderly progress towards the shared goals.

Maintaining good classroom management is at the core of all good teaching. The skills of the teacher in the maintenance of good classroom management are congruent with the nurturing of relationships within the class, and encompass both managerial abilities and personal attributes. Failure to pursue worthwhile learning as a result of classroom management problems is one of the most significant factors contributing to teacher stress, particularly in the case of student teachers. Establishing an appropriate social distance from your learners will occupy a good deal of your initial thoughts and energy. It is commonly noted by observers that student teachers frequently take refuge in two extremes of behaviour: overly strict behaviour and overly natural behaviour.

### 1. Overly Strict Behaviour

The problem with playing the role of the overly strict, aloof teacher is that it may become a permanent habit and inhibit the development of a positive classroom ethos of learners and teacher interacting as a community in a mutually respectful manner. Also, it carries with it the danger of encouraging one to believe that a 'quiet class' is necessarily a 'good class' (Wragg 2005: 39). It is important to reflect on our attitudes to the concept of 'control' in education, particularly since research indicates that learners in autonomy-supportive classrooms engage more positively and attain better educational outcomes than learners with controlling teachers (Reeve and Jang 2006; Ryan and Deci 2000).

### 2. Overly Natural Behaviour

Beginning teachers often associate the qualities of 'niceness' with effectiveness in teaching. The problem confronting teachers who adopt overly familiar approaches to the learners is that when situations arise which necessitate social distance (e.g. when the teacher needs to be more authoritative), both teacher and learners may have difficulty in adapting. Also, learners often expect their teacher to interact with them in defined, recognisable ways, that is, they expect a certain degree of social distance. Understandably, many student teachers often want to be a friend or a pal. While in certain contexts this role may be appropriate, the teacher very often needs to draw upon a wider repertoire of roles and personae, and to remain aware of the 'thin line between friendliness and over familiarity' (Wragg 2005: 30).

## Reviewing Some Practical Approaches to Classroom Management

The following is a list of strategies commonly employed by effective teachers to avoid classroom management problems:

- *Co-operative rule building:* a very effective way to give learners a voice in their classroom is to facilitate them in devising their own classroom rules and learning expectations. This is not only empowering to learners, but the relationship between you and the learners is enriched, and learners will be much less likely to disrupt the learning environment. The outcomes of learning for all should be enhanced. Beginning the term by developing a class set of rules displays to class members your trust in them to have responsibility for their environment, learning and behaviour. Rather than deciding on the rules after a brief discussion, it is recommended that developing the classroom rules be an evolving, ongoing process so that expectations are fully shared and internalised. There are three elements to this process. The first involves co-establishing classroom rules – the set of standards that all your learners agree to follow. The second focusses on co-determining the consequences if these standards are not met – namely, what occurs when rules are not followed. The third implies the identification of rewards – those ways in which adhering to standards are recognised and rewarded (Erwin 2004).

- *Teaching that matches all learners' abilities*: teaching should be at a level that is not too easy for learners, leading to boredom, and not too difficult, leading to frustration. The ideal teaching level is one that is somewhat challenging to the learner and that gives the learner the potential to achieve – consistent with the principle of the zone of proximal development described by Vygotsky (see Chapter 4). If teaching materials are not at the appropriate level for a learner, there is a good possibility that the learner will be frustrated and misbehave. It is important that 'in a differentiated classroom, all students feel safe and secure enough to take risks and express their understanding or lack of understanding' (Gregory and Chapman 2002: 8). Hence, assessing your learners' knowledge levels and identifying teaching materials that will enable them to learn in challenging ways is a key to effective classroom climate and management.

- *Varying the pedagogical approaches used in the classroom*: a valuable strategy for preventing classroom management problems is for you, the teacher, to vary the style of classroom presentation and of classroom activities. If there is a frequent change of pace and if learners have the opportunity to move from one type of learning to another during any class session, it is most likely that inattentiveness and restlessness will be minimised. A more satisfactory learning environment is most likely to occur in a classroom typified by 'appropriate and considered differentiation, scaffolded learning, varied and rich teaching resources' (Siraj and Taggart 2014: 17).

- *Providing a number of learning choices*: carefully planning the organisation of your classroom is essential to supporting differentiated teaching and learning, and facilitates learners in making choices in respect of their learning. According to Fountas and Pinnell, 'an organised and well-designed classroom enables the teacher to observe, support, and meet the learning needs of each child' (1996: 43). Moreover, the work of Howard Gardner (see Chapter 4) indicates that children learn in different ways and presenting them with the opportunity to do so enhances the likelihood of a well-managed classroom. Gardner notes that 'the biggest mistake in teaching is to treat all children as if they were variants of the same individual and thus to feel justified in teaching them all the same subjects in the same ways' (Gardner, cited in Siegel and Shaughnessy 1994: 563).

- *Expecting learners to be responsible for their own learning and behaviour*: a significant report into learner consultation (Pollard and James 2004) stresses that it is important to note that learner consultation is not simple. The two main constraints that teachers talk about in the report are space in the curriculum and time. However, in outlining benefits, many learners report a sense of respect, being listened to, being taken seriously and an 'awareness that your views are having an impact on how things are done, the feeling that you have greater control over how you learn, the scope to talk about your own learning, more confidence about how to improve it, [and] more positive feelings about learning and about school' (12). Hence, if your learners are given ample opportunities to take responsibility for their own learning, there is a far greater likelihood that their learning will be meaningful and purposeful.

- *Recognising that in some instances behaviours that challenge may be associated with a range of additional needs, which require a specific and targeted approach*: it is important to know that most classrooms are generally orderly, that most teacher–learner and learner–learner relationships are positive, and that teaching and learning progress without any major disruption most of the time. Teachers in such classrooms understand the importance of preventing significant behaviour problems and do so through engaging teaching, well-managed classrooms and positive relationships with learners. These fundamental features of a positive environment are the initial step in promoting good behaviour at school. However, some teachers may have a class in which one or a few learners exhibit persistent or significant behavioural problems, and their behaviour may be disruptive, oppositional, distracting or defiant. When a number of learners demonstrate such behaviour, it can create a chaotic classroom environment that is a serious impediment to learning. These behaviours are generally associated with additional needs and it is crucial that you do not develop a sense of failure due to difficulties in dealing with them. Rather, seek help from colleagues in the school or from psychological or other support services to identify and to provide the learner with the kind of assistance necessary to address the problems. Student teachers should consult the class or host teacher and gain an understanding of approaches in use within the class and school.

---

## TASK 10.6: REFLECTING ON STRATEGIES

Achieving and maintaining good classroom management involves an appropriate balance in your teaching style and management skills. The table below lists some commonly used class management techniques.

- Read through the list with a partner and identify the five strategies you consider to be the most useful. Explain your choice.
- Some strategies may be problematic. If so, identify them and develop a critique.
- Are some of these strategies incompatible with the broad principles of classroom management outlined to date in this chapter?
- Suggest contexts in which some of these strategies might be used. If you have used these strategies in your teaching to date, reflect on their effectiveness while taking the specific contextual and situational factors into consideration.

| Classroom Management Strategies |
| --- |
| **Anticipative Planning** |
| This is the ability to see a problem before it arises and to act immediately to avoid a confrontation later. |
| **Limit Definition** |
| Children learn exactly what behaviour is expected of them and what behaviour is beyond limits. |

### Relationship of Trust

Children who sense that they are trusted and valued will respect the teacher and accept that s/he wants to help them.

### Removing Distractions

Remove objects from desks that can distract the learners.

### Signals

A nod or a gesture will often be sufficient to promote appropriate behaviour in the case of most learners.

### Proximity Control

The teacher stands beside a learner who is misbehaving.

### Overlapping

This is the ability to handle two events simultaneously, e.g. to deal with a disruptive learner while not disturbing the other learners at their work.

### Transition Smoothness

Ensuring that learning flows smoothly from one activity or lesson to the next.

### Group Alertness

Keeping a class alert and interested by using appropriate questioning techniques: involving, pausing, prompting and refocussing (see 'Using Questioning to Promote Thinking and Talking at all Primary Levels' in Chapter 9).

### Changing of Routine

When the learners get restless or tired, it is beneficial to break from the normal routine and do something different, e.g. an action rhyme.

### Helping Over Hurdles

When learners are engaged in something they cannot understand, disruption may ensue. Teachers should ensure that they explain clearly and give clear instructions when setting tasks and activities.

### Positive Reinforcement

Praise or reward for work well done is a powerful tool in promoting self-esteem and positive behaviour. It is important to vary the expressions of praise and to praise with sincerity.

### Direct Appeal

Appealing to the learners' sense of reason is often effective, e.g. telling the learners that their behaviour is disturbing others may be sufficient to cause an improvement in behaviour.

**Explaining Misbehaviour**

Getting learners to give reasons for misbehaving may help them to better understand their own behaviour patterns and deter them from negative behaviour in the future.

**Sanctions**

Threatening learners with sanctions is only effective when the teacher is in a position to carry them out.

**Detention**

Usually, this takes the form of 'staying in at break time' or 'being the last person to leave the school at home time'. Problems with insurance, transport deadlines and learner safety limit the potential of this form of sanction.

## Recognising and Responding to Behavioural Challenges

In any classroom, it is understandable that situations will arise that necessitate the use of effective strategies for dealing with problem behaviour. Diagnosing an appropriate response should involve evaluating one's own teaching approaches, the personalities of the learners in the class and a range of contextual factors that may impinge on the situation (e.g. seating, time of day, facilities, grouping, etc.). Dealing with problem behaviour effectively requires skill, sensitivity and appropriate background knowledge of the learner. Sanctions are best used sparingly and should complement skilful teaching. Using sanctions too frequently will lessen their effect and will erode a positive classroom climate. The following represents a range of strategies, by no means exhaustive, which you may find helpful in diagnosing and responding to problems that may arise in your teaching:

*Identify the specifics and details of the problematic behaviour* and particularly the contexts that may trigger and reinforce it. The success of your intervention depends on reviewing problems holistically and identifying the specific conditions that trigger the problem behaviour. It is recommended that teachers carefully observe and reflect on the context in which the problem behaviour is likely to arise or not. Teachers can then employ those reflections to fashion an appropriate set of approaches that respond to the needs of the individual learner within the classroom context. At times, this may involve a re-evaluation of your methods of teaching. Classroom management problems are often the result of inappropriately chosen or pitched lesson content. Learners become frustrated by lesson content that either presents too much or too little challenge, and they may respond by engaging in inappropriate or disruptive behaviour. As your teaching experience widens, it will be to your benefit to contribute to a whole-school approach to behavioural expectations. Differences in expectations between teachers may cause confusion among learners. A school-wide approach to preventing problem behaviours and increasing positive social interactions among learners, and between school staff and learners, can only be of benefit to all in the academic community. A systemic school-wide approach necessitates genuine, open, shared reflection and a candid review on the part of all school personnel.

*Changing the classroom environment can help to alleviate challenging behaviour.* Many interventions aimed at decreasing disruptive behaviour involve either changing or removing issues that prompt them in the first place. These can be varied and involve seating arrangements, timing of certain subjects, arrangements for group and pair work, the distribution of materials, processes of entering or leaving the classroom, etc. Each classroom will be different with different dynamics, personalities and arrangements. However, the reflective teacher can reduce the occurrence of inappropriate behaviour by regularly revisiting organisational features and viewing them in the context of behavioural expectations.

*Highlighting and affirming positive behaviour* strengthens the sense of a positive classroom climate. Not all learners will be attuned to giving appropriate behavioural responses in the classroom and will require guidance and support. Returning regularly and thoughtfully to classroom rules and procedures in this way, and in a spirit of genuine discussion, should ensure that learners understand their basis and perceive them as important for the smooth running of the classroom environment.

The way in which we interact and deal with learners is of great importance. A number of matters should be borne in mind. A key principle is to emphasise that you *object to the misbehaviour, not the learner.* This allows the teacher to transmit a sense of consideration for the learner and provides the learner with a way to avoid repeating such behaviour. 'You need to share the books with others in your group' is far more preferable than 'You are being selfish.' In this way, you avoid personalising negative comments and, if your comments to learners are largely positive, supportive, encouraging, praising, valuing and relaxing, rather than negative, deprecating, harsh, attacking, dominating and anxiety-provoking, this will do much to foster learners' self-esteem and motivation for learning (Kyriacou 2007: 78).

With that in mind, it is preferable to address issues that arise with an emphasis on giving a positive message, e.g. saying something along the lines of, 'I know you can do better than that. How can I help you to do better?' rather than 'That is very poor work!'

Effective teachers *frequently scan the class to monitor what each learner is doing*. While it is not necessary to react to every sign of off-task behaviour or deviation from the established procedure, it is important for learners to know that what they are doing is being monitored. For example, the use of a learner's name in mid-sentence or the act of standing beside her/him is often all that is required to let the learner know that you are aware of what is happening.

*Being consistent, indeed predictable, in class management creates a sense of security for learners.* Creating new expectations without warning and the inconsistent application of sanctions can lead to anxiety and frustration among learners.

*Learners who are sanctioned for their behaviour should be correctly identified as those who have instigated or engaged in the misbehaviour.* Sanctioning the whole class is a strategy that builds resentment and a sense of unfairness. Equally, resentment may also be fostered when one learner's behaviour is highlighted while others' unacceptable behaviours are ignored. The teacher may be perceived as treating certain learners unfairly, and this perception will not be conducive to the building of a positive climate.

*Misconduct on the part of learners should be dealt with sensitively, taking note of personality, background and contextual factors.* Hurtful, deprecating remarks, sarcasm and ridicule erode learners' self-esteem and undermine mutual respect, and should never be used. Public reprimanding may involve the humiliation of the learner and result in deterioration of classroom atmosphere. Reprimands that involve stereotyping or comparisons with others are unfair, unacceptable and should never be used. For example, comparisons with other members of the learner's family – 'Why can't you be more like your sister?' – or denigration of the learner's social, ethnic or religious group – 'Sure, I couldn't expect any more from the likes of you.'

*Emphasise what learners should be doing rather than focussing on the misbehaviour itself.* 'Raymond, what colour is the car in the picture?' is more effective than 'Raymond, stop looking out of the window.' 'You may talk quietly with your partner' is better than 'There is too much noise in here.' However, when correcting problem behaviour, you should be clear and firm in tone. Avoid pleading or implying damage limitation (e.g. 'At least give me one minute of peace and quiet'). When a correction is given, its impact is enhanced by non-verbal cues, such as eye contact and body language. Being sensitive in terms of the messages our body language can send is also important. After correcting the learner, a momentary prolonging of eye contact, together with a slight pause before continuing with the lesson can increase the force of the exchange. This can be done while conveying concern, respect and care in our body language.

*Expressing anger, shouting at learners or losing your temper should never occur.* Very importantly, corporal punishment is prohibited in all contexts.

*Sanctions should be chosen carefully and realistically.* Do not issue reprimands that threaten consequences you cannot, or would not wish to, implement. Learners will consciously or unconsciously internalise empty threats and often ignore them, and this may cause further deterioration in the classroom atmosphere.

## Some Guidelines to Encourage Positive Behaviour

- Setting behavioural expectations, i.e. giving the learners a clear outline of your expectations regarding their behaviour in class, is far more effective than admonishing learners following repeated and prolonged misbehaviour.
- Reprimands should relate to clear and consistently applied expectations. Your correction should convey the concern that the best interests of all learners in the class are being affected by the misbehaviour. A reprimand can usefully consist of a statement of the rule being transgressed together with an explanation of why the rule is required for the benefit of teaching and learning. For example:

*Rule*: Raise your hand and don't speak out of turn.
*Rationale*: Please put up your hand and wait until I ask you to talk so that everyone gets a fair chance.

- It is important to have positive consequences or rewards to recognise good behaviour for both individual learners and for the entire class. These incentives and rewards should be in accordance with sound educational practice and should comply with class and school policy. Positive rewards for individual learners can range from verbal praise to notes to parents praising the learners, to certificates of merit. Whole-class rewards should also be given to recognise the good behaviour of the entire group of learners. These should be earned as a result of good conduct by the class over a period of time and should reward every member of the class.
- Once rules have been established, it is advisable that sanctions be identified for learners who misbehave. In the spirit of the democratic classroom, it is appropriate that the consequences of misbehaviour be negotiated with the learners. This should result in the compilation of a broad range of agreed sanctions for various categories of misbehaviour. In developing disciplinary consequences, it is important that both you and the learners are comfortable with them. They should comply with class and school policy. And, while they are intended to discourage negative behaviour, they should never be psychologically or physically harmful to the learners.
- It is important to address repeated or flagrant breaches of conduct quickly and directly. Ignoring a potentially disruptive situation will rarely cause the problem to diminish or disappear. Usually, in fact, this results in an escalation rather than a diminution.

Teachers who are good classroom managers make classroom standards and rules known to learners at an early stage. These rules are explicit, concrete, clear and functional. In devising classroom rules, the following principles should be borne in mind:

- Decide on a *limited number* of classroom rules.
- Ensure that the rules are *absolutely clear* to all learners.
- Enforce the rules for *all learners*, ensuring that this is done equitably.

## Principles and Rules of Classroom Behaviour

You can establish classroom management rules initially, or you may wish to establish some basic classroom principles with your learners. These principles place rules in a broader context and give them added meaning. They are not designed to be enforced because they are very general. However, they provide a strong foundation for discussing classroom management rules. Examples of such principles are:

- Be respectful of the rights of others.
- Be courteous when others are speaking.
- Be prepared and on time for your class.
- Treat others as you would have them treat you.
- Try to do your best.

With a group of principles such as these as a foundation, a set of specific rules can be established, taking account of different settings and contexts. Many teachers invite their learners to help them in this process. The democratic involvement of the learners has the effect of increasing learners' sense of ownership and responsibility in upholding the rules. We suggest that no more than five to ten classroom rules be established. Equally, we suggest that they are as precise, clear and brief as possible. Finally, it is best if the rules are stated positively and displayed prominently in an attractive and visually appealing manner.

---

**M-LEVEL TASK 10.2: EXPLORING THE CHILD'S PERSPECTIVE**

Interview a number of primary school learners to ascertain their views on appropriate forms of class rewards and sanctions. In reporting back to your peers, try to give voice to the learners' opinions and concerns. As always, ensure the anonymity of the learners and adhere to your institution's ethical guidelines when engaging with learners.

Figure 10.1: Example of Classroom Rules for Early Primary Years

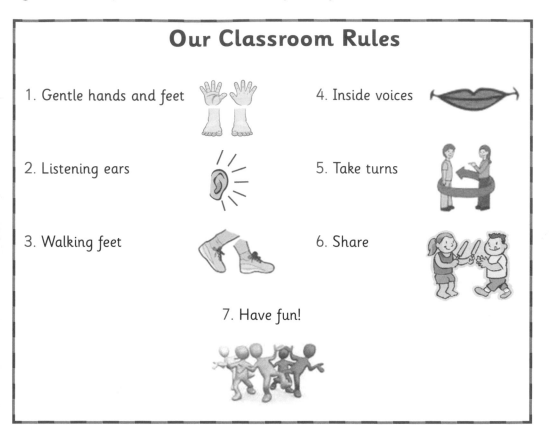

## Class and Lesson Management

Lesson management refers to the preparation and planning involved in the creation of a lesson as well as the efficacy with which the lesson is taught. The more learners are engaged and interested in a lesson, the less likely they are to misbehave (Powell *et al.* 2001: 17).

Effective teachers place great emphasis on planning and lay out a clear roadmap and a set of learning outcomes for each lesson. Lesson planning is undertaken in the context of the curriculum and the teacher's own long-term plans. A structured approach is key, and the planning process usually commences with an overview of the learning outcomes of the lesson, which are linked to previous lessons. An effective teacher communicates the lesson content in various ways, taking account of the different learning styles of learners, and manages the key activities for the duration of the lesson. These are not chance activities. Content is presented and explored in small steps, with opportunities for learners to practise what is being taught subsequent to each step. Each stage of the lesson is usually preceded by clear guidelines for the learners. But a well-planned lesson also acknowledges the varying needs of learners, particularly those with learning difficulties. For learners, all of this provides clarity, a sense of clear direction, and ultimately a sense of outcome and achievement. Effective teachers regularly review lesson objectives, teaching strategies and learning outcomes. The principal focus of any review hinges on learners and the quality of their engagement with learning outcomes.

The key to understanding effective class management may be encapsulated by the word 'simultaneity'. In the classroom, many activities occur simultaneously. There can be little doubt that the range of skills involved in teaching 25 to 30 learners is quite immense. This situation requires a whole range of managerial and organisational competencies in order to ensure effective learning. Successful class and lesson management require you to switch attention and action between several activities to ensure that learning proceeds smoothly. The principal task faced by the teacher is to elicit and maintain learner involvement towards the intended learning outcomes. Class management essentially refers to those skills involved in managing and organising learning activities so that productive involvement in the lesson is maximised.

---

### TASK 10.7: PLANNING FOR CLASS MANAGEMENT

Here are some questions that may assist us in reflecting on our sense of classroom management. In addressing these matters, we can see the considerable range of demands placed on the teacher in ensuring a sense of fluidity and flexibility in our teaching. Other questions will occur to you and will contribute to some worthwhile reflection on the issue of lesson management.

1. Prior to teaching a class, how much preparation have I undertaken with particular attention to the range of learners and their different learning styles?
2. Have I worked with the learners in agreeing a small number of rules and positive behavioural expectations?
3. Do I return to these rules and expectations regularly to ensure full understanding?
4. Are the introductions to my lessons attractive, thought provoking and engaging?
5. How punctual am I in beginning a lesson?
6. Having gained the attention of learners, how do I seek to maintain it throughout the lesson?
7. Do I strive to induce internal motivation among learners or do I rely unduly on external motivation through rewards and sanctions?
8. How much attention do I place on individual learners and their engagement as the lesson progresses?

9. Do I give adequate support to individual learners during the lesson, using praise and assistance appropriately?
10. Are the learners sufficiently comfortable to seek further clarification and explanation in my classroom?
11. When transitions occur within the lesson, such as organising group work, distributing materials or undertaking any activity, have I given adequate attention to the organisational demands involved?
12. What strategies have I in place for learner mobility around the classroom in the course of a lesson?
13. How easily and often am I diverted from the learning outcomes planned for the lesson?
14. When the demands of a lesson become markedly more difficult, do I give sufficient thought to all learners' capabilities?
15. Do I manage the use of teaching equipment, aids, white/blackboard, computers and interactive whiteboard in ways that contribute to the smoothness of the lesson?
16. In bringing a lesson to a conclusion, have I given sufficient thought to the next related lesson, maintaining learners' interest and promoting ongoing engagement, or do my lessons tend to fizzle out?

## Flow

There is little doubt that classroom management can often be described in terms of *flow*. The concept of 'flow' implies the degree of continuity and coherence that can be achieved. It implies movement in a particular direction – movement that is continuous and steady. It seems implicit that we, as teachers, should aim to develop a coherent sense of purpose within our classes, should organise our classrooms in ways that are consistent with those purposes, and should manage the learners, materials and stages of the lesson in order to achieve those purposes:

> Lesson management skills are essential if the learning activities you set up are to take place with sufficient order for learning to occur. Almost any task or activity can lead to chaos unless you give some thought to the organisation of how and when learners are to do what is required of them. Organised control over the logistics of classroom life, whether it be how learners answer questions, collect equipment from cupboards, or form themselves into small groups, requires explicit direction from you, at least until the procedures you expect are followed as a matter of routine. (Kyriacou, 2007: 62)

### Beginnings, Transitions, Crises, Pacing and Endings

Aspects of lessons that can pose challenges to the flow include *beginnings*, *transitions*, *crises*, *pacing* and *endings*.

## Beginnings

The start of a session is important because it sets the tone for the rest of the lesson. Good beginnings introduce and interest the learners in the lesson and provide an advance organiser which prepares the learners for what is to come. Introductions can take many forms, such as the use of an analogy, a demonstration, the posing of an intriguing problem that the learners can solve, etc.

## Transitions

Transitions between lessons and stages of lessons often present management challenges, particularly for the student teacher. This often occurs when expectations and guidelines regarding learner behaviour in one activity are abandoned before the guidelines for the subsequent activity have been established. The key to successful transitions lies in pre-empting problems before they arise and in interesting the learners in the next step so that they are eager to behave appropriately in order to experience it.

## Crises

Classroom crises can be caused by many events – from a child getting sick in class to a minor, or in some cases a more serious, accident. Pollard *et al.* (2014) recommend three simple principles to apply in such circumstances. The first principle is *to minimise the disturbance*. Help from school colleagues, classroom assistants or the school principal should be called for, either to deal with the problem or to supervise the class, thus enabling you to address the problem. The second principle is to *maximise reassurance*. Learners can often be upset when something unexpected happens and, in such circumstances, it may be necessary to provide reassurance and support. A degree of flexibility in the choice of activities for a suitable period afterwards might be desirable. The third principle in dealing with a crisis is to *pause for sufficient thought before making a judgement on how to act*. If you allow yourself some time to think about the wider issues arising from the crisis, it may help you to make a more reflective and appropriate decision.

## Pacing

Pacing involves making judgements, especially about when to take a new initiative. It relies on the teacher's sensitivity to how learners are responding to the lesson activities. Pacing involves making appropriate judgements about the timing and sequence of the various activities and parts of a session, and then taking suitable action. In this context, persisting with a task or a topic for longer than is necessary should be avoided as it results in the loss of lesson pace.

## Endings

Ending a session presents situations that could lead to management issues, such as tidying up materials, learner movement while resuming usual seating arrangements, exiting from the classroom and learners' natural exuberance. The effective teacher will have a range of management strategies appropriate to each of these situations and the interests and age range of the learners in the class. This range will be flexible and develop naturally out of the process of ongoing reflection.

---

### TASK 10.8: ANTICIPATING PROBLEM BEHAVIOUR

Speculate on some of the problem behaviours your future learners might display. In the context of your own present abilities and knowledge, how prepared are you for addressing such problem behaviours? Based on your own school experiences and observations, how will you manage your future classroom? What standards of 'good' behaviour will not be negotiable? Will you be flexible about some things? Share your insights with your peers.

---

## A SUMMARY OF KEY POINTS

Establishing a positive classroom climate:

- Requires teachers to focus reflectively on personal attributes and their interaction with learners.
- Involves a myriad of demands on the teacher in terms of preparation, the creation of a safe and nurturing environment with positive expectations, a sense of differentiation with reasonable expectations, the setting of boundaries, and the nurturing of shared values within the classroom community.
- Implies considerable reflection on learners' backgrounds and on other factors that might influence classroom behaviour.
- Involves employing appropriate incentives and keeping the importance of motivation to the fore.
- Encompasses exemplifying a range of positive standards, behaviours, approaches and values that are expected from learners.
- Involves giving learners a voice in respect of their learning, and the pace and direction of their learning.

# CHAPTER ELEVEN

# Assessment and Learning

How can assessment support learning?

Are there different types of assessment?

How can I encourage learners to self-assess?

Once you have worked through this chapter you will be able to:

- Define assessment.
- Understand that there are different types of assessment for different purposes.
- Appreciate that assessment practices are underpinned by theories of learning.
- Plan for assessment on school placement.

## INTRODUCTION

Assessment is a word that often conjures up unpleasant memories of state or school examinations. Many learners feel that assessment is something that is visited upon them by others to determine or quantify the extent to which certain learning targets have been achieved at the end of a period of learning. However, assessment can also be used to support learning and teaching. It can provide learners with valuable feedback and help teachers to refine their teaching to meet the learners' specific needs. Assessment can then be compared to a GPS navigational system, which accurately identifies the current position of the learner with reference to the desired learning goals, and uses this information to plot the most suitable route to achieving them. If the learner pauses, regresses, meanders or deviates from the highlighted route for any reason, a recalculation of their new location is used to plot the next most appropriate set of directions. Hence, to extend the metaphor, when assessment results are utilised by the teacher to locate the learning co-ordinates of the learner and to chart the direction of future action, all participants become learners. Employed in this way, assessment can be a source of support and empowerment for both learner and teacher.

---

### TASK 11.1: DEFINING ASSESSMENT

Read and discuss the definitions of assessment below. What are the implications of assessment, as defined in these ways, for the teacher?

Assessment is the ongoing process of collecting, documenting, reflecting on, and using information to develop rich portraits of children as learners in order to support and enhance their future learning. (NCCA 2009: 72)

Assessment is the process of gathering, recording, interpreting, using and reporting information about a child's progress and achievement in developing knowledge, skills and attitudes. (NCCA 2007: 7)

---

## RECENT TRENDS IN ASSESSMENT

In recent years, due in large measure to the synthesis conducted by Black and Wiliam in 1998 of over 250 research studies linking assessment and learning, there has been a change in how assessment is perceived and employed within education. Black and Wiliam (1998) based their work on earlier reviews (Crooks 1988; Natriello 1987) and embraced studies of teachers' assessment practices; learners' motivation and self-perception; classroom discourse analysis; assessment practices; and the quality of feedback. To be effective, Black and Wiliam (1998) concluded that assessment should involve all of the following:

- Teachers using assessment evidence to inform and modify learning and teaching
- Learners receiving feedback on their assessments with advice regarding the next steps for them to take to improve
- Learners engaging in self-assessment

There is now a growing appreciation of assessment as a means of informing learning and teaching on an ongoing basis, leading to gains in learning through more appropriately focussed teaching. Such assessment is formative and focusses on the learners as they engage in learning, exploring how learners are thinking and observing what they can do. The teacher uses this information to evaluate the learners' progress and to identify any emerging challenges or problems. The information thus gathered is used to amend or change the learning and teaching activities. Hence, formative assessment is concerned with the everyday classroom processes of learning and teaching. This has come to be known as Assessment for Learning (AfL).

## Assessment in the Primary School

In line with international trends, assessment for learning (AfL) has received considerable attention in recent years in Ireland. The Primary School Curriculum (PSC) 1999 accords a central position to assessment in the teaching and learning process. It states that 'through assessment the teacher constructs a comprehensive picture of the short-term and long-term needs of the child and plans future work accordingly' (NCCA 1999: 17). The PSC 1999 goes on to say:

> Assessment is integral to all areas of the curriculum and it encompasses the diverse aspects of learning: the cognitive, the creative, the affective, the physical and the social. In addition to the products of learning, the strategies, procedures and stages in the process of learning are assessed. Assessment includes the child's growth in self-esteem, interpersonal and intrapersonal behaviour, and the acquisition of a wide range of knowledge, skills, attitudes and values. (NCCA 1999: 18)

In the PSC 1999, assessment is recommended as a means to:

- Monitor learning and ascertain achievement.
- Construct a picture of the short-term and long-term needs of learners.
- Identify specific learning difficulties.
- Assist communication about learners' progress.
- Encourage learners to become more self-aware and develop powers of self-assessment.
- Help to ensure quality in education.

(Adapted from NCCA 1999)

In 2007, the NCCA published *Assessment in the Primary School Curriculum: Guidelines for Schools*. This comprehensive document draws on research, theory and practice to highlight and demonstrate how assessment can be used by the teacher to 'make learning more enjoyable, more motivating and more successful for each child' (8). It states:

> Assessment is about building a picture over time of a child's progress and/or achievement in learning across the Primary School Curriculum. Information about how the child learns (the learning process) as well as what the child learns (the products of learning) shapes the picture. The teacher uses this information to identify and celebrate the child's current learning, and to provide him/her with appropriate support for future learning. (NCCA 2007: 7)

The guidelines focus on two interrelated and complementary approaches to assessment:

* Assessment for Learning (AfL) – the use of evidence on an ongoing basis to inform teaching and learning
* Assessment of Learning (AoL) – the periodic recording of progress and achievement for the purpose of informing parents, teachers and other relevant persons

Assessment?

### Assessment in the Early Primary Years

In 2009, the NCCA published *Aistear: The Early Childhood Curriculum Framework* for the care and education of children in early years settings and in Primary infant classes. As we saw in Task 11.1 above, *Aistear* defines assessment as follows:

> Assessment is the ongoing process of collecting, documenting, reflecting on, and using information to develop rich portraits of children as learners in order to support and enhance their future learning. (NCCA 2009: 72)

*Aistear* highlights the interconnectedness of learning, assessing, reviewing and planning. It provides guidelines that focus on the purpose, methods and uses of assessment during early childhood. *Aistear* prioritises assessment as a key concern within the provision of relevant and meaningful experiences to help young learners:

> Relevant and meaningful experiences make learning more enjoyable and positive for children. On-going assessment of what children do, say and make, and reflection on these experiences helps practitioners to plan more developmentally appropriate and meaningful learning experiences for children. This also enables them to improve their practice. Assessment is about building a picture of children's individual strengths, interests, abilities, and needs and using this to support and plan for their future learning and development. (NCCA 2009: 11)

*Aistear* uses Assessment for Learning (AfL) to celebrate the achievements of children and to direct them to the next steps in their learning.

> Assessment enables the adult to find out what children understand, how they think, what they are able to do, and what their dispositions and interests are. This information helps the adult to build rich stories of children as capable and competent learners in order to support further learning and development. In doing this, he/she uses the assessment information to give on-going feedback to children about how they are getting on in their learning, to provide challenging and enjoyable experiences for them, to choose appropriate supports for them, and to document, celebrate and plan the next steps in their learning. (NCCA 2009:72)

Much assessment takes place through observations, conversations and listening to young learners in a variety of learning situations. Five assessment methods are recommended to gather evidence of learning and development, namely:

- Self-assessment
- Conversations
- Observation
- Setting tasks
- Testing

Figure 11.1: Assessment as Part of Classroom Practice

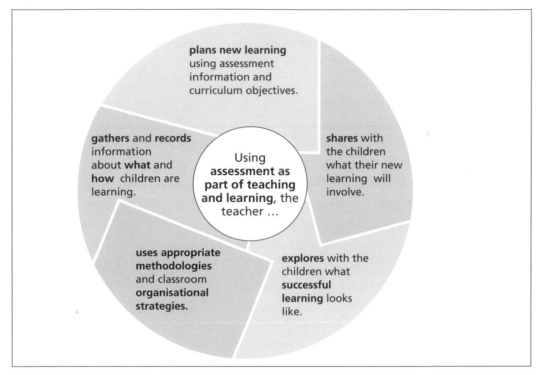

Source: NCCA (2007), *Assessment in the Primary School Curriculum: Guidelines for Schools*, Dublin: National Council for Curriculum and Assessment: 8.

## Assessment of Learners with Special Educational Needs

The Education Act 1998 and the Education for Persons with Special Educational Needs (EPSEN) Act 2004 require schools to ensure that the educational needs of all learners, including those with a disability or other special educational needs, are identified and catered for. Assessment policies within schools are required to highlight the role of diagnostic assessment, and specify the assessment instruments used together with a timeline for assessments. Schools also need to specify procedures for identifying and responding to the needs of exceptionally able children. *Assessment in the Primary School Curriculum: Guidelines for Schools* (NCCA 2007) states that:

Because the early years provide the foundation for subsequent learning it is important to identify children who experience learning difficulties as soon as possible. To facilitate this, the school should implement a screening policy in the second school year, preferably by February of the second term. Screening involves teacher observation of children and the administration of group and individual tests of early literacy, numeracy and developmental skills. The information acquired through screening tests, together with day-to-day observation by the infant class teacher, facilitiates a more accurate assessment of the child's learning strengths and needs. This is particularly important in the case of younger children when learning does not necessarily follow a sequential pattern. (78)

Under the provisions of the EPSEN Act 2004, schools are required to identify when a learner is not progressing and to investigate the reasons for this. The EPSEN Act 2004 has not been fully implemented at this point, and specifically the role of the National Council for Special Education in ensuring that learners' progress is monitored and regularly reviewed has not as yet been commenced. However, it is good practice to ensure that appropriate individualised planning is in place for learners who have been identified as having special educational needs. The learner's parents or guardians, relevant multi-disciplinary personnel and the learner himself or herself should be involved in this planning. Individualised planning should specify the goals for learning and development, include reference to appropriate pedagogical strategies and resources, and be reviewed as agreed. For more information on the assessment of learners with special educational needs, refer to the websites of the National Educational Psychological Service (NEPS) (http://www.education.ie/en/Schools-Colleges/Services/National-Educational-Psychological-Service-NEPS-/NEPS-Home-Page.html); the Special Education Support Service (http://www.sess.ie/); and the National Council for Special Education (http://ncse.ie/).

## Functions of Assessment

The main purposes of assessment are described as follows:

- *Assessment of Learning* – where learners' achievements are measured against established criteria (summative)
- *Assessment as Learning* – where learners reflect on and monitor their own learning in respect of specified learning goals (formative)
- *Assessment for Learning* – where teachers use evidence about learners' progress to inform their teaching (formative)

### Assessment of Learning

Assessment of learning (AoL), also called assessment for summative purposes or summative assessment (Ussher and Earl, 2010), refers to an end-of-period assessment where feedback to learners is usually provided in the form of grades or marks that are sometimes compared to national standards (Krause, Bochner and Duchesne 2003). AoL presents a summary or snapshot of achievement in certain domains of learning and evaluates learners' progress relative to curriculum objectives. Assessment results can be used to provide information to stakeholders that are both internal and external to the school community. Internally, assessment data can be used to track attainment over time and to report to learners and parents. External uses include certification based on the results of externally created tests or examinations (Harlen 2005).

AoL is useful in assessing attainment at particular junctures, but, taken in isolation, it is of little value in advising learners regarding how to improve:

> While these results are useful to the teacher they can be of limited value to the child, unless the teacher identifies the essential information they provide about the child's progress and achievement and communicates this to the child. (NCCA 2007: 9)

AoL should involve more than an appraisal of previous learning. It requires a compilation and analysis of evidence documented over time, which the teacher uses to inform planning to support individual learners (Harlen 2005; Moreland, Jones and Chambers 2001). Utilised in this way, AoL 'helps the teacher to plan future work, to set new targets, and to provide feedback and information for end-of-year assessment' (NCCA 2007: 9).

### Assessment as Learning

Assessment as Learning (AaL) highlights the centrality of the learner in both learning and evaluation. It encourages learners to engage in self- and peer-assessment, and enhances learners' self-confidence through developing metacognitive skills, i.e. an awareness of themselves as learners and their own thinking and learning processes. Learners monitor their learning and use feedback from this monitoring to make adaptations and adjustments to what they understand (Earl 2003). Earl states that

> Effective assessment empowers learners to ask reflective questions and consider a range of strategies for learning and acting. Over time, learners move forward in their learning when they can use personal knowledge to construct meaning, have skills of self-monitoring to realize that they don't understand something, and have ways of deciding what to do next. (2003: 25)

AaL focusses on the learning process as it is uniquely experienced by each learner.

## *Assessment for Learning*

As mentioned above, the term Assessment for Learning (AfL) refers to formative assessment, which involves making judgements about learners' progress, attainments and learning processes, and using these judgements to inform learning and teaching. The purpose of AfL is to use the process of assessment to help learners to improve their learning. AfL occurs as learning is taking place. It involves the teacher observing *how* learning is taking place. Used in a diagnostic role, AfL enables the teacher to identify if a learner has any learning difficulties and to use this information in lesson planning. AfL requires teachers to understand how learners think and feel, and to locate where learners are in respect of learning goals. On the basis of this information, teachers can point out the most appropriate next steps. Providing feedback to learners that helps them to celebrate their achievement and to identify further challenges is central to AfL:

> This level of involvement in shaping their own learning can heighten children's awareness of themselves as learners and encourage them to take more personal responsibility for, and pride in, their learning. (NCCA 2007: 9)

Assessment information is used to inform curriculum planning, which is tailored in response to the needs of individual learners. Learners are informed of what they are expected to learn and how they can identify when they have succeeded in learning. AfL presupposes a collaborative approach to teaching where learners feel free to ask open-ended questions, to construct meaning and to share understandings. Hence, AfL encourages learners and teachers to focus on:

- **Where are** children **now** in their learning?
- **Where are** children **going** in their learning?
- **How** will children get to the **next point** in their learning?

(NCCA 2007: 9)

Planning for assessment is an integral aspect of planning for teaching. AfL requires teachers to:

- Identify where individual learners are in respect of learning goals.
- Share learning intentions and success criteria with learners.
- Uncover learners' prior knowledge, preconceptions, gaps and learning styles.
- Challenge limiting beliefs or ideas that are inhibiting the next stage of learning.
- Use assessment information to differentiate instruction and learning tasks to reinforce and build on productive learning.

- Provide descriptive feedback on specific ways to improve.
- Use self- and peer assessment as key elements of learning and teaching.
- Encourage learners to take greater ownership of learning.
- Engage in ongoing and continuous assessment as part of the learning process.
- Diagnose and address learners' needs.
- Plan assessment as part of the lesson.
- Use a variety of assessment approaches to make judgements on progress and inform the next steps.

AfL encourages learners to:

- Be aware of what they are expected to learn.
- Take more responsibility for their learning and value their own work.
- Use criteria to assess their own work and the work of others.
- Become more resourceful, reflective and effective learners.
- Reflect on the quality of their work and identify how they can improve.
- Recognise that making mistakes and struggling to understand or to do something is a necessary and formative part of learning.

## Sharing the Learning Intentions and Success Criteria

Sharing the learning intentions and explaining the criteria for success are regarded as key features of Assessment for Learning and Assessment as Learning. When learners know what they are expected to learn (the learning intentions) and how they can evaluate when they have been successful (the success criteria), they are empowered to take more responsibility for their own learning. Effective learning intentions are discussed to ensure that learners are clear about what they should know, appreciate or be able to do as a result of a period of learning. Hence, learning intentions focus the learner's attention on what is to be learned rather than just on the activity or task.

Success criteria indicate how learners and teachers can determine that a learning intention has been achieved. Success criteria derive from the learning intentions and are most effective when explored in advance by the teacher and learners.

> Self-assessment is an essential part of AfL. It enables the child to take greater responsibility for his/her own learning. The child can use different strategies when thinking about what he/she has learned and use a set of criteria to make judgements about it. (NCCA 2007: 14)

Dunning, Heath and Suls (2004) state that 'accurate self-assessment is...crucial for education to be a lifelong enterprise that continues far after the student has left the classroom' (85). Learners can learn to assess their own progress by reflecting on some key questions about their learning progress and trajectory:

- Where am I now?
- Where am I trying to go?
- How will I get there?
- How will I know when I have achieved my learning goals?

To help learners respond to the question **'Where am I now?'** teachers can:

- Ensure that learners know the criteria for good work, so that they are able to assess their work relative to that standard as fairly and accurately as possible.
- Help learners to assume gradually more responsibility for their own learning progress by practising self-assessment using strategies such as checklists and rubrics.
- Provide learners with opportunities to discuss their self-assessments with others.

To help learners respond to the question **'Where am I trying to go?'** teachers can:

- Develop, in co-operation with the learners, clear learning targets and examples of desirable work.
- Assist learners in setting learning goals for themselves, ensuring that they are realistic and meaningful.
- Record individual learners' goals as a means of benchmarking progress.

To help learners respond to the question **'How will I get there?'** teachers can:

- Use assessment and observational data to identify strengths and gaps in learning.
- Help learners develop realistic action plans that point out the next steps to take in order to move towards learning goals.
- Monitor learners as they progress through the action plans.

To help learners respond to the question **'How will I know when I have achieved my learning goals?'** teachers can:

- Have learners revisit long-term goals periodically to reflect on their relevance and to make any necessary adjustments.
- Talk with each learner about his or her long-term goals and action plans on an ongoing basis.

- Invite learners to reflect on their strengths and areas for improvement in respect of the learning goals.

---

### TASK 11.2: BENEFITS AND CHALLENGES OF SELF-ASSESSMENT

Read and discuss the quotation below from *Assessment in the Primary School Curriculum: Guidelines for Schools* (NCCA 2007), focussing on the advantages and challenges of developing self-assessment processes in the classroom.

Self-assessment helps the child to recognise the next steps in his/her learning and to become more independent and motivated. As the child develops self-confidence he/she can feel more secure about not always being right. In this way, self-assessment contributes to a positive classroom climate in which making mistakes is considered central to the learning process. (NCCA 2007: 14)

---

## Assessment and Learning Theory

A central tenet of current approaches to assessment is that assessment, both formative and summative, should serve learning. This resonates with constructivist learning theory and with Vygotsky's ideas on scaffolding (see Chapter 4), where the teacher extends the learner's understanding as it develops. Assessment that informs learning and teaching enables teachers and learners to engage consistently in the zone of proximal development (ZPD), the area where learning takes place (Vygotsky 1978). By observing and recording emerging learning, teachers identify what is within the learners' reach and provide them with appropriate experiences to support and extend learning.

Assessment also connects with sociocultural theories of learning, which highlight the role of interaction and joint collective action in the learning process. It involves both teachers and learners in a shared endeavour to advance learning, which is enacted within a community of practice. Teacher and learners participate in the community and assume roles, goals and practices that are intended to support learning. Hargreaves *et al.* paint a vivid picture of how assessment can be used to benefit learning:

In assessment-centred classrooms, assessment is both formative and summative and becomes a tool to aid learning: students monitor their progress over time and with their teachers identify the next steps needed to improve. Techniques such as open questioning, sharing learning objectives and focused marking have a powerful effect on students' ability to take an active role in their learning. There is always sufficient time left for reflection by students. Whether individually or in pairs, students are given the opportunity to review what they have learnt and how they have learnt it.

They evaluate themselves and one another in a way that contributes to understanding. Students know their levels of achievement and make progress towards their next goal. (2005: 17)

## Student Teachers' Use of Assessment on School Placement

In its guidelines for providers of programmes of initial teacher education, *Initial Teacher Education: Criteria and Guidelines for Programme Providers*, the Teaching Council specifies a number of learning outcomes, including the following, which state that graduates of teacher education programmes should be able to

- apply knowledge of the individual potential of pupils, dispositions towards learning, varying backgrounds, identities, experiences and learning styles to planning for teaching, learning and assessment
- use a range of strategies to support, monitor and assess pupils' approach to learning and their progress

(Teaching Council 2011: 27)

However, studies have shown, and our experiences of observing student teachers on school placement corroborate, that student teachers are so preoccupied with managing the day-to-day in the classroom that the crucial area of assessment is often sidelined. This is understandable in the early experiences of school placement. However, as your understanding of learning and teaching develops, it is important that your attention is directed outwards to embrace what and how well your learners are doing. Hammerness *et al.* (2005) noted that 'beginning teachers frequently focus on their teaching practices rather than on what their students are learning' (377). This was corroborated by the Department of Education and Science in their *Learning to Teach* study (2006). This study involved a sampling of 10 per cent (n = 143) of the final year cohort of students of the BEd degree or postgraduate diploma in primary teaching in 2006. The evaluation was carried out during the student teachers' final school placement. As a means of evaluating the range and effectiveness of assessment approaches used by student teachers, the study explored:

- the extent to which a range of systematic and efficient assessment modes, procedures and practices were employed
- the extent to which copybooks and other work samples were corrected and monitored consistently
- the extent to which the outcomes of assessment affected teaching and classroom organisation

- the extent to which records of learners' progress were maintained.

(Department of Education and Science 2006: 29)

The study found that

- Fewer than half the student teachers were given the top ratings in relation to their assessment practices.
- More than a third of the student teachers were considered to be experiencing some difficulty with assessment, and a few were deemed to be ineffective in this aspect of their teaching.

(Adapted from Department of Education and Science 2006)

## Planning for Assessment on School Placement

The Teaching Council's *Guidelines on School Placement* state that school placement should involve the student teacher in Assessment of Learning and Assessment for Learning (Teaching Council 2013: 13). The NCCA in its *Assessment in the Primary School Curriculum: Guidelines for Schools* (2007) provides detailed examples of modes of assessment that encompass AfL and AoL, notably, self-assessment, conferencing, portfolio assessment, concept mapping, questioning, teacher observation, teacher-designed tasks and tests, and standardised testing. Drawing on the NCCA *Guidelines*, we suggest the following approaches as useful starting points as you begin to integrate assessment into your school placement experiences and as a basis for engaging more fully with the range of assessment approaches recommended.

### *Use Classroom Observations to Inform Planning*

Spending time in classrooms as an observer is a valuable learning opportunity for you as a student teacher. In Chapter 7 we presented a detailed overview and range of approaches to classroom observation, including descriptive accounts, critical incident reports, ethnographic records, checklists and analysis of seating. We recommend that you read and reflect on the ideas presented in Chapter 7 and select some methods of observation that will benefit you in coming to know your learners and the context in which your teaching will take place. Utilising classroom observation periods wisely will be of immense benefit to you in planning appropriately for learning, and the ongoing use of observation will assist you in assessing how well your learners are doing and planning the most appropriate next steps.

### Share the Learning Intentions

Research has shown that sharing the learning intentions with learners before they begin an activity or lesson is beneficial to learning (Black and Wiliam 1998; Chappuis and Stiggins 2002; Rolheiser and Ross 2001; White and Frederiksen 1998). We recommend that you take a moment to discuss the learning intention, once you have introduced the topic – hopefully in a creative way – and elicited the learners' relevant prior knowledge. The following points are noteworthy when discussing the learning intentions associated with a new activity or topic with learners:

1.  Explain the focus of the learning, e.g.:
    *'We are learning how to…'*
    *'We are learning about…'*
    *'We are exploring why…'*
2.  Explain why this new learning is important, e.g.: *'We are learning this because…'*
3.  Present the learning intention in language that is learner friendly, e.g.:
    *'We are learning how to set up a fair test.'*
    *'We are learning about life in a Kibbutz.'*
    *'We are learning to use evidence to support an argument.'*
    *'We are learning to ask questions about artefacts to find out about the past.'*
    *'We are exploring why rainbows form in the sky.'*
4.  Write the learning intention on the board and remind learners of the learning intention throughout the activity or lesson.
5.  Write learning intentions as generic statements that will allow learners of all abilities to achieve them. Differentiate the level of challenge of the tasks to enable all learners to experience success.

### Encourage Learners to Self-Assess

While learning intentions draw attention to the learning focus of an activity or lesson, success criteria help learners to recognise whether or not they have been successful in their learning. The following are some key features of success criteria:

1.  They derive from the learning intention.
2.  They are specific to an activity or lesson.
3.  They are discussed and agreed with learners prior to commencing the learning activity.
4.  They provide support and direction to learners as they engage in the activity.
5.  They form the basis of feedback, and self- and peer-assessment.

The following are some strategies to promote learner self-assessment.

## Reflective Prompts

Depending on the age and ability of learners and their level of familiarity with the topic, it may be preferable to encourage the learners to self-assess orally. Prompts such as the following can be helpful to encourage the learners to reflect on their learning:

- The part I found difficult was…
- The part I enjoyed most was…
- The part I was surprised by was…
- I would like to find out more about…
- I need more help with…
- I am still puzzled about…
- What I have learned that is new is…
- What helped me when it got hard was…
- What made me think was…
- I changed my mind about…
- Now I feel…
- I might have learned better if…
- What I would change about this activity to help another class learn is…

## 'I Can' Statements

'I can' statements are a form of self-assessment that can be used at the end of a lesson, unit or theme to allow learners to indicate what they feel they are able to do. With learners in the early years of primary school, 'I can' statements for each learner – e.g. 'I can ask questions about important details in a story' – can be 'ticked' by the teacher on the basis of evidence from observations or interactions with the learners (see Table 11.1).

Table 11.1: 'I Can' Statements in the Early Primary Years

|  | Zara | Jade | Rob | Alejandro | Úna |
|---|---|---|---|---|---|
| I can answer questions about important details in a story. | ✓ | ✗ | ✓ | ✗ | ✓ |
| I can retell a story and include important details. | ✓ | ✓ | ✗ | ✓ | ✗ |
| I can identify characters from a story. | ✓ | ✓ | ✗ | ✗ | ✗ |
| I can identify the setting of a story. | ✓ | ✓ | ✓ | ✓ | ✗ |

'I can' statements are sometimes used by the teacher as a form of 'exit slip', which learners complete and give to the teacher at the end of a lesson or before leaving the classroom. This process allows the teacher to review the learners' responses and determine if there is a correspondence between what the learners can do and the lesson objectives, or if there is a need for refinement, review or revision.

## Rubrics

Rubrics are very helpful in supporting learners' self-assessment because they clearly describe varying levels of quality in a particular piece of work. It is best to use very simple rubrics when you first begin to use this form of self-assessment with a class, e.g. with younger learners, using emoji faces to indicate levels of satisfaction with their own work. 'Children can be helped to assess their own work in very simple ways by verbally commenting on what they have done, saying whether they are pleased with it, what they like or don't like about it, or what they would like to do better next time' (NCCA 2007: 85). More complex rubrics, such as the one presented in Figure 11.2 below, can be used to inform learners of the criteria by which to assess their own work or the work of their peers in self- and peer-assessment.

Figure 11.2: Procedural Writing Rubric

Author's name: _____    Date: _____

My name: _____

|  | 3 | 2 | 1 | THEIR SCORE |
|---|---|---|---|---|
| **Title and date** | Title and date | Title OR date | Neither | |
| **One step on each line** | Each step was on a new line. | Some steps were on a new line. | Steps were not split onto separate lines. | |
| **Capital letters at the start of each step** | Every time | 1–2 omissions | 3+ omissions | |
| **Numbering** | All steps | Some steps | None | |
| **Correct order** | All steps were in the correct order. | Some steps were in the correct order. | The steps were not in the correct order. | |
| **Comprehension** | I fully understand the instructions. | I understand some of the instructions. | I don't understand the instructions. | |
| **Handwriting** | Very neat | OK, could do better | Not very neat | |
| | | | Total: | /21 |

Source: Adapted from http://acrucialweekblogspot.com.

## Task 11.3: Planning for Assessment

Other useful approaches to learner self-assessment are provided in *Assessment in the Primary School Curriculum: Guidelines for Schools* (NCCA 2007: 14–23; 84–85).

Read and review the approaches outlined, which include:

- Rubrics
- Know, want to know, learned (KWL) grids
- Plus, minus and interesting (PMI) diagrams
- Ladders
- Traffic lights
- Talk partners/buddies
- Checklists
- Webs

Consider how you might integrate some of these ideas into your planning for assessment on school placement.

### Use Concept Mapping for AoL and AfL

Concept mapping is a powerful means for learners to organise their conceptual understanding within different domains of learning. While originally intended to help learners organise their understanding of topics that lend themselves to hierarchical categorisation, the method is also useful for topics that are highly interconnected. Concept maps can provide valuable information regarding learners' current level of understanding about a particular issue. This information enables the teacher to identify gaps in knowledge and understanding, and to specify areas of immediate learning need. Concept mapping can also be used as a means of evaluating progress at the end of a period of learning by providing evidence of how experiences or activities have modified or extended learners' thinking. In this way, concept mapping can be used for AoL. See Figure 11.3 for a sample concept map template.

### Develop Your Skills of Teacher Questioning

Teacher and learner questioning is fundamental to all classroom assessment methods. Asking higher-order questions promotes deeper thinking and provides teachers with insight into the degree and level of understanding. Effective questioning engages learners in dialogue, which expands and promotes learning. Questioning strategies should be embedded in your lesson planning. Part of your work in using questioning as an assessment method is to model good questioning. This in turn helps learners to become more skilful at asking good questions to aid their own conceptual development. Chapter 9 explores questioning in detail.

Figure 11.3: Sample Concept Map Template

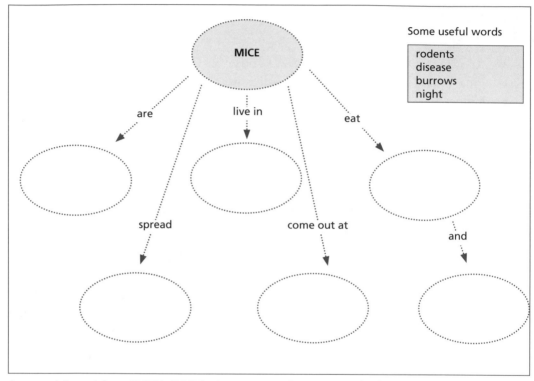

Source: Adapted from NCCA (2007), *Assessment in the Primary School Curriculum: Guidelines for Schools*, Dublin: National Council for Curriculum and Assessment: 37.

## TASK 11.4: REFLECTING ON YOUR ASSESSMENT PLANNING

Use the following questions to evaluate your approach to assessment and to identify how your assessment practices can be improved.

- Are my assessments inclusive of all learners?
- Do I share or develop the criteria for assessment with the learners?
- How can the learners demonstrate their understanding of the assessment process?
- How do I plan to involve learners in self-assessment?
- How do I plan to provide opportunities for learners to identify the next steps in their learning?
- How does my assessment develop learners' metacognitive skills?

# A SUMMARY OF KEY POINTS

- Assessment is an integral part of planning for learning and teaching.
- Assessment evidence is used to inform and modify learning and teaching.
- Assessment involves learners receiving feedback on their assessments along with advice regarding the next steps, and engaging in self-assessment.
- Assessment of Learning (AoL) is a summative form of assessment and involves learners' achievements being measured against established criteria.
- Assessment as Learning (AaL) is a formative form of assessment and involves learners reflecting on and monitoring their own learning with reference to specified learning goals.
- Assessment for Learning (AfL) is a formative form of assessment and involves teachers using evidence about learners' progress to inform planning and teaching.
- A range of techniques should be used to collect assessment information about a learner's progress and attainment.

# CHAPTER TWELVE

# Professional Relationships as a Student Teacher

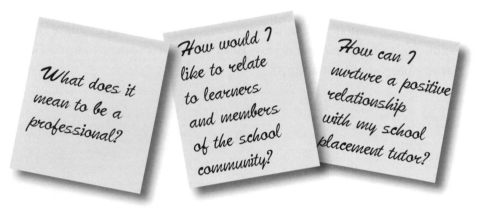

*What does it mean to be a professional?*

*How would I like to relate to learners and members of the school community?*

*How can I nurture a positive relationship with my school placement tutor?*

'Pupils may learn many things when a teacher is not in fact teaching.'

Paul Hirst, 'What Is Teaching?'

**Having studied this chapter, you will be in a position to appreciate:**

- The manner in which teaching and developing worthwhile relationships in the school community are interlinked in very significant ways.
- The significance of concepts such as 'care', 'love', 'respect' and 'trust', and their place in our evolving identities as teachers.
- The significance of relating ethically within the school community.
- The importance of relating professionally on school placement.
- Some of the intricacies and demands involved in reaching ethical decisions.
- The need for reflection and adaptability in our efforts to relate ethically and fairly in the school environment.
- How circle time may provide us with one approach in our wish to promote criticality, positive behaviour and positive relationships within the school community.

> ### TASK 12.1: NURTURING POSITIVE RELATIONSHIPS
>
> In your own experience as a learner, can you recall a teacher who was memorable for the manner in which he or she nurtured positive relationships? If so, in what ways did this teacher cultivate positive relationships? What impact did this climate have on general behaviour and on the quality of learning in the classroom? You might also reflect on other classroom atmospheres that you have encountered.

## INTRODUCTION

Teaching, almost by definition, is an act of relating to learners principally, but also to colleagues, parents, guardians, the community, supervisors, mentors, inspectors and a myriad of others. For that reason, exploring your understanding of what is meant by 'relating' seems crucial in the context of your progression as a student teacher. Many questions can arise in this process, not least whether a single template for the building of relationships is even possible or desirable. Such a question draws us to the issue of our identity and, very significantly, our understanding of relating as part of our unique sense of self. Ayers highlights the relational demands placed on teachers:

> (T)eaching as the direct delivery of some preplanned curriculum, teaching as the orderly and scripted conveyance of information, teaching as clerking, is simply a myth. Teaching is much larger and much more alive than that; it contains more pain and conflict, more joy and intelligence, more uncertainty and ambiguity. It requires more judgment and energy and intensity than, on some days, seems humanly possible. Teaching is spectacularly unlimited. (2001: 5)

## A RELATIONAL MODEL OF TEACHING

Viewed in this way, teaching can be daunting, enthralling, challenging or evoke a myriad of other feelings. Teaching engages our human qualities such as care, love, understanding, empathy and support. These qualities and others have received attention in education discourse in recent times in the context of building meaningful and sustainable relationships in schools. Such a perspective on teaching, which has been called a relational model or lens, places the quality of relationships to the fore. It has a long tradition, though not necessarily a prime position, in teaching practice. Socrates may well have been an early advocate. He viewed teaching as a journey of co-exploration between learners and teacher in the pursuit of truth, and declared, 'I cannot teach anybody anything. I can only make them think.'

Götz (2001) has a similar view of teaching: '[To be] a teacher, then, is not merely to learn to know when and where and how unconcealment is to take place, to learn to listen to the call of Being, to learn to answer, correspond and converse; to be a teacher means above all to learn to let others learn' (93). The relational quality of teaching is also argued by Buber (1947). For Buber, however, the teacher can only teach if he or she is capable of building a relationship based on authentic dialogue with learners and on a profound sense of inclusion and mutuality. He refers to this type of engagement as an 'I-Thou' relationship. This dialogue can only occur if the learner develops trust in the educator and if the learner feels totally accepted. In the absence of such trust, attempts to educate will lead to rebellion and disinterest. According to Buber:

> Everything depends on the teacher as a man, as a person. He educates from himself, from his virtues and his faults, through personal example and according to circumstances and conditions. His task is to realize the truth in his personality and to convey this realization to the pupil. (Buber, cited in Hodes 1972: 146)

More recent work in the same vein views education (in its broadest sense) as being central to the creation of caring in society (Noddings 1992). Noddings believes that the 'main aim of education should be to produce competent, caring, loving and lovable people' (8). She describes education as 'a constellation of encounters, both planned and unplanned, that promote growth through the acquisition of knowledge, skills, understanding and appreciation' (2002: 283). Noddings gives a central role to the concept of care in education. She argues that personal manifestations of care are probably more significant in learners' lives than any particular curriculum or style of pedagogy (1984: 60).

---

### TASK 12.2: THE RELATIONAL VIEW OF TEACHING

Read and think about the quotations below.
   Identify your two favourite quotations and consider their implications for teaching. What do your two chosen quotations have in common?

We carry with us habits of thought and taste fostered in some nearly forgotten classroom by a certain teacher. (Bruner 1996: 24)

I do not need to establish a deep, lasting, time-consuming personal relationship with every student. What I must do is to be totally and non-selectively present to the student – to each student – as he addresses me. The time interval may be brief but the encounter is total. (Noddings 1984: 180)

Your first duty is to be humane. Love childhood. Look with friendly eyes on its games, its pleasures, its amiable dispositions. Which of you does not sometimes look back regretfully on the age when laughter was ever on the lips and the heart free of care? Why steal from the little innocents the enjoyment of a time that passes all too quickly? (Rousseau 1762, Vol. 2: 70)

One looks back with appreciation to the brilliant teachers, but with gratitude to those who touched our human feelings. The curriculum is so much necessary raw material, but warmth is the vital element for the growing plant and for the soul of the child. (Jung 1954: 144).

How can I be an educator if I do not develop in myself a caring and loving attitude toward the student, which is indispensable on the part of one who is committed to teaching and to the education process itself. (Freire 1998: 65)

The kids sense it right away when you don't like what you're doing. So many people went into teaching, and their hearts weren't in it, and they became what you call disciplinarians. Well, that's the last refuge of a bad teacher, being a disciplinarian. (McCourt 2007)

The themes touched on in the quotations in Task 12.2, namely, care, dialogue and our own evolving sense of self and self-awareness, are central to this chapter and we explore them further below.

## Relating to Learners

A great deal of research has been undertaken in the sphere of the teacher–learner relationship and a survey of insights is useful. It is clear that cultivating learners' relationships with their teachers has significant, affirmative and enduring consequences for learners' personal, academic and social development. Learners who have affirming, understanding and supportive relationships with their teachers tend to realise higher levels of achievement than those learners who don't (Rimm-Kaufman and Sandlios 2015).

More specifically, affirmative teacher–learner relationships, as demonstrated by low levels of conflict and high incidences of closeness and care, have been shown to assist learners' initial adjustment to the school environment, augment social skills, advance academic performance and nurture learners' capabilities in academic performance (Battistich, Schaps and Wilson 2004; Birch and Ladd 1997; Hamre and Pianta 2001). Learners who have close relationships with teachers display higher attendance rates, are more self-directed and cooperative, and are more engaged in learning (Birch and Ladd 1997; Klem and Connell 2004).

Interestingly, learners who enjoy a warm relationship with their teachers are more likely to indicate a liking for school and a diminished sense of isolation or loneliness. This positive connection with school, in the context of positive teacher–learner relationships, also results in enhanced achievement in tests of academic accomplishment and school readiness (Birch and Ladd 1997). Moreover, teachers who employ more learner-centred approaches (i.e. approaches that differentiate among learners, promote inclusive decision-making and recognise learners' needs) report much higher levels of motivation than teachers who do not (Daniels and Perry 2003; Perry and Weinstein 1998).

Research indicates that the quality of teacher–learner relationships in the early school years has an enduring effect. In situations where greater levels of conflict exist between teachers and learners, and where higher levels of dependency are also manifested in the early school years, learners tend to have lower levels of achievement and more behavioural issues as they progress in school (Hamre and Pianta 2001). Conversely, research indicates that learners with a greater degree of closeness to and who are in less conflictual relationships with their teachers go on to display higher levels of social skills as they progress through school (Berry and O'Connor 2009).

Having reviewed the research in this area, Rimm-Kaufman and Sandlios present the following general indicators of positive classroom relationships:

- Teachers enjoy their interactions with learners.
- Teachers interact with learners in a responsive and respectful manner.
- Teachers offer learners help in achieving academic and social objectives (e.g. answering questions in a timely manner, offering support that matches the learners' needs).
- Teachers help learners to reflect on their thinking and learning skills.
- Teachers know and demonstrate knowledge about individual learners' backgrounds, interests, emotional strengths and academic levels.
- Teachers seldom show irritability or aggravation toward learners.

(Adapted from Rimm-Kaufman and Sandlios 2015)

Campbell (2014) offers further evidence-based guidance on building relationships with learners and places considerable importance on creating environments where the safety and security of learners are valued, their sense of self-worth is nurtured, a real sense of belonging is present, a purposeful sense of direction is promoted and the cultivation of self-esteem is paramount.

The discourse on education offers numerous examples in respect of building relationships with learners. Ostrosky and Jung advise teachers to:

- Engage in one-to-one interactions with learners.
- Get on the learner's level for face-to-face interactions.
- Use a pleasant, calm voice and simple language.
- Follow the learner's lead and interest during play.
- Help learners to understand classroom expectations.
- Redirect learners when they engage in challenging behaviour.
- Listen to learners and encourage them to listen to others.
- Acknowledge learners for their accomplishments and effort.

(Adapted from Ostrosky and Jung 2015)

Stage and Quiroz propose that teachers can effect a good working classroom climate by employing approaches such as the following:

1. Using a wide variety of verbal and physical reactions to students' misbehavior such as moving closer to offending students and using a physical cue, such as a finger to the lips, to point out inappropriate behavior.
2. Cuing the class about expected behaviors through prearranged signals, such a raising a hand to indicate that all students should take their seats.
3. Providing tangible recognition of appropriate behavior, with tokens or chits, for example.
4. Employing group contingency policies that hold the entire group responsible for behavioral expectations.
5. Employing home contingency techniques that involve rewards and sanctions at home.

(Stage and Quiroz 1997, cited in Ahmad 2010: 178)

In this brief discussion, an apparent dilemma might be evident and may be developed into several questions:

- How significant is the individual personality of the teacher in bringing about an effective classroom relationship and climate?
- Should issues of teacher identity and self matter to any great extent or impact on the development of a positive climate in our classrooms?
- Can a uniform imposition of a set of techniques achieve worthwhile and nurturing classroom relations for all involved, regardless of varying contexts and personalities?

In the context of this discussion, can we discern some significance for the less tangible qualities of 'care', 'dialogue', 'identity' and 'self-awareness'? If so, what implications arise for the development of our own appropriate techniques or approaches when we factor in these less concrete considerations? How can we as teachers incorporate our own reflected-upon experiences in developing our own sense of positive classroom relationship, a sense that reflects our identity as persons interacting with our learners? In the context of developing classroom relations and the possibility of implementing a singular applicable method, what are we to make of Palmer's view that 'good teaching cannot be reduced to technique; good teaching comes from the identity and integrity of the teacher' (1998: 10)?

It is clear that drawing on established research and the advice of practitioners can offer us valuable insights into our own evolving practice. However, Palmer cautions about developing a dependency on external advice to the detriment of our own hard-earned reflectivity. Equally, Noddings argues for an educational atmosphere beyond the capacity of mere technique, an atmosphere that she roots in the inherently human concept of care. In her view, caring is at the heart of being an educator, and the context of caring in the educational relationship becomes the model of moral ethics for learners. The learner becomes a daily witness to an adult who strives to live out an ethic of care. Living out an ethic of care seems to demand much more of us as teachers than just the implementation of impersonal and generally applicable techniques or methods for maintaining classroom control (Noddings 2002).

## Engaging Ethically as a Professional

It is clear that relationships are rooted deeply in our overall ethical disposition towards learners and, very importantly, towards others in the educational encounter, including colleagues, parents and ancillary staff. Recent years have seen the publication of the *Code of Professional Conduct for Teachers* (CPCT) (Teaching Council 2012) and the *Guidelines on School Placement* (Teaching Council 2013). School placement is undertaken within the framework of these guidelines. School placement opportunities have been built on many years of cooperation with a broad range of schools.

Hence, working within the standards and expectations outlined in the *CPCT*, teachers collaborate with student teachers in the interests of supporting, nurturing and developing good, innovative practice. Schools seek to provide worthwhile developmental opportunities for aspiring teachers and strive to make the experience as beneficial as possible.

The guidelines should provide you with a rich and thought-provoking window as you prepare for your school placement. A number of insights from the *CPCT* merit some further insight and scrutiny. To the forefront, the document places emphasis on the values of respect, care, integrity and trust, and claims that these 'are reflected throughout the

Code' (Teaching Council 2012: 3). These values are afforded high significance as 'these core values underpin the work of the teacher in the practice of his or her profession' (3).

Based on the fundamental premise that 'the role of the teacher is to educate,' the *CPCT* gives each one of these values some clarity. With regard to the core value of 'respect', teachers are exhorted to uphold 'human dignity and promote equality and emotional and cognitive development' (Teaching Council 2012: 5). Moreover, in their work teachers are encouraged to 'demonstrate respect for spiritual and cultural values, diversity, social justice, freedom, democracy and the environment'. Equally, teachers are expected to embed 'care' as a core value in their practices so that their engagements are 'motivated by the best interests of the pupils/students entrusted to their care'. This key value is best shown 'through positive influence, professional judgement and empathy in practice'. The value of integrity is depicted in terms of 'honesty, reliability and moral action' and best demonstrated through teachers' 'professional commitments, responsibilities and actions'. Finally, 'trust' is located at the centre of the range of relationships that characterise teaching. These relationships with all our learners, 'colleagues, parents, school management and the public are based on trust' (Teaching Council 2012: 4–8).

---

**M-LEVEL TASK 12.1: STATEMENT OF VALUES**

Devise a statement of values for students in your class group.

Work within a small group to develop a refined list of six values for presentation to the larger class group:

1. Brainstorm: within your small group, list all the values you come up with. Keep in mind that values are multi-dimensional and often overlap.
2. Refine: reduce your list to a manageable size (five to seven values). Do this by rewording, synthesising, combining, eliminating and placing specific values under more general ones. Do your best to make your list comprehensive and representative.
3. Share your list with the entire class group.
4. Revise: make any last-minute changes.
5. Combine: one member of the class organises the lists into a combined list of discrete values.
6. Vote: each person ranks their top six values.

Reflect on the overall exercise and consider how this exercise has prompted you to review your own values.

The *CPCT* then addresses six further areas of concern:

- Professional Values and Relationships
- Professional Integrity
- Professional Conduct
- Professional Practice
- Professional Development
- Professional Collegiality and Collaboration

(Teaching Council 2012: 6–8)

An example for each sphere may help us understand some of the intentions and concerns of the Teaching Council. Reading the *CPCT* in full will undoubtedly broaden our understanding. In the case of professional values and relationships, the Teaching Council advises that

> teachers should be committed to equality and inclusion and to respecting and accommodating diversity including those differences arising from gender, civil status, family status, sexual orientation, religion, age, disability, race, ethnicity, membership of the Traveller community and socio-economic status, and any further grounds as may be referenced in equality legislation in the future. (2012: 6)

In the second sphere of concern, that of professional integrity, it is explicitly stated that 'teachers should act with honesty and integrity in all aspects of their work' (2012: 6). One of the core concerns mentioned within the sphere of professional conduct is the need and requirement for teachers to 'communicate effectively with pupils/students, colleagues, parents, school management and others in the school community in a manner that is professional, collaborative and supportive, and based on trust and respect' (2012: 7). Among the requirements regarding professional practice, we find the expectation that teachers should 'act in the best interest of pupils/students' (2012: 7). Professional development on the part of teachers is also a key requirement to the extent that teachers should reflect on and critically evaluate 'their professional practice, in light of their professional knowledge' (2012: 8). Finally, professional collegiality and collaboration are seen as central and teachers should seek to 'work in a collaborative manner with pupils/students, parents/guardians, school management, other members of staff, relevant professionals and the wider school community, as appropriate, in seeking to effectively meet the needs of pupils/students' (2012: 8).

While these are extracts from a more comprehensive document, they may prompt us to further questioning and discussion. Before we embark on a more in-depth reading of the entire *CPCT* we might engage with the questions and exercises in Task 12.3.

---

### TASK 12.3: EXPLORING THE CODE OF PROFESSIONAL CONDUCT FOR TEACHERS

Some questions and exercises:

- Is the idea of a general set of ethical guidelines being applicable to all teachers a feasible one?
- Can the uniqueness or individuality of teachers thrive within such general requirements?
- In the case of each of the six areas addressed in the *CPCT* (and listed above), could you outline other possible concerns that may merit attention?
- Draw on your own experience in education in order to express the need for such a code, or indeed otherwise.
- Critique the code and consider what merits deletion and/or addition.
- Compare the changes you propose with those of your fellow students.

---

## Relating Professionally on School Placement

The positive relationships with learners, school personnel and parents you build while on school placement will set the foundation for future worthwhile professional relationships. In its *Guidelines on School Placement*, the Teaching Council highlights the importance of fostering positive professional relationships:

> Relationships based on mutual respect, trust and inclusion are paramount to the success of the placement. In that context, it is important that student teachers are included and supported by all partners during their school placement. In turn, student teachers must recognise and respect the role of school personnel and have due regard for the policies, protocols and characteristic spirit that underpin the day-to-day life of the school. (2013: 10)

Hence, as a student teacher with privileged access to placement settings, you are expected to display a level of professionalism and a sense of responsibility commensurate with those of the teaching profession. It is your responsibility to know, and to adhere to, the policies and procedures of your teacher education institution and the school to which you are assigned.

The *Guidelines on School Placement* state that student teachers on school placement should:

- Engage constructively and collaboratively in a broad range of professional experiences as part of the school placement process.
- Meet with the principal and co-operating teacher(s) to plan the placement.

- Recognise their stage in the learning-to-teach process and how this should inform their interactions with the school community.
- In collaboration with the co-operating teacher and other teachers in the school as appropriate, seek and avail of opportunities to observe and work alongside other teachers.
- Take a proactive approach to their own learning and seek to avail of support as a collaborative practitioner.
- Prepare and deliver lessons to a standard commensurate with their stage of development and in line with HEI [Higher Education Institute] requirements and the policies of the host school (in particular homework, assessment and other relevant teaching and learning policies).
- Be familiar with the school's Code of Behaviour, Child Protection Policy and other relevant policies.
- Always be conscious that learners' needs are paramount and that a duty of care obtains.
- Engage with constructive feedback from HEI tutors, co-operating teachers and principals.
- Engage with other student teachers in the context of peer learning, insofar as practicable.
- Work towards becoming critically reflective practitioners.
- Engage with all in the school community in a respectful and courteous manner.
- Recognise that they have much to contribute to the school community.
- Support the characteristic spirit (ethos) of the school.
- Have due regard for the ethical values and professional standards which are set out in the Teaching Council's *Code of Professional Conduct for Teachers*.
- Respect the privacy of others and the confidentiality of information gained while on placement.
- Participate fully in each placement to develop their teaching skills and meet the placement requirements of their HEI.

(Teaching Council 2013: 19)

The fostering of relationships, based on mutual respect, trust and inclusion, is vitally important for effective school placement. Clear and open communication between all partners is essential. In particular, effective communication with parents is

[C]ritical.... In all communications, student teachers, cooperating teachers, principals, HEI placement tutors and all partners in the school placement process should respect the privacy of others and the confidentiality of information gained in the course of school placement. (Teaching Council 2013: 11)

Experiences and information relating to the school and its community to which you have privileged access while on school placement should not be shared with other audiences. It is essential that you respect the confidentiality of information that you receive about learners and their families. In addition, you also need to be respectful in the manner in which you share the experiences you encounter in the school with those outside of that environment. Confidentiality is a professional attribute that you need to cultivate at all times.

You may have an opportunity to engage with parents during your student teaching experience. It is a good practice to have your cooperating teacher present if conferring with parents.

### Observations of Your Teaching

While many student teachers find the prospect of being observed while teaching daunting at first, it usually becomes less stressful over time.

As you develop positive relationships with your placement tutor and cooperating teacher, you will experience observation as a rich dialogue and a positive learning experience that affirms the unique and positive aspects of your teaching and alerts you to areas of further growth and professional development. This support is central to all school placement experiences and has been underlined by the Teaching Council as follows:

> The provision of structured support for the student teacher is a key element of school placement. The HEI placement tutor has primary responsibility for the provision of such support and is also responsible for assessment for grading purposes. Co-operating teachers and school principals will also provide structured support to student teachers, having regard to capacity. The role of the co-operating teacher in providing structured support and guidance to student teachers is pivotal, though it is not evaluative, in terms of assessing the student teacher's work on behalf of the HEI. (2013: 15)

### Pre-Placement Meeting with School Placement Tutor

Prior to embarking on your school placement, a meeting with your placement tutor is usually scheduled. This is a valuable opportunity to introduce yourself to your placement tutor, to discuss your goals and aspirations for the placement, and to raise any questions or concerns you may have in relation to any aspect of the forthcoming placement. The following are indicative of the types of questions that your placement tutor may ask during your pre-placement meeting:

- What do you know about the learners?
- What do you know about the school and the community it serves?
- How do you intend to take the abilities, interests and needs of the learners into consideration in your planning?
- How will you know if the learners have attained the objectives you have set?
- Are you familiar with college guidelines and expectations for this school placement?
- What are you hoping to learn during this school placement?
- What teaching strengths do you want to consolidate?
- What new understandings/methods/strategies/insights are you hoping to develop?
- How can I, as your school placement tutor, be of assistance to you in achieving your learning goals?
- What is an appropriate time and place for discussion following the lesson?
- Do you have any questions or observations that you would like to share?

## During the Observation

When you are being observed during your school placement, your placement tutor will try to make their presence as unobtrusive as possible. To facilitate this, ensure that there is a place for your placement tutor to sit where there is ready access to folders containing all of the requisite documentation, including lesson plans, schemes, reflections, etc.

During your lesson observation, as with all lessons, keep your focus of attention on the learners. The placement tutor will be fully engaged with and focussed on reviewing your preparation, planning folders, reflections and other documentation. Do not try to interpret their body language, or the amount of time they spend reading through your documentation or writing notes as being either positive or negative. Engaging in teaching observation is intense work that requires simultaneous concentration on what is unfolding moment by moment in the classroom as well as on reading documentation and writing evaluative observations and constructive recommendations. In fact, it is best if you do not pay any attention to the placement tutor at all. As placement tutors we have both had the uncomfortable experience of being 'taught' by the student teacher, receiving all the eye contact and attention that should have been directed to the learners!

## Post-Observation Discussion

Following an observation of one of your lessons, your placement tutor will normally request to meet with you as soon as possible to help you review and reflect on the lesson.

During the post-observation discussion, your placement tutor will encourage you to reflect on what transpired during the observation period and may ask questions such as the following:

- What aspects of the lesson/session were you pleased with today?
- What went according to expectations?
- How well did you achieve your objectives? How do you know?
- Think of a strategy that worked well with a particular group of learners (e.g. those with English as a foreign/additional language, those with special education needs, the gifted and talented, members of the travelling community, etc.)? Why do think this was? How might you develop this strategy?
- What aspects do you feel did not go well? Why? What surprised you?
- How can you tell that all learners are learning?
- As you think about this lesson, what are some of the outcomes you want to have happen again?
- As you think about the results you got, what were some of the ways you designed the lesson to make sure the results would be achieved?
- When you think about what you had planned and what actually happened, what were the similarities and what were the differences?
- If you were to teach this lesson again, what would you change? What would you keep the same?
- What have you learned about teaching and learning from this lesson?
- What have you learned about your learners?
- Reflecting on your experiences today, what are the next steps for you in improving your teaching?
- How do you feel I can best support you?

In asking questions such as those outlined above, your placement tutor will endeavour to provide a context in which you can maximise the reflective learning opportunities presented by your teaching experiences. It is important that you engage honestly, and not defensively, with the question asked. Student teachers who can demonstrate that they have learned from their experiences can benefit from all teaching encounters. Different aspects of any lesson can be reviewed, discussed, revisited and adapted for more worthwhile engagements in teaching and learning in the future.

## Criticality and Relating Positively to Learners

As critical autonomy and independent thinking have emerged as key concerns in this book, it is necessary to speculate briefly on how the development of positive class relationships might be entirely congruent with the dispositions involved in critical thinking. These dispositions have been set out and argued by many theorists but, in general, the discernible outcomes appear compatible with inclusive and encouraging learning environments.

Many researchers have cited a wide set of related benefits and attributes accruing from the encouragement of critical thinking. One of the most commonly mentioned attributes is that of open-mindedness (Bailin *et al.* 1999; Ennis 1985; Facione 1990, 2000; Halpern 1998). Equally, a sense of fair-mindedness is encouraged and nurtured (Bailin *et al.* 1999; Facione 1990). Significantly, an inclination to seek reason has also been recognised (Bailin *et al.* 1999; Ennis 1985; Paul 1992), along with a sense of inquisitiveness (Bailin *et al.* 1999; Facione 1990, 2000). The desire to be well-informed (Ennis 1985; Facione 1990) in a context of flexibility (Facione 1990; Halpern 1998) also emerges as significant. Moreover, respect for and willingness to entertain others' viewpoints is a recurring finding in much of the research (Bailin *et al.* 1999; Facione 1990). Perhaps by way of summary, Facione (2000) defines a core characteristic of critical thinking as the 'consistent internal motivation to act toward or respond to persons, events, or circumstances in habitual, yet potentially malleable ways' (64).

Significant attempts have been initiated in classrooms in order to give more practical expression to the benefits of criticality in tandem with developing positive relationships in schools. Among such programmes we can find initiatives such as circle time, which is one of the most widely employed socio-emotional approaches (Ballard 1982; Mosley 1993). Circle time is extensively employed in connection with aspects of citizenship education within the SPHE curriculum (Mosley and Tew 1999). Throughout your engagement in teacher education and your further development as teachers, encounters with circle time will undoubtedly arise. A brief outline of circle time here might offer you the opportunity to explore some of its possibilities in terms of the development of positive relationships in the context of schooling.

As the name implies, circle time involves non-traditional seating arrangements, and is often typified by speaking prompts, opening games, communal songs and chants, positive peer reporting where learners talk about each other in positive terms, and other rituals deemed to nurture collaboration. A key objective is to promote the enhancement of learners' competencies in recognising, comprehending and articulating their own emotions, and perceiving the validity of others' thoughts and emotional responses. Very often, circle time is of a whole-school nature, with unconditional positive support as a key characteristic. Learners within the structure of circle time are encouraged to discuss, share, resolve, explore and empathise with their peers in an atmosphere of respect. Rules and procedures for circle time are often collaboratively designed by learners and teachers with an emphasis on giving all learners opportunities to voice concerns, and share their thoughts, ideas, insights, doubts and preferences in a safe and nurturing context.

It is important to note that circle time requires considerable more research as to its impact in a broad range of spheres: emotional, behavioural and academic (Collins, 2013). However, it may prove insightful to you as a significant, current and popular approach in schools, which strives to promote positive behaviour, self-discipline and the creation of positive relationships (Mosley 1993, 1996, 1998, 2006).

Circle Time

---

**M-LEVEL TASK 12.2: BENEFITS OF AND POSSIBLE ISSUES WITH CIRCLE TIME**

Download and study the following research report by Collins and Kavanagh (2013). Evaluate the benefits of circle time as laid out in the report. Discuss the research methodology used and critique the findings of the study.

Collins, B. and Kavanagh, A.M. (2013), *Student Teachers' Experiences of Circle Time: Implications for Practice*, Limerick: DICE Project, available from: http://www. diceproject.ie/research/papers-reports/.

---

## A SUMMARY OF KEY POINTS

- Teaching and the development of meaningful relationships within the school community are inextricably linked.
- Concepts such as 'care', 'love', 'respect' and 'trust' require our attention as our teaching identities evolve.
- Relating ethically to all partners in education is of key significance.
- Reaching ethical decisions requires reflection, adaptability and ongoing attention.
- Circle time is one of many evolving approaches to the nurturing of criticality, positive behaviour and positive relationships within the school community.

# Glossary

**Action research:** A form of inquiry generally undertaken by teacher researchers with the intention of improving practice. It usually involves the systematic gathering of data about one's own practice for the purpose of improvement.

**Agency:** Where learners exercise choice in their learning, undertake initiatives, contribute to discussions and develop their decision-making capacities.

**Assessment as Learning:** A form of assessment that highlights the centrality of the learner in both learning and evaluation. It encourages learners to engage in self- and peer-assessment, and enhances learners' self-confidence through developing metacognitive skills.

**Assessment for Learning** (also called **formative assessment**): Involves making judgements about learners' progress, attainments and learning processes, and using these judgements to inform learning and teaching.

**Assessment of Learning** (also called **summative assessment**): Refers to an end-of-period assessment where feedback to learners is usually provided in the form of grades or marks that are sometimes compared to national standards.

**Behaviourism:** Is principally concerned with observable behaviour. It is believed that such observable behaviours can be objectively assessed and measured.

**Beliefs:** The conclusions we reach based on our experiences over time, which inform how we think and behave.

**Co-construction:** Arises when learners and teachers, while working together, construct insight and knowledge about the environment. This involves assisting learners in exerting control over their learning, and nurturing their abilities in the selection of content, the sequencing of material, and in choosing ways of learning and assessment.

**Cognition:** The mental or cognitive process inherent in gaining knowledge and understanding. It includes remembering, thinking, judging, problem-solving, intuition, awareness, perception and reasoning.

**Collaborative learning:** A social form of learning, based in social contexts and reliant upon environmental resources. Collaborative learning is based on the belief that knowledge can be generated within a group or a class, or between a pair of learners, particularly where all learners actively cooperate by sharing understandings and embracing different roles.

**Critical friends:**  Learners who offer support, insight and constructive critique to their peer learners.

**Critical incident:** A significant event, which was unanticipated, that is intensely remembered and influences understanding of learning and teaching.

**Critical reflection:** The conscious, deliberate and sustained consideration of the moral and ethical implications of classroom practice for learners.

**Didactic:** A form of teaching that relies heavily on instruction as a key method.

**Differentiation:** The manner in which a teacher responds to the range of learner needs. Teachers differentiate by adjusting the challenge levels of what is being taught (content), how it is taught (process) and how learners demonstrate their learning (outcomes).

**Empirical:** Modes of thinking and research that rely on or are intrinsically related to observation and the verification or otherwise of hypotheses, with a reliance on experimentation and the assessment of derived evidence. Empirical experiences relate chiefly to sense experiences and are viewed to be empirical if they have origins in, or may be established by, sensory observation.

**Hypothesis:** A provisional explanation of a phenomenon, problem or observation that is subject to further testing, scrutiny and investigation.

**Identity:** A sense of self that provides a degree of consistency and continuity to each person over time, but is subject to reflection, change and modification as life progresses.

**Inclusion:**  The integration of learners from a wide and diverse spectrum of religions, beliefs, non-belief, ethnic origins, learning needs and socio-economic backgrounds.

**Inquiry stance:** A position in which one actively searches for understanding and meaning.

**Inter-subjectivity:** A shared understanding that may be reached by people based on communication.

**Metacognition:** An awareness or analysis of one's own learning or thinking processes. Metacognition is often referred to as 'thinking about thinking'.

**Metaphor:** A figure of speech that acts as a means of depicting objects, processes, data, etc. by means of a comparison. It is normally devised in order to assist understanding of one kind of phenomenon in terms of another.

**Objective reality:** Having an existence independent of and external to the mind and based on phenomena that are observable.

**Ontology:** A form of philosophical inquiry into the nature of being; a branch of metaphysics. Ontology comprises the investigation into being, or attempts to establish a theory of being.

**Open-mindedness:** Being open to the viewpoints of others, awareness of alternative perspectives and recognising our own capacity to make errors.

**Paradigm:** A collection of viewpoints, concepts and assumptions that define a perspective on reality, and are found within a community sharing a common interest, e.g. scholars within a specific discipline.

**Pedagogical content knowledge:** A form of professional understanding that brings together content knowledge and knowledge about pedagogy. It is based on an understanding of how best to organise and present ideas, and adapt them in response to the diverse interests and abilities of learners.

**Pedagogy of mutuality:** A viewpoint that recognises that both learner and teacher bring different insights to the learning encounter and that, by means of discussion, a mutual frame of understanding can be built. This leads to an interchange of insights between the learner and the practitioner.

**Pluralism:** A belief that argues that people who come from different contexts such as religions, ethnic backgrounds and social classes, while living harmoniously within society, should also be supported in maintaining their distinctive traditions.

**Positivist:** A theoretical framework that is guided by the search for the objective truth, often using scientific approaches. Positivist approaches tend to view true inquiry in terms of engaging with empirical and often quantifiable facts.

**Readiness:** Related to the manner in which the child passes through a sequence of developmental stages. According to some developmental psychologists, a child should be 'ready' to progress to the next stage of development and should not be introduced to material beyond his or her stage of development.

**Realist:** A believer in philosophical realism is one who inclines towards the representation of phenomena in very concrete terms, and claims to be devoid of illusions and not subject to the deceptions of wishful thinking.

**Reflection-in-action:** Thinking about events in the classroom as they occur in order to make immediate adjustments to one's practice.

**Reflection-on-action:** Thinking back on one's practice in order to gain more profound insight into events and occurrences that transpired.

**Reflective inquiry:** A systematic and disciplined approach to addressing problems, gaining insight, applying solutions and evaluating outcomes.

**Reflective teaching:** A perspective on teaching as a cyclical process in which teachers continually evaluate, monitor, adjust and revise their own practice.

**Reflective thinking:** Involves nurturing the attitudes of open-mindedness, criticality, responsibility and dedication.

**Reframe:** To view an experience in a different way or place it in a new frame; to view it from a different angle or perspective and perhaps to perceive aspects of the experience that weren't observable from the first vantage point.

**Reposition:** To adjust your perception by broadening your perspective and developing new structures and processes for interpreting experience.

**Representation:** According to Bruner, modes of representation are the process by which information and data are stored and encoded in memory.

**Responsibility:** Being accountable for the outcomes of your actions and their impact on learners.

**Scaffolding:** Providing guidance and support to learners as they progress from one level of competence to another.

**Schema:** A cognitive structure of predefined ideas that provides a means by which to represent aspects of the environment and organise new experiences.

**Self-reflection:** Exploring how one's values, beliefs, outlooks and expectations, family influences, and cultural habituation impact on learners and their learning.

**Sociocultural theories:** A group of theories, developed with a basis in the work of Vygotsky, which place an emphasis on the influence of social and cultural factors on learners' development and learning.

**Subjective:** Reliant upon or occurring in a person's mind rather than in the external world.

**Taxonomy:** The systematic identification and organisation of attributes, qualities, characteristics, objectives or traits in a hierarchical manner, which displays the connections between them and the degree of progression from one to the next within the sequence.

**Teacher efficacy:** A teacher's belief in his or her ability to organise and execute courses of action necessary to bring about desired results.

**Teacher narratives:** Stories written or narrated by and about teachers, which can be drawn upon as data within a context of inquiry.

**Values:** Deeply held views about what we think is worthwhile.

# Bibliography

Abbott, S. (ed.) (2014), 'Hidden Curriculum' in *The Glossary of Education Reform,* available from: http://edglossary.org/hidden-curriculum (accessed 7 May 2015).

Abel, E.M. and Campbell, M. (2009), 'Student-Centred Learning in an Advanced Social Work Practice Course: Outcomes of a Mixed Methods Investigation,' *Social Work Education,* 28(1): 23–8.

Acheson, K.A. and Gall, M.D. (1987), *Techniques in the Clinical Supervision of Teachers* (2nd ed.), New York: Longman.

Adler, P.A. and Adler, P. (1994), 'Observational techniques' in N.K. Denzin and Y.S. Lincoln (eds.), *Handbook of Qualitative Research,* Thousand Oaks, CA: Sage Publications: 377–92.

Ahmad, M. (2010), 'Application of Classroom Management Strategies in Public and Private Sector at School Level in Pakistan,' *International Journal of Library and Information Science,* 2(9), 177–83.

Alberto, P.A. and Troutman, A.C. (2006), *Applied Behaviour Analysis for Teachers* (7th ed.), New Jersey: Pearson Merrill Prentice Hall.

Alexander, R. (2001), *Culture and Pedagogy: International Comparisons in Primary Education,* Oxford: Blackwell.

Alexander, R. (2004), 'Dialogic Teaching and the Study of Classroom Talk,' 4th International Conference keynote address, *Literacy,* 44(3): 103–111.

Alexander, R. (2006), *Towards Dialogic Teaching: Rethinking Classroom Talk* (3rd ed.), Cambridge, UK: Dialogos.

Alexander, R. (2010), *Dialogic Teaching Essentials,* Singapore: National Institute of Education.

Anderson, L.W., Krathwohl, D.R., Airasian, P.W., Cruikshank, K.A., Mayer, R.E. *et al.* (eds) (2001), *A Taxonomy for Learning, Teaching, and Assessing: A Revision of Bloom's Taxonomy of Educational Objectives* (complete edition), New York: Longman.

Argyris, C. and Schön, D. (1974), *Theory in Practice: Increasing Professional Effectiveness,* San Francisco: Jossey-Bass.

Ayers, W. (2001), *To Teach: The Journey of a Teacher,* New York: Teachers College Press.

Bailin, S., Case, R., Coombs, S. and Daniels, L.B. (1999), 'Conceptualizing Critical Thinking,' *Curriculum Studies,* 31 (3): 285–302.

Baker, L. (2006), 'Observation: A Complex Research Method,' *Library Trends*, 55(1): 171–89.

Ballard, J. (1982), *Circle Time*, New York: Irvington Publishers.

Balsley, H.L. (1970), *Quantitative Research Methods for Business and Economics*, New York: Random House.

Barnes, D. (1975), *From Communication to Curriculum*, London: Penguin.

Barnes, D. (2008), 'Exploratory talk for learning,' in N. Mercer and S. Hodgkinson (eds), *Exploring Talk in Schools*, London: Sage Publications: 1–16.

Barnes, D. and Todd, F. (1995), *Communication and Learning Revisited: Making Meaning through Talk*, Portsmouth, NH: Boynton/Cook Publications.

Bartlett, S. and Burton, D. (2006), 'Practitioner research or descriptions of classroom practice? A discussion of teachers investigating their classrooms,' *Educational Action Research*, 14(3): 395–405.

Bartlett, S. and Burton, D. (2012), *Introduction to Education Studies*, London: Sage Publications.

Batten, M., Marland, P. and Khamis, M. (1993), *Knowing How to Teach Well: Teachers Reflect on Their Classroom Practice*, Hawthorn, Vic: ACER.

Battistich, V., Schaps, E. and Wilson, N. (2004), 'Effects of an elementary school intervention on students' "connectedness" to school and social adjustment during middle school,' *The Journal of Primary Prevention*, 24(3), 243–62.

Battistich, V., Solomon, D., Watson, M. and Schaps, E. (1997), 'Caring school communities,' *Educational Psychologist*, 32(3): 137–51.

Belvel, P.S. (2010), *Rethinking Classroom Management: Strategies for Prevention, Intervention, and Problem Solving* (2nd ed.), Thousand Oaks, CA: Corwin Press.

Berry, D. and O'Connor, E. (2009), 'Behavioral risk, teacher–child relationships, and social skill development across middle childhood: A child-by-environment analysis of change,' *Journal of Applied Developmental Psychology*, 31(1): 1–14.

Birch, S.H. and Ladd, G.W. (1997), 'The teacher–child relationship and early school adjustment,' *Journal of School Psychology*, 55(1): 61–79.

Black, P.J. and Wiliam, D. (1998), 'Inside the Black Box: Raising Standards through Classroom Assessment,' *Phi Delta Kappan*, 80: 139–48.

Blaxter, L., Hughes, C. and Tight, N. (1996), *How to Research*, Buckingham: Open University Press.

Bloom, B.S., Engelhart, M.D., Furst, E.J., Hill, W.H. and Krathwohl, D.R. (1956), *Taxonomy of Educational Objectives: The Classification of Educational Goals. Handbook I: Cognitive Domain*, New York: David McKay Company.

Bond N. (2011), 'Preparing Preservice Teachers to Become Teacher Leaders,' *The Educational Forum*, 75(4): 280–97.

Boud, D. and Walker, D. (1998), 'Promoting Reflection in Professional Courses: The Challenge of Context,' *Studies in Higher Education*, 23(2): 191–206.

Boyer, E. (1990), *Scholarship Reconsidered*, Princeton, NJ: The Carnegie Foundation for the Advancement of Teaching.

Brahier, Daniel J. (2009), *Teaching Secondary and Middle School Mathematics*, Boston: Pearson Education.

Brookfield, S.D. (1990), 'Using critical incidents to explore learners' assumptions' in J. Mezirow (ed.), *Fostering Critical Reflection in Adulthood*, San Francisco: Jossey-Bass.

Brookfield, S.D. (1998), 'Critically Reflective Practice,' *The Journal of Continuing Education in the Health Professions*, 18: 197–205.

Brookfield, S.D. (2006), *The Skillful Teacher: On Technique, Trust and Responsiveness in the Classroom* (2nd ed.), San Francisco: Jossey-Bass.

Brookfield, S.D. (2015), *The Skilful Teacher*, San Francisco: Jossey-Bass.

Brown, G. and Wragg, E.C. (1993), *Questioning*, London: Routledge.

Bruner, J.S. (1957), *Going Beyond the Information Given*, New York: Norton.

Bruner, J.S. (1960), *The Process of Education*, Cambridge, Mass.: Harvard University Press.

Bruner, J.S. (1961), 'The Act of Discovery', *Harvard Educational Review*, 31: 21–32.

Bruner, J.S. (1966), *Toward a Theory of Instruction*, Cambridge, Mass.: Belkapp Press.

Bruner, J.S. (1996), *The Culture of Education*, Cambridge, Mass.: Harvard University Press.

Bruner, J.S., Ross, G. and Wood, D. (1976), 'The Role of Tutoring in Problem Solving,' *Journal of Child Psychiatry and Psychology*, 17(2): 89–100.

Bryant, A. and Charmaz, K. (2007), 'Qualitative Research and Grounded Theory: Complexities, Criticisms, and Opportunities' in A. Bryant and K. Charmaz (eds), *The SAGE Handbook of Grounded Theory*, London: SAGE Publications Ltd: 417–36.

Buber, M. (1947, 2002), *Between Man and Man*, trans. R.G. Smith, London: Kegan Paul.

Burbules N. and Berk, B. (1999), 'Critical Thinking and Critical Pedagogy: Relations, Differences and Limits' in Thomas S. Popkewitz and Lynn Fendler (eds), *Critical Theories in Education*, New York: Routledge: 45–66.

Campbell, D.E. (2003), 'Building Positive Relationships' in D.E. Campbell (ed.), *Choosing Democracy: A Practical Guide to Multicultural Education*, 3rd ed., Boston: Pearson Allyn Bacon Prentice Hall.

Campbell, D.E. (2014), *Building Positive Relationships*, Boston: Pearson Allyn Bacon Prentice Hall, available from: http://www.education.com/reference/article/building-positive-relationships-students/ (accessed 18 March 2015).

Carey, S., Collins, G., Greer, J., McNamara, M., O' Donoghue, E. and Timoney, A., (2008), *Understanding the Challenges of Immigration for Education Provision*, Dublin: Oireachtas Library and Research Spotlight Series.

Carr, D. (2003), *Making Sense of Education: An Introduction to the Philosophy and Theory of Education and Teaching*, London: Routledge Falmer.

CCL (2006), 'Why Is High-Quality Child Care Essential? The link between Quality Child Care and Early Learning,' *Lessons in Learning*, Ottawa: Canadian Council on Learning.

CECDE (2006), *Síolta: The National Quality Framework for Early Childhood Education*, Dublin: Centre for Early Childhood Development and Education.

Centre for Inclusive Child Care (2011), 'Factors that Influence Behaviour', tipsheet, Saint Paul, MN: Concordia University.

Chapman, G. and Chapman, C. (2002), *Differentiated Instructional Strategies: One Size Doesn't Fit All*, Thousand Oaks, CA: Corwin Press.

Chappuis, S. and Stiggins, R.J. (2002), 'Classroom Assessment for Learning,' *Educational Leadership*, 60(1): 40–3.

Cheng, S.T. (1999), 'Perception of Classroom Environment in Hong Kong: Differences between Students in Junior and Senior Forms,' *Adolescence*, 34 (136), 793–8.

Churton, M.W., Cranston-Gingras, A. and Blair, T.R. (1998), *Teaching Children with Diverse Abilities*, Boston: Allyn & Bacon.

Cochran-Smith, M. (2004), *Walking the Road: Race, Diversity and Social Justice in Teacher Education*, New York: Teachers College Press.

Cochran-Smith, M. and Lytle, S.L. (1993), *Inside/Outside: Teacher Research and Knowledge*, New York: Teachers College Press.

Cochran-Smith, M. and Lytle, S.L. (2009), *Inquiry as Stance: Practitioner Research for the Next Generation*, New York: Teachers College Press.

Cohen, L., Manion, L. and Morrison, K. (2000), *Research Methods in Education*, London: Routledge/Falmer.

Collier, S.T. (1999), 'Characteristics of Reflective Thought during the Student Teaching Experience,' *Journal of Teacher Education*, 50(3):173.

Collins, B. (2013), 'Empowerment of children through circle time: myth or reality?' *Irish Educational Studies*, 32(4): 421–36.

Collins, B. and Kavanagh, A.M. (2013), *Student Teachers' Experiences of Circle Time: Implications for Practice*, Limerick: DICE Project.

Condon, J. (2015), 'The multicultural classroom: how can our schools ensure a more stable, diverse society?' *Irish Times*, 24 February.

Connell, J.P. and Wellborn, J. (1991), 'Competence, Autonomy and Relatedness: A Motivational Analysis of Self-System Processes' in M. Gunnar and A. Sroufe (eds), *Self-Processes in Development: Minnesota Symposium on Child Psychology*, Vol. 23, New Jersey: Erlbaum: 43–77.

Coolahan, J. and O'Donovan, P.F. (2009), *A History of Ireland's School Inspectorate, 1831–2008*, Dublin: Four Courts Press.

Corra, M. (2007), 'Stereotype threat: Male and female students in advanced high school Courses,' *Journal of Women and Minorities in Science and Engineering*, 13: 95–118.

CREET (n.d.), *Thinking Together in the Primary Classroom*, Milton Keynes: Centre for Research in Education and Educational Technology and the Open University, available from: http://www.open.ac.uk/creet/main/sites/www.open.ac.uk.creet.main/files/08%20Thinking%20Together.pdf (accessed 2 October 2015).

Cremin, T. and Arthur, J. (eds) (2014), *Learning to Teach in the Primary School* (3rd ed.), Abingdon: Routledge.

Creswell, J.W. (2003), *Research Design: Qualitative, Quantitative and Mixed Methods Approaches* (2nd ed.), Thousand Oaks, CA: Sage Publications.

Creswell, J.W. (2009), *Research Design: Qualitative, Quantitative and Mixed Method Approaches* (3rd ed.), London: Sage Publications.

Creswell, J.W. (2013), *Qualitative Enquiry and Research Design: Choosing Among Five Approaches* (3rd ed.), London: Sage Publications.

Crooks, T.J. (1988), 'The Impact of classroom evaluation on students,' *Review of Educational Research*, 58: 438–81.

Cullingford, C. (2003), *The Best Years of Their Lives? Pupils' Experiences of School*, London: Routledge Falmer.

Curwin, R. and Mendler, A. (1988), *Discipline with Dignity*, Alexandria, VA: Association for Supervision and Curriculum Development.

Daniels, D.H. and Perry, K.E. (2003), '"Learner-centered" according to children,' *Theory Into Practice*, 42(2): 102–108.

Danielson L. (2009), 'Fostering Reflection,' *How Teachers Learn*, 66(5): 5–9.

Darling-Hammond, L., Austin, K., Orcutt, S. and Rosso, J. (2001), 'Introduction – How people learn,' *How People Learn: Introduction to Learning Theories*, Stanford, CA: Stanford University School of Education, available from: http://www.stanford.edu/class/ed269/hplintrochapter (accessed 17 February 2015).

Darling-Hammond, L. and Bransford, J. (2007), *Preparing Teachers for a Changing World: What Teachers Should Learn and Be Able To Do*, San Francisco: Jossey-Bass.

Day, C., Sammons, P., Stobart, G., Kington, A. and Gu, Q. (2007), *Teachers Matter: Connecting Lives, Work and Effectiveness*, Maidenhead: Open University Press.

Day, C., Stobart, G., Sammons, P., Kington, A., Gu, Q., Smees, R. and Mujtaba, T. (2006), *Variations in Teachers' Work, Lives and Effectiveness*, London: DfES.

Department of Children and Youth Affairs (2011), *Children First: National Guidance for the Protection and Welfare of Children*, Dublin: Government Publications.

Department of Children and Youth Affairs (2012), *Guidance for Developing Ethical Research Projects Involving Children*, Dublin: Department of Children and Youth Affairs.

Department of Education (1971), *Primary School Curriculum (Curaclam na Bunscoile)*, *Vols 1 and 2*, Dublin: Government of Ireland Publications.

Department of Education and Science (2006), *Learning to Teach: Students on Teaching Practice in Irish Primary Schools*, Dublin: Government Publications.

Dewey, J. (1897), 'My Pedagogic Creed,' *The School Journal, LIV* (3): 77–80.

Dewey, J. (1900), *The School and Society*, Chicago: University of Chicago Press.

Dewey, J. (1902), *The Child and the Curriculum*, Chicago and London: University of Chicago Press.

Dewey, J. (1916), *Democracy and Education: An Introduction to the Philosophy of Education*, New York: Macmillan.

Dewey, J. (1916, 1961), *Democracy and Education*, New York: Macmillan.

Dewey, J. (1933), *How We Think: A Restatement of the Relation of Reflective Thinking to the Educative Process*, Boston: D.C. Heath.

Dewey, J. (1934), 'The Need for a Philosophy of Education,' in *John Dewey on Education: Selected Writings*, Chicago: Chicago University Press: 3–14.

Dewey, J. (1938), *Experience and Education*, New York: Collier.

Dewey, J. (2008), 'The relation of theory to practice in education' in J.A. Boydston (ed.), *The Middle Works of John Dewey 1899–1924, Vol. 3*, Carbondale IL: Southern Illinois University Press: 249–72.

Dodd-Nufrio, A.T. (2011), 'Reggio Emilia, Maria Montessori, and John Dewey: Dispelling teachers' misconceptions and understanding theoretical foundations,' *Early Childhood Education Journal*, 39(4): 235–7.

Dooly, M. (2008), 'Constructing Knowledge Together' in M. Dooly (ed.), *Telecollaborative Language Learning. A Guidebook to Moderating Intercultural Collaboration Online*, Bern: Peter Lang: 21–45.

Duncan, P. (2015), 'We have allowed segregation to happen,' *Irish Times*, 24 February.

Dunning, D., Heath, C. and Suls, J.M. (2004), 'Flawed Self-assessment Implications for Health, Education, and the Workplace', *Psychological Science in the Public Interest*, 5(3): 69–106.

Earl, L. (2003), *Assessment as Learning: Using Classroom Assessment to Maximize Student Learning*, Thousand Oaks, CA: Corwin Press.

Education Scotland (2005), *Let's Talk about Pedagogy: Towards a Shared Understanding for Early Years Education in Scotland*, Edinburgh: Learning and Teaching Scotland.

Eisner, E. (1994), *The Educational Imagination: On the Design and Evaluation of School Programs*, New York: Macmillan.

Elliott, J. (1990), 'Educational Research in Crisis: Performance Indicators, and the Decline in Excellence,' *British Educational Research Journal*, 16(1): 3–18.

Elliott, J. (1991), *Action Research for Educational Change*, London: Open University Press.

Ennis, R.H. (1985), 'A Logical Basis for Measuring Critical Thinking Skills,' *Educational Leadership*, 43(2): 44–8.

Epstein, M., Atkins, M., Cullinan, D., Kutash, K. and Weaver, R. (2008), *Reducing Behavior Problems in the Elementary School Classroom: A Practice Guide,* Washington, DC: National Center for Education Evaluation and Regional Assistance, Institute of Education Sciences, US Department of Education.

Eraut, M. (2004), 'The Practice of Reflection,' *Learning in Health and Social Care*, 3(2): 47–52.

Erwin, J.C. (2004), *The Classroom of Choice: Giving Students What They Need and Getting What You Want*, Alexandria, Virginia: Association for Supervision and Curriculum Development.

Evertson, C.M. and Weinstein C.S. (eds) (2013), *Handbook of Classroom Management: Research, Practice and Contemporary Issues*, New York: Routledge.

Facione, P.A. (1990), *Critical Thinking: A Statement of Expert Consensus for Purposes of Educational Assessment and Instruction*, Millbrae, CA: The California Academic Press.

Farrell, Thomas S.C. (2011), '"Keeping SCORE": Reflective Practice through Classroom Observations,' *RELC Journal*, 42(3): 265–72.

Flanders, N.A. (1968), 'Interaction analysis and in-service training,' *The Journal of Experimental Education*, 37(1): 126–33.

Fletcher, S. (1997), 'Modelling Reflective Practice for Pre-service Teachers: The Role of Teacher Educators,' *Teaching and Teacher Education*, 13(2): 237–43.

Fountas, I.C. and Pinnell, G.S. (1996), *Guided Reading: Good First Teaching for all Children*, Portsmouth, NH: Heinemann.

Francis, D. (1995), 'The Reflective Journal: A Window to Preservice Teachers' Practical Knowledge,' *Teaching and Teacher Education*, 11(3), May: 229–41.

Frankfort-Nachmias, C. and Nachmias, D. (1992), *Research Methods in the Social Sciences* (4th ed.), New York: St Martin's Press.

Fraser, B.J. (2002), 'Learning Environments Research: Yesterday, Today and Tomorrow' in S.C. Goh and M.S. Khine (eds), *Studies in Educational Learning Environments: An International Perspective*, London: World Scientific: 1–25.

Freire, P. (1998), *Pedagogy of Freedom: Ethics, Democracy and Civic Courage* (Critical Perspectives Series), Lanham, MD: Rowman & Littlefield Publishers.

Fullan, M. (2013), *Great to Excellent: Launching the Next Stage of Ontario's Education Agenda*, Toronto, ON: Ministry of Education.

Furrer, C. and Skinner, E. (2003), 'Sense of Relatedness as a Factor in Children's Academic Engagement and Performance,' *Journal of Educational Psychology*, 95(1): 148–62.

Gall, M., Gall, J. and Borg, W. (2003), *Educational Research*, Boston: Pearson Education.

Galton, M., Hargreaves, L., Comber, C., Wall, D. and Pell, A. (1999), 'Changes in patterns of teacher interaction in primary classrooms: 1976–96,' *British Educational Research Journal*, 25(1), 23–37.

Gardner, H. (1983), *Frames of Mind: The Theory of Multiple Intelligences*, New York: Basic Books.

Gardner, H. (1993), *Multiple Intelligences: The Theory in Practice*, New York: Basic Books.

Gardner, H. (2011), 'Multiple Intelligences: The First Thirty Years', Harvard Graduate School of Education, available from: www.multipleintelligencesoasis.org (accessed 9 November 2015).

Gaudelli, W. and Ousley, D. (2009), 'From Clothing to Skin: Identity Work of Student Teachers in Culminating Field Experiences,' *Teaching and Teacher Education*, 25: 931–9.

Gibbs, G. (1988), *Learning By Doing: A Guide to Teaching and Learning Methods*, London: Further Education Unit.

Giuliano, F.J. (1997), 'Practical professional portfolios,' *Science Teacher*, 64(1): 42–4.

Glaser, B. and Strauss, A. (1967), *The Discovery of Grounded Theory: Strategies for Qualitative Research*, Chicago: Aldine.

Glazzard, J., Denby, N. and Price, J. (2014), *Learning To Teach*, Maidenhead: Open University Press.

Glendenning, D. (1999), *Education and the Law*, Dublin: Butterworths.

Golafshani, N. (2003), 'Understanding Reliability and Validity in Qualitative Research,' *The Qualitative Report*, 8(4): 597–607.

Gold, R.L. (1958), 'Roles in Sociological Field Observations,' *Social Forces*, 217–223.

Goodyear, G. and Allchin, D. (1998), 'Statements of teaching philosophy,' *To Improve the Academy*, 17: 103–121.

Götz, I. (2001), *Technology and the Spirit*, Westport, CT: Praeger.

Government of Ireland (2000), *National Children's Strategy: Our Children – Their Lives*, Dublin: Government of Ireland Publications.

Gregory, G. and Chapman, C. (2002), *Differentiated Instructional Strategies: One Size Doesn't Fit All*, Thousand Oaks, CA: Corwin Press.

Halpern, D.F. (1998), 'Teaching Critical Thinking for Transfer across Domains: Dispositions, Skills, Structure Training, and Metacognitive Monitoring,' *American Psychologist*, 53(4): 449–55.

Hammerness, K., Darling-Hammond, L., Bransford, J., Berliner, D., Cochran-Smith, M., McDonald, M. (2005), 'How teachers learn and develop,' in L. Darling-Hammond and J. Bransford (eds), *Preparing Teachers for a Changing World*, San Francisco, CA: Jossey-Bass: 358–89.

Hammersley, M. (2012), 'Methodological Paradigms in Educational Research,' British Educational Research Association on-line resource, available from: https://www.bera.ac.uk/researchers-resources/publications/methodological-paradigms-in-educational-research (accessed 15 June 2015).

Hammersley, M. and Atkinson, P. (2007), *Ethnography: Principles in Practice* (3rd ed.), London: Routledge.

Hammersley, M. and Traianou, A. (2012), 'Ethics and Educational Research,' British Educational Research Association on-line resource, available from: https://www.bera.ac.uk/researchers-resources/publications/ethics-and-educational-research (accessed 28 June 2015).

Hamre, B.K. and Pianta, R.C. (2001), 'Early teacher–child relationships and the trajectory of children's school outcomes through eighth grade,' *Child Development*, 72, 625–38.

Hargreaves, A. (1994), *Changing Times, Changing Teachers*. London: Cassell.

Hargreaves, D. (1996), 'Teaching as a research-based profession: possibilities and prospects,' The Teacher Training Agency Annual Lecture, London: TTA.

Hargreaves, D., Beere, J., Swindells, M., Wise, D., Desforges, C., *et al.* (2005), *About Learning: Report of the Learning Working Group*, London: DEMOS.

Harlen, W. (2005), 'Teachers' summative practices and assessment for learning – tensions and synergies,' *Curriculum Journal*, 16(2): 207–223.

Harris, K. and Alexander, P. (1998), 'Integrated, Constructivist Education: Challenge and Reality,' *Educational Psychology Review*, 10(2): 116.

Hatton, N. and Smith, D. (1995), 'Reflection in Teacher Education: Towards Definition and Implementation,' *Teaching and Teacher Education*, 11(1): 33–49.

Heacox, D. (2002), *Differentiating Instruction in the Regular Classroom: How to Reach and Teach all Learners, Grades 3–12*, Minneapolis, MN: Free Spirit.

Heinich, R., Molenda, M., Russell, J. and Smaldino, S. (2001), *Instructional Media and Technologies for Learning*, Englewood Cliffs: Prentice Hall.

Hilgard, E.R. and Bower, G.H. (1975), *Theories of Learning*, Englewood Cliffs, NJ: Prentice Hall, Inc.

Hillier, Y. (2005), *Reflective Teaching in Further and Adult Education*, London: A&C Black.

Hodes, A. (1972), *Encounter with Martin Buber*, London: Allen Lane/Penguin.

Hollingsworth, S. (1989), 'Prior Beliefs and Cognitive Change in Learning to Teach,' *American Educational Research Journal*, 26(2): 160–89.

hooks, bell (1994), *Teaching to Transgress: Education as the Practice of Freedom*, London: Routledge.

hooks, bell (2009), *Teaching Critical Thinking: Practical Wisdom*, New York, London: Routledge.

Horgan, K. (2015), 'A Longitudinal Analysis of the Beliefs about Teaching and Learning of Undergraduate and Post-Graduate Student Teachers,' paper presented at the European Conference on the Scholarship of Teaching and Learning, University College Cork, June.

Horne, M. and Lownsbrough, H. (2005), *About Learning – Report of the Learning Working Group*, London: Demos Group.

Horner, S.B., Fireman, G.D. and Wang, E.W. (2010), 'The Relation of Student Behavior, Peer Status, Race, and Gender to Decisions about School Discipline Using CHAID Decision Trees and Regression Modeling,' *Journal of School Psychology*, 48(2): 135–161.

Husbands, C. and Pearce, J. (2012), *What Makes Great Pedagogy? Nine Claims from Research*, Nottingham: National College for School Leadership.

Indiana University Bloomington (2015), 'Six Principles for Teacher Education', School of Education, available from: http://education.indiana.edu/undergraduate/six-principles.html (accessed 7 March 2015).

Inglis, F. (1985), *The Management of Ignorance: a Political Theory of the Curriculum*, Oxford: Blackwell.

Institute for Humane Education (2015), 'Scrubbing our Assumptions about our Students', available from: http://humaneeducation.org/blog/2012/09/17/scrubbing-our assumptions-about-our-students/ (accessed 25 February 2015).

Intel® Teach Program (2007), 'Designing Effective Projects: Thinking Skills Frameworks. Bloom's Taxonomy: A New Look at an Old Standby,' CA: Intel Foundation, available from: http://download.intel.com/education/Common/in/Resources/DEP/skillsBloom.pdf (accessed 6 October 2015).

INTO (2004), 'Intercultural Education in the Primary School' in *Proceedings of the INTO Consultative Conference on Education*, Kilkenny: INTO Publications.

Iram, S. and Taggart B. (2014), *Exploring Effective Pedagogy in Primary Schools: Evidence from Research*, London: Pearson.

Jay, J.K. and Johnson, K.L. (2002), 'Capturing Complexity: A Typology of Reflective Practice for Teacher Education,' *Teaching and Teacher Education*, 18(1): 73–85.

Johns, C. (2000), *Becoming a Reflective Practitioner: A Reflective and Holistic Approach to Clinical Nursing, Practice Development and Clinical Supervision*, Monograph Collection (Matt-Pseudo).

Johnson, D.W. and Johnson, F.P. (2009), *Joining Together: Group Theory and Group Skills*, Boston: Allyn & Bacon.

Johnson, D.W. and Johnson, R.T. (1998), *Active Learning: Cooperation in the College Classroom*, Edina, MN: Interaction Book Company.

Johnson, D.W., Johnson, R.T. and Stanne, M.B. (2000), 'Cooperative Learning Methods: A Meta-Analysis,' University of Minnesota, available from: http://www.researchgate.net (accessed 17 May 2015).

Johnson, R.B. and Onwuegbuzie, A.J. (2004), 'Mixed Methods Research: A Research Paradigm Whose Time Has Come,' *Educational Researcher*, 33(7): 14–26.

Jung, Carl (1933), *Psychological Types*, New York: Harcourt, Brace.

Jung, Carl (1954), 'The Development of Personality' in H. Read, M. Fordham and G. Adler (eds), *Collected Works of Carl Jung*, New York: Routledge and Kegan Paul.

Kealey, D.J. and Protheroe, D.R. (1996), 'The effectiveness of cross-cultural training for expatriates: An assessment of the literature on the issue,' *International Journal of Intercultural Relations*, 20(2): 141–65.

Kellaghan, T. (2002), *Preparing Teachers for the 21st Century: Report of the Working Group on Primary Preservice Teacher Education*, Dublin: Department of Education and Science.

Kemp, S. (2011), 'Constructivism and Problem-based Learning', Learning Academy, available from: http://www.tp.edu.sg/staticfiles/TP/files/centres/pbl/pbl_sandra_joy_kemp.pdf (accessed 6 October 2015).

Kerawalla, L., Petrou, M. and Scanlon, E. (2010), 'Talk Factory: The Use of Graphical Representations to Support Argumentation around an Interactive Whiteboard in Primary School Science,' Computer-Based Learning in Science Conference, 7–10 July, Warsaw, Poland.

Kington, A., Regan, E., Sammons, P. and Day, C. (2012), 'Effective Classroom Practice: A Mixed-Method Study of Influences and Outcomes,' *Jubilee Press Occasional Papers*, School of Education, University of Nottingham: The Nottingham Jubilee Press.

Kirova, A. and Emme, M. (2009), 'Immigrant Children's Bodily Engagement in Accessing Their Lived Experiences of Immigration: Creating Poly-Media Descriptive Texts,' *Phenomenology and Practice*, 3(1): 59–79.

Klem, A.M. and Connell, J.P. (2004), 'Relationships matter: Linking teacher support to student engagement and achievement,' *Journal of School Health*, 74(7), 262–73.

Knowles, G. and Holt-Reynolds, D. (1991), 'Shaping Pedagogies through Personal Histories in Preservice Teacher Education,' *The Teachers College Record*, 93(1): 87–113.

Korthagen, F.A. (1985), 'Reflective Teaching and Preservice Teacher Education in the Netherlands,' *Journal of Teacher Education*, 36(5): 11–15.

Korthagen, F.A. and Wubbels, T. (1995), 'Characteristics of Reflective Practitioners: Towards an Operationalization of the Concept of Reflection,' *Teachers and Teaching: Theory and Practice*, 1(1): 51–72.

Kounin, J. (1970, 1977), *Discipline and Group Management in Classrooms*, New York: Holt, Rinehart and Winston.

Krasnor, L.R. and Pepler, D.J. (1980), 'The study of children's play: Some suggested future directions' in K.H. Rubin (ed.), *New Directions for Child Development: Children's Play*, San Francisco: Jossey-Bass: 85–95.

Krause, K., Bochner, S. and Duchesne, S. (2003), *Educational Psychology for Learning and Teaching*, Victoria: Thomson Learning.

Kyriacou, C. (2007), *Essential Teaching Skills* (3rd ed.), Cheltenham: Nelson Thornes.

Labaree, R.V. (2002), 'The risk of "going observationalist": Negotiating the hidden dilemmas of being an insider participant observer,' *Qualitative Research*, 2(1): 97–122.

Lai, E.R. (2011), 'Critical Thinking: A literature Review,' research report, Pearson Assessments, available from: http://www.pearsonassessments.com/hai/images/tmrs/ CriticalThinkingReviewFINAL.pdf (accessed 15 February 2015).

Larrivee, B. and Cooper, J. M. (2006), *An Educator's Guide to Teacher Reflection*, Boston: Houghton Mifflin.

Larson, J. and Peterson, S.M. (2003), 'Talk and Discourse in Formal Learning Settings,' in N. Hall, J. Larson, and J. Marsh (eds), *Handbook of Early Childhood Literacy*, London: Sage Publications.

Lee, H.J. (2005), 'Understanding and Assessing Preservice Teachers' Reflective Thinking,' *Teaching and Teacher Education*, 21(6): 699–715.

Levine, T. and Donitsa-Schmidt, S. (1996), 'Classroom Environment in Computer-Integrated Science Classes: Effects of Gender and Computer Ownership,' *Science and Technological Education*, 14(2): 163–78.

Lomak, P. (1999), 'Working together for educative community through research,' presidential address, *British Educational Research Journal*, 25(1): 5–21.

Looney, A. (2001), 'Curriculum as policy: Some implications of contemporary policy studies for the analysis of curriculum policy, with particular reference to post-primary curriculum policy in the Republic of Ireland,' *The Curriculum Journal*, 12(2): 149–62.

Lortie, D. (1975), *Schoolteacher: A Sociological Study*, Chicago: University of Chicago Press.

Lovat, T.J. (2003), 'The Role of the "Teacher": Coming of Age?', discussion paper, Victoria, Australia: Australian Council of Deans of Education.

Lyons, N. (1999), 'How portfolios can shape emerging practice,' *Educational Leadership*, 56(8): 63–5.

Lyons, N. (ed.) (1998), *With Portfolio in Hand: Validating the New Teacher Professionalism*, New York: Teachers College Press.

Lyons, N., Hyland, A. and Ryan, N. (eds) (2002), *Advancing the Scholarship of Teaching and Learning through a Reflective Portfolio Process: The University College Cork Experience*, Cork: UCC.

McCourt, F. (2007), 'Frank McCourt Reflects on Teaching Career' in Ellen R. Delisio (ed.), *Education World*, available from: http://www.educationworld.com/a_issues/ chat/chat163.shtml (accessed 17 March 2015).

McCoy, S., Smyth, E. and Banks, J., (2012), *The Primary Classroom: Insights from the Growing Up in Ireland Study*, Dublin: The Economic and Social Research Institute.

McCulloch, G. and Richardson, W. (2000), *Historical Research in Educational Settings*, Buckingham and Philadelphia: Open University Press.

Mack, L. (2010), 'The Philosophical Underpinnings of Educational Research,' Polyglossia, 19: 5–11.

McKechnie, L. (E.F.) (2000), 'Ethnographic observation of preschool children,' *Library & Information Science Research*, 22(1): 61–76.

McLeod, J., Fisher, J. and Hoover, G. (2003), *The Key Elements of Classroom Management: Managing Time and Space, Student Behavior and Instructional Strategies*, Virginia: Association for Supervision and Curriculum Development.

McNiff, J. (2001), 'Action Research and the Professional Learning of Teachers,' unpublished paper presented at the Qattan Foundation, Palestine, January.

McNiff, J. and Whitehead, J. (2002), *Action Research: Principles and Practices*, London and New York: Routledge/Falmer.

Marzano, R. and Marzano, J. (2003), 'The Key to Classroom Management,' *Building Classroom Relationships*, 61(1): 6–13.

Marzano, R.J., Marzano, J.S. and Pickering, D.J. (2003), *Classroom Management that Works*, Alexandria, VA: Association for Supervision and Curriculum Development.

Maynes, N., Allison, J. and Julien-Schultz, L. (2012), 'International practical experiences as events of influence in a teacher candidates' development,' *McGill Journal of Education*, 47(1): 69–91.

Mehta, S. (2002), *Multiple Intelligences and How Children Learn: An Investigation in One Preschool Classroom*, unpublished thesis, Virginia Polytechnic Institute and State University, Blacksburg, VA.

Mercer, N. (1993), 'Neo-Vygotskian theory and education' in B. Stierer and J. Maybin (eds.), *Language, Literacy and Learning in Educational Practice*, Clevedon: Multilingual Matters.

Mercer, N. (1995, 2000), *The Guided Construction of Knowledge: Talk amongst Teachers and Learners*, Clevedon: Multilingual Matters Ltd.

Mercer, N. and Dawes, L. (2008), 'The Value of Exploratory Talk' in N. Mercer and S. Hodgkinson (eds), *Exploring Talk in School: Inspired By the Work of Douglas Barnes*, London: Sage: 55–71.

Mercer, N. and Hodgkinson, S. (eds) (2008), *Exploring Talk in School*, London: Sage.

Mercer, N. and Littleton, K. (2007), *Dialogue and the Development of Children's Thinking*, London: Routledge.

Mercer, N., Warwick, P., Kershner, R. and Staarman, J.K. (2010), 'Can the interactive whiteboard help to provide "dialogic space" for children's collaborative activity?' *Language and Education*, 24(5), 367–84.

Mercer, N. and Wegerif, R. (1999), 'Is "exploratory talk" productive talk?' in P. Light and K. Littleton (ed.), *Learning with Computers: Analysing Productive Interaction*, London: Routledge.

Michaels, S., O'Conner, M.C. and Hall, M.W., with Resnick, L.B. (2002), *Accountable Talk: Classroom Conversation that Works*, 3 CD-ROM set, Pittsburgh, PA: University of Pittsburgh.

Moon, J. (1999), *Reflection in Learning and Professional Development*, Abingdon, Oxon: RoutledgeFalmer.

Moon, J. (2001), 'Learning through Reflection' in F. Banks and A. Shelton Mayes (eds), *Early Professional Development for Teachers*, London: David Fulton Publishers: 364–78.

Moon, J. (2005), 'The Higher Education Academy Guide for Busy Academics No. 4: Learning through reflection', available from: http://www.nursing-midwifery.tcd.ie/assets/director-staff-edu-dev/pdf/Guide-for-Busy-Academics-No1-4-HEA.pdf (accessed 13 May 2015).

Moore Johnson, S. and Donaldson, M.L. (2007), 'Overcoming the Obstacles to Leadership,' *Educational Leadership*, 65(1): 8–13.

Moreland, J., Jones, A. and Chambers, M. (2001), 'Enhancing student learning in technology through enhancing teacher formative interactions,' *Set: Research Information for Teachers*, 3: 16–19.

Mosley, J. (1993), *Turn Your School Round*, Cambridge: LDA.

Mosley, J. (1996), *Quality Circle Time in the Primary Classroom: Your Essential Guide to Enhancing Self-esteem, Self-discipline and Positive Relationships*, Wisbech, Cambridgeshire: Lda.

Mosley, J. (1998), *More Quality Circle Time*, Wisbech, Cambridgeshire: Lda.

Mosley, J. (2006), *Step-by-Step Guide to Circle Time for SEAL*, Trowbridge: Positive Press.

Mosley, J and Tew, M. (1999), *Quality Circle Time in Secondary School: A Handbook of Good Practice*, London: David Fultion.

Murdock, T.B. and Miller, A. (2003), 'Teachers as sources of middle school students' motivational identity: Variable-centered and person-centered analytic approaches,' *The Elementary School Journal*, 13(4), 383–99.

Natriello, G. (1987), 'The impact of evaluation processes on students,' *Educational Psychologist*, 22: 155–75.

NCCA (n.d.), 'Diversity and Inclusion', available from: http://www.ncca.ie/en/Curriculum_and_Assessment/Inclusion/Diversity_and_inclusion.pdf (accessed: 9 March 2015).

NCCA (n.d.), 'Practitioners and children talking and thinking together', Aistear tipsheet, available from: http://www.ncca.ie/en/file/aistearsiolta/65-415-Thinking-and-talking-tipsheet.pdf (accessed 7 October 2015).

NCCA (1999), *Primary School Curriculum Introduction*, Dublin: National Council for Curriculum and Assessment.

NCCA (1999a), *Primary School Curriculum: Geography – Social, Environmental and Scientific Education*, Dublin: National Council for Curriculum and Assessment.

NCCA (1999b), *Primary School Curriculum: Social, Personal and Health Education*, Dublin: National Council for Curriculum and Assessment.

NCCA (1999c), *Primary School Curriculum: History*, Dublin: National Council for Curriculum and Assessment.

NCCA (2005), *General Guidelines on Intercultural Education in the Primary School*, Dublin: National Council for Curriculum and Assessment.

NCCA (2007), *Assessment in the Primary School Curriculum: Guidelines for Schools*, Dublin: National Council for Curriculum and Assessment.

NCCA (2007a), *Exceptionally Able Students: Draft Guidelines for Teachers*, Dublin: National Council for Curriculum and Assessment.

NCCA (2008), *Primary Curriculum Review*, final report, Dublin: National Council for Curriculum and Assessment.

NCCA (2009), *Aistear: The Early Childhood Curriculum Framework*, Dublin: National Council for Curriculum and Assessment.

NIPT (2013), *Short-Term Planning: Draft Guidelines*, The National Induction Programme for Teachers, available from: http://www.nccaplanning.ie/support/pdf/short_term_planning.pdf (accessed 7 October 2015).

Noddings, N. (1984), *Caring: A Feminine Approach to Ethics and Moral Education*, Berkeley: University of California Press.

Noddings, N. (1992), *The Challenge to Care in Schools: An Alternative Approach to Education*, New York: Teachers College Press.

Noddings, N. (2002), *Starting at Home: Caring and Social Policy*, Berkeley: University of California Press.

Noddings, N. (2003), *Happiness and Education*, Cambridge: Cambridge University Press.

Noddings, N. (ed.) (2005), *Educating Citizens for Global Awareness,* New York: Teachers College Press.

Nosek, B., Smyth, F., Sriram, N., Lindner, N., Devos, T. *et al.* (2009), 'National Differences in Gender – Science Stereotypes Predict National Sex Differences in Science and Math Achievement,' *Proceedings of the National Academy of Sciences in the USA*, 106(26): 10593–7.

Opdenakker, M.C. and Van Damme, J. (2006), 'Teacher Characteristics and Teaching Styles as Effectiveness Enhancing Factors of Classroom Practice,' *Teaching and Teacher Education,* 22(1): 1–21.

Osterman, K.F. and Kottkamp, R.B. (2004), 'Reflective Practice for Educators,' available from http://www.fgse.nova.edu/edl/secure/mats/rdgelach2.pdf (accessed 16 November 2015).

Ostrosky, M. and Jung E. (2005), 'Building Positive Teacher–Child Relationship,' Center on the Social and Emotional Foundations for Early Learning, Washington: US Department of Health and Human Service.

Palmer, Parker J. (1998), *The Courage to Teach: Exploring the Inner Landscape of a Teacher's Life,* San Francisco: Jossey-Bass.

Patton, A., Robbin, J. (2012), *Work that Matters: The Teacher's Guide to Project-Based Learning*, London: Paul Hamlyn Foundation.

Paul, R.W. (1992), 'Critical Thinking: What, Why, and How?' *New Directions for Community Colleges*, 1992(77): 3–24.

Paul, R. and Elder, L. (2009), *The Miniature Guide to Critical Thinking Concepts and Tools*, California: Foundation for Critical Thinking Press.

Peddiwell, J.A. and Benjamin, H.R.W. (1939), *The Saber Tooth Curriculum and Other Essays*, New York: McGraw-Hill.

Perry, K.E. and Weinstein, R.S. (1998), 'The social context of early schooling and children's school adjustment,' *Educational Psychologist*, 33(4): 177–194.

Pirsig, R.M. (1974), *Zen and the Art of Motorcycle Maintenance: An Inquiry into Values*, New York: Morrow & Co.

Plato (1956), *Meno*, trans. W.K.C. Gutherie, London: Penguin.

Platz, D. and Arellano, J. (2011), 'Time tested early childhood theories and practices,' *Education*, 132(1): 54–63.

Pollard, A., Anderson, J., Maddock, M., Swaffield, S., Warin, J. and Warwick, P. (2008), *Reflective Teaching: Evidence Informed Professional Practice* (3rd ed.), London: Continuum.

Pollard, A., Black Hawkins, K., Cliff Hodges, G., Dudley, P., James, M., Linklater, H. *et al.* (2014), *Reflective Teaching in Schools*, London: Bloomsbury.

Pollard, A. and James M. (eds.) (2004), *Personalised Learning: A Commentary by the Teaching and Learning Research Programme*, London: ESRC.

Pollard, A. and Tann, S. (1993), *Reflective Teaching in the Primary School: A Handbook for the Classroom*, London: Cassell.

Pollard, A., Triggs, P., Broadfoot, P., McNess, E. and Osborne, M. (2000), *What Pupils Say: Changing Policy and Practice in Primary Education*, New York: Continuum.

Pontecorvo, C. and Sterponi, L. (2002), 'Learning to Argue and Learning to Reason through Discourse in Educational Settings', in G. Wells and G.L. Claxton (eds.), *Learning for Life in the 21st Century: Sociocultural Perspectives on the Future of Education*, Oxford: Blackwell.

Popper, K. (1963), *Conjectures and Refutations: The Growth of Scientific Knowledge*, London: Routledge and Kegan Paul.

Powell, R.R., McLaughlin, H.J., Savage, T.V. and Zehm, S. (2001), *Classroom Management: Perspectives on the Social Curriculum*, Upper Saddle River, NJ: Merrill/Prentice Hall.

Reeve, J. and Jang, H. (2006), 'What Teachers Say and Do to Support Students' Autonomy During a Learning Activity,' *Journal of Educational Psychology*, 98, 209–218.

Resnick, L.B., Michaels, S. and O'Connor, C. (2010), 'How (Well Structured) Talk Builds the Mind' in D. Preiss and R. Sternberg (eds), *Innovations in Educational Psychology: Perspectives on Learning, Teaching and Human Development*, New York: Springer: 163–194.

Richards, J.C. and Farrell, T.S.C. (2005), *Professional Development for Language Teachers: Strategies for Teacher Learning*, New York: Cambridge University Press.

Richert, A.E. (1992), 'Writing Cases: A Vehicle for Inquiry into the Teaching Process,' *Case Methods in Teacher Education*, 155–174.

Richmond, W.K. (1970), *Readings in Education: A Sequence*, London: Methuen.

Rimm-Kaufmann, S. and Sandilos, L. (2015), 'Improving Students' Relationships with Teachers to Provide Essential Supports for Learning,' *American Psychological Association,* available from: http://www.apa.org/education/k12/relationships.aspx (accessed 18 March 2015).

Ring, E. (2010), 'An Evaluation of the Effects of an Autistic Spectrum Disorder-Specific Post-Graduate Certificate Continuing Professional Development Programme on Practice in Six Schools,' unpublished doctoral dissertation, Dublin City University.

Ring, E. (2015), 'Early Years Education Focused Inspections: A Reason to Celebrate,' *Children's Research Digest,* 2(2), in press.

Ring, E., Mhic Mhathúna, M., Moloney, M., Hayes, N., Breatnach, D. *et al.* (2015), *An Examination of Concepts of School-Readiness among Parents and Educators in Ireland,* Dublin: Department of Children and Youth Affairs, in press.

Rolfe, G., Freshwater, D. and Japser, M. (2001), *Critical Reflection for Nursing and the Helping Professions: A User's Guide*, New York: Palgrave.

Rolheiser, C. and Ross, J. A. (2001), 'Student Self-Evaluation: What Research Says and What Practice Shows' in R.D. Small and A. Thomas (eds), *Plain Talk about kids,* Covington, LA: Center for Development and Learning: 43–57.

Rousseau, Jean-Jacques (1762, 1979), *Emile, Vols I–V,* trans. Allan Bloom, New York: Basic Books.

Rubin, K., Fein, G. and Vandenberg, B. (1983), 'Play,' in E.M. Hetherington (ed.), *Handbook of Child Psychology: Socialization, Personality, Social Development, Vol. 4,* New York: Wiley: 694–759.

Ryan, R. and Deci, E. (2000), 'Self-Determination Theory and the Facilitation of Intrinsic Motivation, Social development, and Well-Being,' *American Psychologist,* 55: 68–78.

Sachs, J. (2005), 'Teacher Education and the Development of Professional Identity: Learning to Be a Teacher' in P. Denicolo and M. Kompf (eds), *Connecting Policy and Practice: Challenges for Teaching and Learning in Schools and Universities,* Oxford: Routledge.

Sahlberg, P. (2013), 'Leveraging Teacher Leadership: Teachers as Leaders in Finland,' *Educational Leadership,* 71–2: 36–40.

Sanderson, R. (2010), *Towards a New Measure of Playfulness: The Capacity to Fully and Freely Engage in Play,* unpublished dissertation, Loyola University, Chicago.

Sanford, A.J. and Garrod, S.C. (1981), *Understanding Written Language: Explorations of Comprehension beyond the Sentence,* New York: Wiley.

Santrock, J.W. (2008), *A Topical Approach to Life-Span Development*, 4th ed., New York: McGraw-Hill.

Savery, J.R. (2006), 'Overview of Problem-based Learning: Definitions and Distinctions,' *Interdisciplinary Journal of Problem-Based Learning*, 1(1): 9–20.

Savoie, J. and Hughes, A. (1994), 'Problem-Based Learning as Classroom Solution', *Strategies for Success*, 52(3): 54–7.

Schön, D. (1983), *The Reflective Practitioner: How Professionals Think in Action*, New York: Basic Books.

Schon, D. (1995), 'The New Scholarship Requires a New Epistemology,' *Change*, 27: 27–34.

Scrivener, J. (2005), *Learning Teaching*, 2nd ed., Oxford: Macmillan Education.

SESS (n.d.), 'Differentiation in the Classroom for Children with Special Education Needs,' PowerPoint presentation, Cork: Special Education Support Service, available from: http://www.sess.ie/resources/teaching-methods-and-organisation (accessed 5 October 2015).

Shellard, E. and Protheroe, N. (2000), *Effective Teaching: How Do We Know It When We See It?* Arlington, VA: Educational Research Service.

Sheridan, L. and Moore, C.L. (2009), 'Staff perceptions of desirable "teacher qualities" for pre-service teachers,' paper presented at AARE 2009 International Education Research Conference, University of Canberra, Australia.

Shumow, L. and Schmidt, J.A. (2013), 'Academic Grades and Motivation in High School Science Classrooms among Male and Female Students: Associations with Teachers' Characteristics, Beliefs, and Practices' in R. Haumann and G. Zimmer (eds.), *Handbook of Academic Performance: Predictors, Learning Strategies and Influences of Gender*, New Jersey: Nova Science Publishers: 53–72.

Siegel, J. and Shaughnessy, M. (1994), 'An Interview with Howard Gardner: Educating for Understanding,' *Phi Delta Kappan*, 75(7): 563–6.

Silver, D. (2011), 'Using the "Zone" to Help Reach Every Learner,' *Kappa Delta Pi Record*, 47: 28–31.

Silver, H.F., Strong, R.W. and Perini, M.J. (1997), 'Integrating Learning Styles and Multiple Intelligences,' *Educational Leadership*, 55(1): 22–7.

Silver, H.F., Strong, R.W. and Perini, M.J. (2000), *So Each May Learn: Integrating Learning Styles and Multiple Intelligences*, Alexandria, WV: Association for Supervision and Curriculum Development.

Siraj, I. and Taggart, B. (2014), *Exploring Effective Pedagogy in Primary Schools: Evidence from Research*, London: Pearson.

Smith, F., Hardman, F., Wall, K. and Mroz, M. (2004), 'Interactive Whole-Class Teaching in the National Literacy and Numeracy Strategies,' *British Educational Research Journal*, 30(3): 395–411.

Spencer, J. (2003), 'Learning and Teaching in the Clinical Environment' in P. Cantillon, L. Hutchinson and D. Wood (eds), *ABC of Learning and Teaching in Medicine*, London: BMJ Publishing Group.

Spradley, J.P. (1980), *Participant Observation*, New York: Holt, Rinehart and Winston.

Stage, S.A. and Quiroz, D.R. (1997), 'A meta-analysis of interventions to decrease disruptive classroom behavior in public education settings,' *School Psychology Review*, 26(3), 333–8.

Stake, R.E. (2008), 'Qualitative Case Studies' in N.K. Denzin and Y.S. Lincoln (eds), *Strategies of Qualitative Inquiry*, Los Angeles: Sage: 119–49.

Stenhouse, L. (1975), *An Introduction to Curriculum Research and Development*, London: Heinemann.

Stenhouse, L. (1984), 'Artistry and Teaching: The Teacher as Focus of Research and Development' in D. Hopkins and M. Wideen (eds.), *Alternative Perspectives on School Improvement*, London: Lewes Falmer Press.

Stepien, W.J. and Gallagher, S.A. (1993), 'Problem-based Learning: As Authentic as it Gets,' *Educational Leadership*, 50(7): 25–8.

Stoecker, R. (1991), 'Evaluating and rethinking the case study,' *The Sociological Review,* 39(1): 88–121.

Strauss, A. and Corbin, J. (1990), *Basics of Qualitative Research: Grounded Theory Procedures and Techniques,* Newbury Park, CA: Sage.

Strauss, A. and Corbin, J. (1994), 'Grounded Theory Methodology' in N.K. Denzin and Y.S. Lincoln (eds.), *Handbook of Qualitative Research*, Thousand Oaks, CA: Sage: 273–85.

Sylva, K., Melhuish, E., Sammons, P., Siraj-Blatchford, I. and Taggart, B. (2004), 'The Effective Provision of Pre-School Education (EPPE) Project: Findings from Pre-school to end of Key Stage 1,' available from: https://www.ioe.ac.uk/RB_Final_Report_3-7.pdf (accessed 28 July 2015).

Takona, J. (2002), *Pre-Service Teacher Portfolio Development*, Bloomington, IA: Writers Club Press, Universe Inc.

Teaching Council (2011), *Initial Teacher Education: Criteria and Guidelines for Programme Providers*, Athlone: Teaching Council.

Teaching Council (2011a), *Policy on the Continuum of Teacher Education*, Dublin: Teaching Council.

Teaching Council (2012), *Code of Professional Conduct for Teachers*, Athlone: Teaching Council.

Teaching Council (2013), *Guidelines on School Placement*, Maynooth: Teaching Council, available from: http://www.teachingcouncil.ie/en/Publications/Teacher-Education/Guidelines-for-School-Placement-.pdf (accessed 16 April 2015).

Teaching Council (2013a), *Final Report of the Review Panel to the Teaching Council following a review of the reconceptualised degree programme submitted for accreditation by Mary Immaculate College*, Maynooth: Teaching Council.

Teaching Council (2013b), *Final Report of the Review Panel to the Teaching Council following a review of the reconceptualised degree programme submitted for accreditation by St Patrick's College, Drumcondra*, Maynooth: Teaching Council.

Teaching Council (2013c), *Final Report of the Review Panel to the Teaching Council following a review of reconceptualised programmes of initial teacher education, Professional Master of Education (submitted for accreditation by University College Cork) and Professional Master of Education Art and Design (submitted for accreditation jointly by University College Cork and Crawford College of Art and Design/Cork Institute of Technology: Cork, UCC and CIT)*, Maynooth: Teaching Council.

Tedlock, B. (2001), 'Ethnography and Ethnographic Representation' in N. Denzin and Y. Lincoln (eds), *The Handbook of Qualitative Research*, Thousand Oaks, California: Sage.

Tharp, R. and Gallimore, R. (1988), *Rousing Minds to Life*, New York: Cambridge University Press.

Tobin, K. and Gallagher, J.J. (1987), 'What happens in high school science classrooms?' *Journal of Curriculum Studies*, 19(6): 549–60.

Training and Development Agency UK (2007), *Professional Standards for Teachers*, London: UK Training and Development Agency for Schools.

Tripp, D. (1993), *Critical Incidents in Teaching*, London: Routledge.

Ussher, B. and Earl, K. (2010), '"Summative" and "formative": Confused by the assessment terms?' *New Zealand Journal of Teachers' Work*, 7(1): 53–63.

van Manen, M. (1977), 'Linking Ways of Knowing with Ways of Being Practical,' *Curriculum Inquiry*, 6(3), 205–228.

van Manen, M. (1995), 'On the Epistemology of Reflective Practice,' *Teachers and Teaching: Theory and Practice*, 1(1): 33–50.

Vygotsky, L.S. (1978), 'Interaction between learning and development,' trans M. Lopez Morillas, in M. Cole, V. John-Steiner, S. Scribner and E. Souberman (eds.), *Mind in Society: The Development of Higher Psychological Processes*, Cambridge, MA: Harvard University Press: 79– 91.

Wajnryb, R. (1992), *Classroom Observation Tasks*, Cambridge: Cambridge University Press.

Walsh, P. (1993), *Education and Meaning: Philosophy and Practice*, New York: Cassell.

Weber, J.A. (1997), 'Preparing the Portfolio: A Personal View' in P. Seldin (ed.), *The Teaching Portfolio: A Practical Guide to Improved Performance and Promotion/Tenure Decisions*, 2nd ed., Bolton, MA: Anker.

Wegerif, R. (1996), 'Using computers to help coach exploratory talk across the curriculum,' *Computers and Education,* 26(1–3): 51–60.

Wei, L. and Elias, H. (2011), 'Relationships between students' perceptions of classroom environment and their motivation in learning English language,' *International Journal of Humanities and Social Science,* 1(21): 240–50.

West Kentucky School of Teacher Education (2015), 'Components and Objectives,' Western Kentucky University, available from: http://www.wku.edu/ste/objectives/components.php (accessed 14 July 2015).

White, B.Y. and Frederiksen, J.R. (1998), 'Inquiry, modelling and metacognition: Making science accessible to all students,' *Cognition and Instruction,* 16(1): 18–31.

Whitehead, J. (1998), 'Developing research-based professionalism through living educational theories,' Keynote presentation to the Action Research and the Politics of Educational Knowledge Conference, Trinity College Dublin, 27 November, in J. McNiff, G. McNamara and D. Leonard (eds) (2000), *Action Research in Ireland,* Dorset: September Books.

Wiggins, G. and McTighe, J. (1998), *Understanding by Design,* Alexandria, VA: Association for Supervision and Curriculum Development.

Willig, C. (2008), *Introducing Qualitative Research in Psychology: Adventures in Theory and Method,* London: Open University Press.

Wilson, J. (1975), *Educational Theory and the Preparation of Teachers,* Windsor: NFER Publishers.

Wilson, L.O. (2013), 'A succinct discussion of the revisions to Bloom's classic cognitive taxonomy by Anderson and Krathwohl and how to use them effectively,' available from: http://thesecondprinciple.com/teaching-essentials/beyond-bloom-cognitive-taxonomy-revised/ (accessed 5 October 2015).

Winch, C. (2006), *The Philosophy of Human Learning,* London and New York: Taylor & Francis.

Wolf, K. and Dietz, M. (1998), 'Teaching portfolios: purposes and possibilities,' *Teacher Education Quarterly,* 25(1): 9–22.

Woolfolk, A. (2004), *Educational Psychology,* 9th ed., Boston, MA: Allyn & Bacon.

Wragg, E.C. (2005), *The Art and Science of Teaching and Learning: The Selected Works of Ted Wragg,* London: Routledge Falmer.

Yin, R.K. (2005), 'Introduction,' in R.K. Yin (ed.), *Introducing the World of Education: A Case Study Reader,* Thousand Oaks, CA: Sage: xiii–xxii.

Zeichner, K.M. and Liston, D.P. (2014), *Reflective Teaching: An Introduction,* New York: Routledge.

Zeichner, K.M. and Noffke, S. (2001), 'Practitioner research' in V. Richardson (ed.), *Handbook of Research on Teaching,* 4th ed., Washington, DC: American Educational Research Association: 298–330.

Zimmerman, B.J. (2000), 'Attaining Self-Regulation: A Social Cognitive Perspective' in M. Boekarts, P. Pintrich and M. Zeidner (eds), *Self-Regulation: Theory, Research and Applications*, Orlando Florida Academic: 13–39.